Understanding Diaspora Development

Melissa Phillips • Louise Olliff
Editors

Understanding Diaspora Development

Lessons from Australia and the Pacific

palgrave
macmillan

Editors
Melissa Phillips ⓘD
Western Sydney University
Penrith, NSW, Australia

Louise Olliff
School of Regulation and Global Governance
Australian National University
Canberra, ACT, Australia

ISBN 978-3-030-97865-5   ISBN 978-3-030-97866-2   (eBook)
https://doi.org/10.1007/978-3-030-97866-2

© The Editor(s) (if applicable) and The Author(s), under exclusive licence to Springer Nature Switzerland AG 2022
This work is subject to copyright. All rights are solely and exclusively licensed by the Publisher, whether the whole or part of the material is concerned, specifically the rights of translation, reprinting, reuse of illustrations, recitation, broadcasting, reproduction on microfilms or in any other physical way, and transmission or information storage and retrieval, electronic adaptation, computer software, or by similar or dissimilar methodology now known or hereafter developed.
The use of general descriptive names, registered names, trademarks, service marks, etc. in this publication does not imply, even in the absence of a specific statement, that such names are exempt from the relevant protective laws and regulations and therefore free for general use.
The publisher, the authors and the editors are safe to assume that the advice and information in this book are believed to be true and accurate at the date of publication. Neither the publisher nor the authors or the editors give a warranty, expressed or implied, with respect to the material contained herein or for any errors or omissions that may have been made. The publisher remains neutral with regard to jurisdictional claims in published maps and institutional affiliations.

Cover illustration: © Alex Linch shutterstock.com

This Palgrave Macmillan imprint is published by the registered company Springer Nature Switzerland AG.
The registered company address is: Gewerbestrasse 11, 6330 Cham, Switzerland

CONTENTS

1 Introduction   1
Louise Olliff and Melissa Phillips

Part I   Long-distance Activism   11

2 Long-Distance Refugee Activism: Commemorating, Recreating and Reimagining Post-Genocide Communities in Diaspora   13
Hariz Halilovich

3 The Co-Construction of the Myanmar Diaspora in Australia   37
Susan Banki

Part II   Transnational Belongings   59

4 Transnational Economic Engagements: The Africa-Australia Nexus   61
Farida Fozdar, David Mickler, Sarah Prout Quicke, Mary B. Setrana, Muhammad Dan Suleiman, and Dominic N. Dagbanja

vi CONTENTS

5 From Resettled Refugees to Humanitarian Actors: The Transformation of Transnational Social Networks of Care 87
Louise Olliff

Part III Responding to War, Conflict and Disaster 109

6 Pacific Diaspora Humanitarianism: Diasporic Perspectives 111
Jeevika Vivekananthan and Phil Connors

7 Diaspora Peacebuilding Through Inter-Ethnic Harmony: The South Sudanese and Sri Lankan Diasporas in Australia 137
Atem Atem, Jennifer Balint, Denise Cauchi, and Shyama Fuad

8 South Sudanese Australians: Transnational Kinship During Conflict and Economic Crisis 161
Sara Maher, Nicki Kindersley, Freddie Carver, and Santino Atem Deng

Part IV Future Imaginings 185

9 Interrogating Diaspora and Cross-Border Politics in Ukrainian Migration to Australia 187
Olga Oleinikova

10 Diaspora Policy: A Missing Plank in Australia's Multicultural Policy Portfolio 207
Melissa Phillips

Index 225

NOTES ON CONTRIBUTORS

Atem Atem is a PhD candidate at the Australian National University, examining the structural barriers experienced by South Sudanese in Western Sydney who are in the process of settlement and challenging the concept of settlement as a binary—success or failure. He has at least ten years of experience supporting refugee and migrant settlement through provision of direct support and services, sector planning and advocacy. In addition, he supports refugee communities in a voluntary capacity through community organising and is the President of NSW Refugee Communities Advocacy Network (RCAN).

Jennifer Balint is Associate Professor of Socio-Legal Studies and Head of the School of Social and Political Sciences at The University of Melbourne. She teaches and writes on post-conflict justice, accountability for state crime and access to justice. Her most recent book is *Keeping Hold of Justice: Encounters between Law and Colonialism.*

Susan Banki is a Senior Lecturer at the University of Sydney. She writes on refugees, migrants and transnational activism, with particular attention to refugees from Bhutan and Myanmar.

Freddie Carver has a background working with international NGOs and the British Government's aid department has informed his research, which focuses on the unintended consequences and politics of aid in the Horn of Africa. He has a particular focus on forced displacement and migration amongst South Sudanese communities.

viii NOTES ON CONTRIBUTORS

Denise Cauchi is a consultant with 12 years of experience in the field of diaspora-led development, humanitarianism, peacebuilding and human rights. She was co-founder and Executive Director of Diaspora Action Australia, and authored *Long-distance Peacebuilding: The Experiences of the South Sudanese and Sri Lankan Diasporas in Australia*.

Phil Connors is Associate Professor and Founding Director of the Centre for Humanitarian Leadership, Deakin University. He has a background in community development and a PhD in Community Economic Development. His recent research projects include exploring how localising leadership can better meet the needs of affected communities in humanitarian contexts.

Dominic N. Dagbanja is a Senior Lecturer in Law at The University of Western Australia Law School and a Research Fellow, African Procurement Law Unit, Department of Mercantile Law, Stellenbosch University, South Africa. He is also the Director of Research of the Organisation of African Communities in Western Australia Inc. and Associate Director (Community Engagement) in UWA Africa Research & Engagement Centre.

Santino Atem Deng is an experienced counsellor, educator/trainer, researcher, and specialised in mental health, family/parenting, and he works as Director, researcher, educator and counsellor in different capacities. He holds a PhD, Master of Education/Counselling and BA. His primary area of research interest includes refugee/migrant resettlement/settlement, diaspora, family/parenting, social inclusion, education and mental health. Atem Deng has written widely for various publications.

Farida Fozdar is Professor, Social Sciences, Curtin University, and Research Fellow in the UWA Africa Research & Engagement Centre (AfREC). Her research focuses on race relations and migrant settlement, nationalism and cosmopolitanism. She has written widely on African settlement in Australia, and issues of employment, identity and mental health.

Shyama Fuad is a registered psychologist working in the field of mental health and wellbeing, reconciliation and community engagement. He facilitates mental health resilience and psychoeducational programs and also volunteers with Bridging Lanka, a diaspora-led not-for-profit organisation involved in community development and reconciliation initiatives in Australia and Sri Lanka.

Hariz Halilovich is Professor of Global Studies and ARC Future Fellow at RMIT University. His research has focused on place-based identity politics, conflict and migration. His published works include *Places of Pain* (2013/2015); *Writing After Srebrenica* (2017); and *Monsters of Modernity* (co-authored with Julian C.H. Lee *et al*) (2019).

Nicki Kindersley is Lecturer in History at Cardiff University, formerly Harry F Guggenheim Research Fellow at Pembroke College, University of Cambridge, and Fellow of the Rift Valley Institute in South Sudan.

Sara Maher is a specialist in the gendered and systemic oppression of former refugee women in Australian post-settlement. Her research has focused on the South Sudanese Australian community looking at the relationship between pre-migration and post-settlement experiences for women, the criminalisation of young people and the dynamics of transnationality.

David Mickler is a Senior Lecturer in Foreign Policy & International Relations and inaugural Director of the Africa Research & Engagement Centre (AfREC) at The University of Western Australia. Mickler was previously Co-Chair of the Worldwide Universities Network's Global Africa Group. His research explores Africa's international relations, including Africa-Australia relations.

Olga Oleinikova is a Senior Lecturer and Director of the Ukraine Democracy Initiative in the School of Communication at the University of Technology Sydney, Australia. She is named among Forbes Top 40 Global Ukrainians, Forbes 30 Under 30 in Asia and is a finalist for Australia's Council of Humanities, Arts and Social Sciences Future Leader Award. She is the author of *Achiever or Survivor? Life Strategies of Migrants from Crisis Regimes* (Palgrave, 2020) and editor of *Democracy, Diaspora, Territory: Europe and Cross-Border Politics* (2019). She also holds an Honorary Research title with the School of Political and Social Sciences, Sydney Democracy Network, University of Sydney.

Louise Olliff is a Senior Policy Advisor for the Refugee Council of Australia, an Adjunct Fellow with Western Sydney University's Humanitarian and Development Research Initiative (HADRI), and a Post doctoral Research Fellow at the Australian National University's School of Regulation and Global Governance (RegNet) working on the Australian Research Council Linkage Project, *Diaspora Humanitarians: How Australia-based migrants help in crises abroad.*

NOTES ON CONTRIBUTORS

Melissa Phillips is a Lecturer in the School of Social Sciences at Western Sydney University. Her research focuses on migration, diaspora, migrant and refugee settlement and multiculturalism. She has a background in working for international NGOs and currently serves on the Board of the Australian Red Cross and the International Detention Coalition.

Sarah Prout Quicke is a Senior Lecturer in Geography at The University of Western Australia and a Research Fellow in the UWA Africa Research & Engagement Centre (AfREC). Her research examines population, development and social policy issues in Indigenous Australia and Africa, with particular focus on population mobility and migration.

Mary B. Setrana is a Senior Lecturer at the Centre for Migration Studies, University of Ghana, Legon; and a Research Associate, Faculty of Humanities, University of Johannesburg, South Africa. She has published widely including on migration decisions to Europe, gender, transnational migration and diasporas and return migration and reintegration.

Muhammad Dan Suleiman is a Research Fellow in the Africa Research & Engagement Centre (AfREC) at The University of Western Australia. He is a 2020 Fellow of the United Nations' Fellowship Program for People of African Descent, and Vice President of Ghana Muslims' Association, Perth. His research interests include international politics of Africa, Australia-Africa relations, international security and decolonial thought.

Jeevika Vivekananthan is a researcher in migration-development-humanitarianism nexus. As a social researcher, she is interested in different worldviews, looking beyond mainstream for untold stories and attempting to overcome the epistemological injustices of colonialism.

LIST OF FIGURES

Fig. 5.1   Refugee diasporas in Australia   95
Fig. 5.2   RDO characteristics   99
Fig. 6.1   A Model for understanding diaspora humanitarianism   121

CHAPTER 1

Introduction

Louise Olliff and Melissa Phillips

Societies that rely on migration create diasporas. This may be the unintended consequence of both temporary and permanent migration in countries of large-scale immigration. It is arguably the most tangible impact of decades of immigration in a country such as Australia, whereby the descendants of migrants go on to settle locally while in many cases maintaining ties with their country of origin. Cumulatively this can result in strong, rich diaspora communities with deep contextual knowledge of their home countries, well-maintained transnational connections and a unique perspective on countries of emigration. Diaspora members and diaspora communities contend with this lived reality. From a wider societal perspective, understanding the many dimensions of diaspora development is critical for matters of integration, multiculturalism, international relations and foreign policy, and social cohesion.

L. Olliff (✉)
School of Regulation and Global Governance, Australian National University, Canberra, ACT, Australia
e-mail: louise.olliff@anu.edu.au

M. Phillips
Western Sydney University, Penrith, NSW, Australia
e-mail: melissa.phillips@westernsydney.edu.au

© The Author(s), under exclusive license to Springer Nature
Switzerland AG 2022
M. Phillips, L. Olliff (eds.), *Understanding Diaspora Development*,
https://doi.org/10.1007/978-3-030-97866-2_1

Understanding processes of diasporization—of people who reside primarily outside a self-defined 'home-land' coming together through the construction of a shared identity—and what this means for societal transformation ('development'), is an area that is marked by conceptual challenges (Tölölyan, 2007). Debates and tensions about the utility of the diaspora concept are well worn, and relate to how we understand a phenomenon that appears both simple and observable—population dispersion across time and space shapes identities and culture (Hage, 2021) and transnational social networks (Glick Schiller, 2012) with implications for the everyday lives of people and societies in an 'age of migration' (de Haas et al., 2019) and 'super-diversity' (Vertovec, 2007). Yet, diaspora can also be a rather amorphous, broad and unsatisfactory term for conceptualizing the richly diverse and nuanced experiences and effects of and on individuals and groups who identify in such ways.

This book is a response to such questions posed by diaspora formation and development. Given the significant cultural and linguistic diversity in Australia, it has been selected as a case study through which to explore diaspora communities from political, economic, social and cultural perspectives. Chapters demonstrate and grapple with the usefulness of 'diaspora' as a concept to explore the experiences of migrant and refugee communities in Australia. They showcase a wide range of diaspora experiences and bring a grounded, temporal and territorialised understanding to notions of diasporic engagement, and foster further understanding on the peacebuilding, conflict, economic, humanitarian and political engagements of diaspora communities in Australia. The lessons gleaned from the Australian case studies provide useful examples as well as raise questions of policy and practice that are relevant to other contexts and diaspora communities in similarly multicultural regions. The insights and findings from the breadth of research showcased shed light on broader debates about diasporas, migration and development, and transnationalism.

The book is divided into four parts. In the first part on long-distance activism, Hariz Halilovich writes of 'Bosnians downunder' who are enmeshed in vibrant trans-local communities and where efforts to commemorate the 1995 genocide at Srebrenica in Australia is central to creating a shared narrative of the Bosnian diaspora as a displaced but resilient people. In Chap. 3, Susan Banki looks more closely at diaspora activism in response to more recent events, the February 2021 coup in Myanmar. In this chapter, Banki illustrates the skilful political theatre and public art of diaspora activists trying to draw attention to injustices perpetrated in their homeland. Both Banki and Halilovich explore how actors from conflict-affected and refugee diasporas draw on the knowledge of lived experience to connect, identify and influence. Both consider diaspora activists as having the potential to shift and deepen understanding within the broader Australian public and polity about conflict, genocide and the kind of world we wish to live in.

In the second part on transnational belongings, Farida Fozdar, David Mickler, Sarah Prout Quicke, Mary Setrana, Muhammad Dan Suleiman and Dominic Dagbanja present findings from a Delphi study that explores the transnational economic engagements of the Kenyan and Ghanaian diaspora, describing the political economy of the Australia-Africa nexus (Chap. 4). These authors identify challenges and avenues for a more robust two-way relationship between the two continents that would benefit actors at different levels, including diaspora members engaged in trade and investment, establishing businesses, remittance flows, and other economic activities. In Chap. 5, Louise Olliff considers how refugee diasporas as a sub-set of diasporas are involved in acts of helping 'their people' living in displacement contexts overseas. This chapter offers an analysis of how Australia's long-standing Refugee and Humanitarian Program and the integration context structures and enables refugee diaspora humanitarianism with implications for the global refugee regime.

Following on from this, in the third part on Responding to War, Conflict and Disaster, Jeevika Vivekananthan and Phil Connors hone in on the ways in which diaspora communities in Australia respond to disasters in Pacific Island countries (Chap. 6). These authors call for a decolonizing of both knowledge and practices of humanitarianism, pointing to the potential role that diaspora leaders can play in bridging local and international understandings and practices in response to crises. In Chap. 7, Atem Atem, Jennifer Balint, Denise Cauchi and Shyama Fuad explore the role diaspora play in peacebuilding through case studies of the South Sudanese and Sri Lankan diasporas. The authors argue that the work done to foster inter-ethnic harmony in the Australian context plays a significant role in conflict resolution and peace-making in countries of origin for diaspora who are extended or trans-local members of 'homeland' communities. In Chap. 8, Sara Maher, Nicki Kindersley, Freddie Carver and Santino Atem Deng continue this thread by looking at the interplay of transnational kinship systems and conflict among the South Sudanese community in Melbourne and Juba and at how this 'thick' transnationalism can have both positive and negative effects.

In the final section on future imaginings, Olga Oleinikova considers the crucial role diasporas play in processes of democratization, focusing on the Ukrainian experience to think through diaspora and democracy as post-territorial phenomena. This chapter finds that Ukraine's democratic development has happened not just inside the country, but also from abroad (Chap. 9). In the final chapter, Melissa Phillips turns our attention to the Australian public policy environment and how this enables or ignores diaspora as an outcome of the country's approach to both migration and multiculturalism. In this, Phillips reviews how diaspora communities are considered and engage with government institutions and the policy landscape and what Australia might learn about diaspora engagement from other parts of the world.

Before detailing further the findings from these interconnected and rich explorations of diaspora engagement, it is necessary to set the scene for the understandings of diaspora today. Diaspora is a contested and dynamic concept. A recent large-scale synthesis of literature on diaspora (Grossman, 2019) highlights the ongoing contestations about the concept and the term 'diaspora' in scholarly research. Grossman points to unresolved contestation, the foremost ontological debate being between 'those who view diasporas as discrete entities or groups—something that is "out there" and can be explicitly defined and measured—and those who regard diaspora as a social construction—a process through which spokespersons create and appropriate diasporic discourse, consciousness and identity and use them to claim and mobilize putative constituencies' (pp. 2-3). At the same time, Grossman offers a definition that he posits can go some way toward bridging this divide: 'Diaspora is a transnational community whose members (or their ancestors) emigrated or were dispersed from their original homeland but remain oriented to it and preserve a group identity' (p. 5). By seeking to come up with a 'de-contested' definition of diaspora, Grossman draws attention to the need for concepts to provide explanatory power that can be used to bring researchers, policy-makers and others in dialogue with each other to explain or theorize the phenomenon.

The terms diaspora and transnationalism have often accompanied one another and transnationalism is a key term in Grossman's recent definition. Indeed, the intersections of diaspora and the experience and effects of migration, globalization, state pluralism and governance, have been a robust area of exploration and elaboration in recent years. Key areas of discussion focusing on diaspora transnationalism have taken place within a range of disciplinary and interdisciplinary debates, including those of migration and development studies (Glick Schiller & Salazar, 2013; Cohen, 2008; Nyberg-Sørensen, 2007; Vertovec & Cohen, 1999); peace and conflict studies (Gamlen, 2014; Budabin, 2014; Spear, 2006); economics, particularly relating to remittances and trade (see e.g. Fullilove, 2008; Monsutti, 2004; Singh, 2012); sociology, anthropology and political science, including around identity, race, long-distance nationalism and its effects (see e.g. Phillips, 2013; Betts & Jones, 2016; Halilovich, 2012) and gender studies on transnational families and social networks of care (Al-Sharmani, 2010; Baak, 2015). Fozdar et al reaffirm in Chap. 4 that transnationalism can be defined as the 'regular and sustained' cross-border activities of individuals (Portes et al., 1999) as a condition where 'transmigrants … maintain, build, and reinforce multiple linkages with their countries of origin' (Glick-Schiller et al., 1995, p. 52). These linkages may take a range of forms, including social, cultural, political and economic engagements.

As explored in Chaps. 4, 5 and 6, transnationalism has multiple and shifting attributes, the outcomes of which are mixed. Nevertheless, it is a critical dimension of diaspora belonging that brings forth what Halilovich describes as the 'complex social realities … where they meet their social needs and perform their 'Bosnian' identities' (Chap. 2). Unlike diaspora groups in the past, that were prevented (or banned) from maintaining active connections with their original homelands, the contemporary diaspora groups described in this volume use both real and virtual space to transcend the 'diaspora-homeland' boundaries—posed by space, time, culture and politics—to (re)create and sustain a sense of belonging to both their old and their new homelands. That sense of belonging is not purely symbolic but manifests itself in a variety of concrete ways—from long-distance political activism to economic exchange and philanthropy—and represents a real and often unacknowledged potential for development.

While the ground may be fertile, there is also much more to be explored through research on how the Australian context enables or constrains diaspora communities and diaspora transnationalism in its many and varied forms. This is an area that has significant policy relevance and is the focus of Chap. 10. In its 2017 Foreign Policy White Paper, the Australian Government made reference to the role of diaspora communities, stating:

These communities often have the connections, language skills and cultural understanding to assist Australia to deepen ties with other countries. They help to facilitate trade and investment, including by sharing information on overseas markets and customs. Diaspora communities can also influence how Australia is perceived internationally. Our diaspora communities often contribute to developing countries through remittances. They also have the knowledge and networks to help improve our understanding of development and humanitarian issues in other countries. The Government is committed to working with diaspora communities to promote Australia's image and reputation, to encourage trade and investment and, where appropriate, to support our development assistance program. (Commonwealth of Australia, 2017, p. 107)

As Chap. 10 details, there is limited evidence of this commitment having since been translated into policy or programmatic outcomes. There is preliminary work being conducted by community organizations and international non-government organizations to enable and amplify the transnational engagements and impacts of diaspora communities in particular areas of peacebuilding, development and humanitarian action (see Danish Refugee Council, 2017; Diaspora Action Australia, 2018). This has not been widely explored in the fields of diaspora studies and international relations, despite a large body of research in similar migrant-receiving countries, such as the United States of America and the United Kingdom. One particular element emerging from the policy domain is the relationship between the state and diasporas, and the role of diasporas in democratic processes in their home country. This is the focus of Chap. 9 which considers the context in Ukraine, to raise important questions about territory matters and connectivity between diasporas and sending countries.

Question of how diaspora communities are transformed by living in a world of heightened virtual connectivity is a recurring theme throughout this volume. The connectivity enabled by social media and other communication technologies and its implications for identities and social networks are made clear in many of the chapters. From Halilovich's description of the 'simultaneous' events commemorating genocide in Srebrenica and Prijedor online and onsite moving and connecting Bosnians across the world in both time and space, to Maher et al.'s exploration of online information-sharing practices within South Sudanese transnational kinship networks that are both an important means for affected communities to keep track of conflict, but also act as a source of re-traumatization, these windows into contemporary diaspora experiences are telling.

While the influence of Australian migration and diaspora policies on development in countries of origin has been considered (Hugo, 2005), there is a need to continually monitor the policy landscape and its impact on development, especially in strategic regions such as the Pacific (Pyke et al., 2012). Chapter 6 provides a timely focus on Pacific diaspora humanitarianism through a diaspora-centered perspective that calls to attention the critical value of diaspora support, particularly in areas affected by climate change. Diaspora humanitarianism is a growing area of research to which the Australian context has lessons to offer, as Chap. 5 also indicates. This latter chapter reminds us that approaching diaspora transnationalism through a simplified dichotomy of 'homelands' and 'hostlands' overlooks the webs of connections of forcibly displaced communities, whose transnational engagements and practices may be focused on sites of displacement even where their orientation is toward a different 'home' (Koinova, 2021).

A temporal approach has also been lacking following the formation and transformation of more newly arrived diaspora communities, such as the South Sudanese, Bhutanese and Hazara, and also considering how diasporic association transforms over time (Goodman, 2000; Betts & Jones, 2016). In Chap. 7, Atem et al review peacebuilding activities undertaken by South Sudanese and Sri Lankan refugees and migrants from an Australian base, approaching diasporas as a category of practice and an identity. Building on this, Chapter 8 takes the view from Australia to look at South Sudan's global diaspora network and explores how conflict (and concomitant economic crises) significantly increased regional demand for diaspora personal and financial support, and also how it re-politicized kinship systems and personal actions, placing social and familial networks under considerable strain. In this chapter, Maher et al illustrate the complex dynamics where transnationalism can clearly have both positive and negative effects, which pose questions for national and international policy-makers as to how their approach could help bring out the best features of globally connected diaspora communities and mitigate the more problematic elements.

This book provides a timely contribution to the development of research-informed policy, both in the Australian context and more broadly. Its contributions build on the understanding of the complex drivers and domains of diaspora transnationalism and its implications for countries and people striving to develop human capabilities in a globally interconnected but also fractured world.

The Editors would like to acknowledge the especially challenging conditions under which this book has been completed, with authors contending with multiple prolonged lockdowns during the Covid-19 pandemic.

REFERENCES

Al-Sharmani, M. (2010). Transnational Family Networks in the Somali Diaspora in Egypt: Women's Roles and Differentiated Experiences. *Gender, Place & Culture: A Journal of Feminist Geography, 17*(4), 499–518. https://doi.org/1 0.1080/0966369X.2010.485843

Baak, M. (2015). Transnational Families, Remittances, Cieng and Obligation for Dinka Women in Australia. *Emotion, Space and Society, 16*, 123–129.

Betts, A., & Jones, W. (2016). *Mobilising the Diaspora: How Refugees Challenge Authoritarianism.* Cambridge University Press.

Budabin, A. (2014). Diasporas as Development Partners for Peace? The Alliance Between the Darfuri Diaspora and the Save Darfur Coalition. *Third World Quarterly, 35*(1), 163–180. https://doi.org/10.1080/01436597.2014.868996

Cohen, R. (2008). *Global Diasporas: An Introduction* (2nd ed.). New York: Routledge.

Commonwealth of Australia. (2017). *Foreign Policy White Paper.* Retrieved 13 September 2021, from https://www.dfat.gov.au/publications/minisite/2017-foreign-policy-white-paper/fpwhitepaper/index.html

Danish Refugee Council (2017). *Split Loyalties: Mixed Migration and the Diaspora Connection.* RMMS Discussion Paper 4. DRC.

Diaspora Action Australia (2018). *Understanding Diaspora-led Development & Peace-Building.* Melbourne: Diaspora Action Australia.

Fullilove, M. (2008). *World Wide Webs: Diasporas and the International System.* Lowy Institute for International Policy.

Gamlen, A. (2014). Diaspora Institutions and Diaspora Governance. *International Migration Review, 48*(1), 180–217.

Glick Schiller, N. (2012). Transnationality, Migrants and Cities. In A. Amelina, D. Nergiz, T. Faist, et al. (Eds.), *Beyond Methodological Nationalism: Research Methodologies for Cross-Border Studies* (pp. 23–40). Routledge.

Glick Schiller, N., & Salazar, N. B. (2013). Regimes of Mobility Across the Globe. *Journal of Ethnic and Migration Studies, 39*(2), 183–200.

Glick-Schiller, N., Basch, L., & Blanc, C. (1995). From Immigrant to Transmigrant: Theorizing Transnational Migration. *Anthropological Quarterly, 68*(1), 48–63.

Goodman, J. (2000). Marginalisation and Empowerment: East Timorese Diaspora Politics in Australia. *Communal/Plural, 8*(1), 25–46. https://doi.org/10.1080/13207870050001448

Grossman, J. (2019). Toward a Definition of Diaspora. *Ethnic and Racial Studies, 42*(8), 1263–1282. https://doi.org/10.1080/01419870.2018.1550261

de Haas, H., Castles, S., & Miller, M. J. (2019). *The Age of Migration* (6th ed.). Red Globe Press.

Hage, G. (2021). *The Diasporic Condition: Ethnographic Explorations of the Lebanese in the World.* The University of Chicago Press.

Halilovich, H. (2012). Trans–local Communities in the Age of Transnationalism: Bosnians in Diaspora. *International Migration, 50*(1), 162–178.

Hugo, G. (2005). The New International Migration in Asia: Challenges for Population Research. *Asian Population Studies, 1*(1), 93–120. https://doi.org/10.1080/17441730500125953

Koinova, N. (2021). *Diaspora Entrepreneurs and Contested States.* Oxford University Press.

Monsutti, A. (2004). Cooperation, Remittances, and kinship Among the Hazaras. *Iranian Studies, 37*(2), 219–240.

Nyberg-Sørensen, N. (2007). In International Organization for Migration (Ed.), *Living Across Worlds: Diaspora, Development and Transnational Engagement.*

Phillips, M. (2013). Migration and Australian Foreign Policy Towards Africa: The Place of Australia's African Transnational Communities. In D. Mickler & T. Lyons (Eds.), *New Engagement: Contemporary Australian Foreign Policy Towards Africa* (pp. 176–192). Melbourne University Press.

Portes, A., Guarnizo, L. E., & Landolt, P. (1999). The Study of Transnationalism: Pitfalls and Promise of an Emergent Research Field. *Ethnic and Racial Studies, 22*(2), 217–237.

Pyke, J., Francis, S., & Ben-Moshe, D. (2012). *The Tongan Diaspora in Australia: Current and Potential Links With the Homeland.* Report from ARC Linkage Project.

Spear, J. (2006). *The Potential of Diaspora Groups to Contribute to Peace Building: A Scoping Paper.* University of Bradford, Peace Studies.

Singh, A. (2012). The Diaspora Networks of Ethnic Lobbying in Canada. *Canadian Foreign Policy Journal, 18*(3), 340–357.

Tölölyan, K. (2007). The Contemporary Discourse of Diaspora Studies. *Comparative Studies of South Asia, Africa, & the Middle East, 27,* 647–655.

Vertovec, S. (2007). Super-diversity and Its Implications. *Ethnic and Racial Studies, 30*(6), 1024–1054.

Vertovec, S., & Cohen, R. (1999). *Migration, Diasporas and Transnationalism.* Cheltenham/Northampton.

PART I

Long-distance Activism

CHAPTER 2

Long-Distance Refugee Activism: Commemorating, Recreating and Reimagining Post-Genocide Communities in Diaspora

Hariz Halilovich

INTRODUCTION

In 2011, the Parliament of Australia adopted a special motion, acknowledging the events of the 1995 genocide at Srebrenica, Bosnia and Herzegovina (hereafter: Bosnia). The motion, or the 'Srebrenica Resolution' as it is popularly known, comprises eight points stating clearly what happened at Srebrenica, who were the victims and who were the perpetrators. The full text of the resolution reads:

(1) on 11 July 1995, the Bosnian town of Srebrenica which was at that time proclaimed a Protected Zone by a United Nations Security Council Resolution of 16 April 1993, fell into the hands of the Army of Republika

---

H. Halilovich (✉)
RMIT University, Melbourne, VIC, Australia
e-mail: hariz.halilovich@rmit.edu.au

© The Author(s), under exclusive license to Springer Nature   13
Switzerland AG 2022
M. Phillips, L. Olliff (eds.), *Understanding Diaspora Development*,
https://doi.org/10.1007/978-3-030-97866-2_2

Srpska, led by General Ratko Mladic and under the direction of the then President of the Republika Srpska, Radovan Karadzic;

(2) from 12 July 1995, the Army and the Police of Republika Srpska separated men aged 16 to approximately 60 or 70 from their families;

(3) Bosnian Serb forces killed over 7000 Bosnian Muslim men following the takeover of Srebrenica in July 1995;

(4) all the executions systematically targeted Bosnian Muslim men of military age, regardless of whether they were civilians or soldiers;

(5) the acts committed at Srebrenica were committed with the specific intent to destroy in part, the group of Muslims of Bosnia and Herzegovina;

(6) these were acts of genocide, committed by members of the Army of Republika Srpska in and around Srebrenica from about 13 July 1995;

(7) these findings have been confirmed by the International Court of Justice and the International Criminal Tribunal for the former Yugoslavia through final and binding judgments; and

(8) the anniversary of the Srebrenica genocide, 11 July, should serve as a time to remember the victims. (Parliament of Australia, 2011)

While to some people it might look somewhat unusual, or even irrelevant, that the Parliament of a country on a different hemisphere, 16,000 kilometres away from Bosnia, would be concerned with something that happened in a small, faraway town in the Balkans seventeen years earlier, none of the Australian Parliamentarians felt that way; they adopted the motion solemnly and unanimously. Their motivation to spend time drafting, debating and voting such a resolution came not so much from a sense of a retrospective moral obligation, but foremost as a response to an expectation to do so by their fellow citizens (and voters); some 50,000 naturalised Australians of Bosnian background, including about 2000 survivors and people directly affected by the Srebrenica genocide who live in Australia today. They, like most of the Bosnian Australians, came to Australia as refugees during the 1990s and early 2000s.

This chapter discusses the origins, settlement patterns and political activism of the Bosnian diaspora in Australia. It is based on extensive fieldwork over the last 15 years, involving a variety of ethnographic approaches and engagements with the Bosnian diaspora communities in Australia, particularly in Melbourne, Sydney, Brisbane and Adelaide, where the bulk of the Bosnian diaspora resides. The ethnographic research has been complemented by reviewing different reports and statistical data, including those by the Australian Government's Census of Population, the Department of Home Affairs (Australia), and the Ministry of Human Rights and Refugees (Bosnia and Herzegovina).

As described in this chapter, expelled from their homes and homeland during the brutal 1992–1995 war, displaced Bosnians followed the trajectories of similar refugee groups in modern history, such as Afghans, Chileans, Vietnamese, East Timorese, Syrians and others (Day, 2017; Valenta et al., 2020): they organised themselves primarily as a political diaspora, a transnational community of Bosnian citizens with clear translocal organisational patterns, usually emerging as informal community networks and associations. While this political diaspora intersected with other forms of community making, the fact that most Bosnians ended up in Australia because of political persecution and genocide made them act and organise themselves as political émigrés rather than labour migrants, for instance. What brought and kept them together in the new faraway destination was their experiences of migration and resettlement and the shared memories of violence, genocide, flight and a homeland they might have lost forever. It can be argued that members of the Bosnian diaspora in Australia, like other similar displaced groups, need each other not only to socialise in the present and to confirm who they are now, but also to reaffirm, through shared memories, who they were in the past. The shared memories of home back in the past are complemented by the lived experiences of home—the new home, here and now, in Australia.

BOSNIANS DOWNUNDER

While in most European countries Bosnians who migrated for economic reasons or were forcibly displaced during the 1992–1995 war were regarded and 'tolerated' as temporary guest workers or refugees, who would eventually—willingly or unwillingly—go 'back home', those who arrived in Australia throughout the twentieth century, and especially during the 1990s and early 2000s, have been treated as and saw themselves as immigrants in search of a permanent resettlement (Halilovich, 2012; Valenta & Ramet, 2011). The so-called chain migration—with migrants assisting family members, friends and neighbours to migrate and join them in desired destinations—has been a key feature of Bosnian migration to Australia. In effect, to paraphrase Paul Gilroy (1995), people's roots have become their routes. Their shared 'local' origins, kinship, networks and loyalties have played an important role in the morphology of the (re)constructed diaspora groups in Australia, with the formation of distinct 'trans-local' *zavičaj* communities (Halilovich, 2013).

It is possible to identify three waves of immigration from Bosnia to Australia, each including a distinct group of people in the search of a safer life: (1) political migrants after World War II; (2) economic migrants between the 1960s and the 1980s; and (3) refugees and 'humanitarian entrants' during and after the 1992–1995 war in Bosnia (Halilovich et al., 2018). In many regards, each of the three migration waves has different social, demographic and economic characteristics. However, it is only after 1992 that we can speak about a distinct and organised Bosnian diaspora in Australia. Before the early 1990s, the immigrants from Bosnia in Australia were not only relatively small in terms of numbers, but also divided between the Yugoslav diaspora, the Croatian diaspora and the Serb diaspora, and some met their social and cultural needs within religious organisations (Jupp, 2011). Many also chose to leave the 'old' identities behind and assimilate into the mainstream Anglo-Celtic culture by residing in 'non-immigrant' neighbourhoods, cutting off their links with any diasporic groups from the region, intermarrying with people from non-Yugoslav background and changing their names to blend better into the dominant culture (Voloder, 2017).

Most of today's Australian Bosnians arrived in Australia on refugee and humanitarian visas (visa subclass 200, 202 and 204) in the mid to late 1990s and early 2000s. Their visa applications were processed in a 'transit country', such as Germany, Austria, Netherlands, Slovenia, Croatia and Serbia. A majority of those who came as part of the refugee resettlement programme had a 'proposer' who assisted them in the migration process. Usually, the 'proposer' was someone they knew (family member, former neighbours, compatriots they met in transit countries) or belonged to the Bosnian community in Australia from earlier migration waves. Some had different charities acting as their proposers. About 1000 of those with non-Bosnian proposers ended up initially in Tasmania, Australia's only island state. Most of them then relocated onshore to places like Melbourne, Adelaide and Sydney. A majority of them continue to live in the same places where they arrived or moved to shortly after their arrival. Similar relocations from one place to another—for example, from Adelaide to Melbourne, from Melbourne to Brisbane, Perth to Melbourne, or Canberra to Sydney—were not unusual during the first months and years after resettlement, but are hardly existent now. Over the last two decades, most Bosnian migrants have developed a sense of belonging to the cities and suburbs they live in. Those who move are usually younger people who follow their career paths or marry into a Bosnian community in a different city (Halilovich et al., 2018).

The refugees from Bosnia—arriving in Australia initially in dozens in 1992, then in hundreds and thousands throughout the mid and late 1990s—brought with them their emotional baggage of personal and collective trauma that inspired solidarity and patriotism among the Bosnian immigrants from the earlier migration waves. The refugees also brought knowledge and practical skills enabling them to organise politically and promote the 'Bosnian' cause. Many of them were directly involved in setting up Bosnian clubs, societies, humanitarian organisations and media outlets.

Profiling a Diaspora Community: From Bosnian Refugees to Australian Citizens

Most of the former Bosnian refugees who resettled in Australia have completed their migration cycle, not by returning to their pre-war places, but by becoming Australian citizens, settling in the 'Bosnian' suburbs and neighbourhoods and to various degrees integrating into the Australian multicultural society—socially, economically and culturally. The Bosnian diaspora organisations in Australia, such as the Australian Union of Bosnian-Herzegovinian Associations in Australia and its predecessor the Australian Council of Bosnian Organisations, estimate that the number of people with the Bosnian-Herzegovinian ancestry in Australia is somewhere around 100,000, while different conservative estimates, including those by the ABS Census data, estimate that the total number of Bosnians living in Australia is about 50,000 (ABS, 2011, 2016). Regardless of their actual number—which is somewhere between 50,000 and 100,000 people of Bosnian ancestry—today the Bosnian diaspora in Australia is a relatively well-established migrant community which has been a subject of growing interest by many researchers across different disciplines, including anthropology, history, sociology, demography, gender studies and economics (cf. Adams, 2008; Colic-Peisker, 2003, 2005; Halilovich, 2012, 2013; Haveric, 2009; Markovic & Manderson, 2002; Voloder, 2017; Vujcich, 2007; Waxman, 1999).

In Australia, as in many other countries of settlement, the Bosnian refugees were seen as immigrants with 'high integration potential' (Valenta & Strabac, 2013). Their European background, educational levels and skills have been significant factors for such a positive reception of the Bosnian refugees in Australia (Colic-Peisker, 2005). However, while these factors might have been helpful to the migrants and refugees from Bosnia in the initial stages of their settlement in Australia, they have not necessarily been directly translated into a competitive advantage in the Australian labour market, where Bosnians coming from a non-English speaking background and having a high proportion of women often ended up in low-paid jobs for which they were overqualified (Colic-Peisker, 2003; Halilovich, 2013).

The gender ratio, relating to a higher percentage of women than men in the Bosnian diaspora in Australia, was captured by the Census statistics in 2006, 2011 and 2016, with the overall gender ratio 97.1 males per 100 females (ABS, 2006, 2011, 2016). The statistics also reveal a generational pattern showing that women outnumber men for all age groups between 35 and 55 years of age. These statistics can be directly linked to the 1992–1995 war that took the lives mostly of men, while many women became war widows. Several thousand war widows and their families from Bosnia migrated to Australia in the aftermath of the war. The reason why so many of the war widows migrated to Australia can be found in Australia's Humanitarian and Refugee Program, which gave preference to applicants under the 'Women at Risk' category (Halilovich, 2019).

While the immigration and integration policies of each individual host country have affected the integration patterns of the Bosnian refugees and migrants into the host societies, in Australia shifting their legal status from refugees to Australian citizens has been a quite straightforward process, as almost all of some 35,000 Bosnians who arrived on permanent humanitarian visas in the 1990s were eligible to apply for Australian citizenship after two years of residence in the country (Department of Home Affairs, 2016).[1] Factors such as age, level of education, social networks and socioeconomic background have influenced the degree of Bosnians' integration into mainstream Australian society upon their settling in the country, but not their access to citizenship. Australian citizenship for Bosnian refugees and migrants has had primarily a practical purpose, enabling them, as bearers of Australian passports, to travel freely to most countries across the

---

[1] Since then, this has changed to four years of living in Australia on a permanent resident visa.

world without the need for visas, something they were deprived of with their Bosnian travel documents. The dual citizenship, Bosnian and Australian, increasingly reflects Australian Bosnians' dual sense of belonging. That sense of dual belonging is not only represented by the official documents or private sentiments, but also corresponds with their social relationships in both countries as almost Australian Bosnians have close family and friends back in Bosnia, with whom they regularly keep in touch via phone and social media, and whom they visit whenever circumstances and finances allow.

Australian citizenship has enabled Bosnian refugees also to access subsidised higher education, apply for certain government jobs and become active participants in the political life in their adopted country. In the meantime, a number of Bosnians have joined Australian political parties and some of them have run as candidates for local and state governments. Most of the politically active migrants from Bosnia are members of or vote for the centre-left Australian Labour Party (ALP), while a significant number of them are aligned closely with the centre-right Liberal Party (LPA). Both dominant political parties in Australia have among their ranks elected members with Bosnian ancestry. In 2010, one of them, Ed Husic, an ALP member, became the 'first Muslim elected to the Australian Federal Parliament and the first MP sworn in by the Chief Justice of the High Court with his hand on a copy of the Koran' (Wilson, 2010). Another prominent Bosnian-born politician is Inga Peulich, an LPA member, who served in the Legislative Council in the Parliament of Victoria as Member for the South-eastern Metropolitan Region for 12 years (2006–2018). At a popular level, members of the Bosnian diaspora have displayed some pride in having given two 'Miss Australia' in recent years: in 2014 Monika Radulović and in 2017 Esma Voloder. Similarly, when playing well and not creating any controversies, the Australian tennis player Bernard Tomic (born to Bosnian-Croatian refugee parents in Germany) gets claimed by both the Bosnian and the Croatian diaspora.

The achievements of Bosnians in Australia might give the impression that Bosnian refugees have had a smooth integration into the Australian multicultural society. To a degree, compared to the earlier refugee waves, this is true as the official policy of multiculturalism adopted by the Australian Government in the 1970s has been very favourable to Bosnian and other emerging ethnic and national migrant communities in Australia. The Australian Government continues to allocate substantial resources to support language, cultural, social and recreational programmes of migrant and refugee communities and their organisations. While, for instance, some older migrant communities in Australia, such as the Maltese, took several decades to develop their own community infrastructure, the Bosnian diaspora achieved this within a decade (York, 1998). They followed the paths paved by the older migrant communities in Australia and established their community organisations, sports clubs, language schools, places of worship and other essential infrastructure needed for a community to make itself visible and meet its specific cultural and social needs. Thanks to the activities of these diaspora organisations, community activists and prominent individuals coming from the Bosnian background, Bosnians in Australia enjoy generally a good reputation, while many Australians have learned about Bosnia through their friends, colleagues and neighbours of Bosnian background.

The Diaspora's Role in Post-war Recovery and Development Initiatives 'Back Home'

While the Bosnian refugees in Australia have developed a strong diaspora infrastructure and integrated relatively well into the Australian society, the situation in their original homeland continues to be dominated by the legacies of the 1992–1995 war in Bosnia. In many ways, the country continues to rely on its diaspora's support and remittances (Williams & Efendic, 2019). The physical distance between Bosnia and Australia has not been a deterrent for the members of the Bosnian diaspora to engage with various humanitarian, development and business initiatives in their first homeland. Most of such development initiatives relate to the localities and regions where they originally come from, but Bosnians in Australia have also supported broader initiatives, such as collecting donations for flood-affected regions in Bosnia or responding to charitable initiatives relating to places and people they do not know. Among others, major charitable activities have included collecting funds for rebuilding schools and community infrastructure destroyed in the war; supporting various ad-hoc humanitarian initiatives; and providing scholarships to students in many parts of the country. Australian Bosnians also regularly respond to public appeals and make donations for various causes not directly relating to Bosnia or Australia, including the recent series of refugee crises across the world (Halilovich et al., 2018).

2 LONG-DISTANCE REFUGEE ACTIVISM: COMMEMORATING, RECREATING... 21

In terms of the visible development initiatives, there are several examples involving Australian-Bosnians' investments in the development of their local communities back in Bosnia. They range from rebuilding homes and local infrastructure to running long-distance businesses in Bosnia from Australia. Such examples include: a truck tyre business based in Bihać, run by two Bosnians from Bihać living in Melbourne; a family from the eastern Bosnian town of Žepa living in Adelaide who have built a very impressive (and the only) hotel with a restaurant in their original hometown, operating throughout the year despite the owners' absence for most of the year; a Bosnian businesswoman living in Sydney who has expanded her business in real estate and the building industry to Bosnia; a businesswoman from Melbourne who established the first commercial research centre in post-war Sarajevo; and many others. There is also a reverse example of a returnee from Australia who has continued managing his business in the education sector based in Sydney—from his home in Sarajevo. Similar is a story featured in the *Australian Financial Review* of a Bosnian businessman who has established a factory near Sarajevo, producing special building material (façade) for the regional and international markets (Bleby, 2017). There are many other examples involving returnees and part-time returnees to Bosnia, from those running small- and medium-size businesses to those using their properties acquired in Australia to generate rental income which sustains their often quite comfortable lifestyles in Bosnia (Halilovich et al., 2018). These and similar examples are evidence of an increasing number of members of the Bosnian diaspora living and working transnationally and being involved in an ongoing mobility, enabled by their dual citizenship.

Along with the traditional migrant remittances, which about 65 per cent of Bosnian diaspora in Australia continue to send to Bosnia, the most significant form of development support comes from the actual visits to Bosnia by the 'Bosnian Australians' (Halilovich et al., 2018). While their earlier visits were mostly motivated by visiting close relatives, their behaviour has been increasingly matching the patterns of international tourists. This especially applies to the diaspora-born Australian Bosnians, who in addition to visiting the local places of their parents and grandparents also spend time travelling through Bosnia and visiting tourist and other destinations across the country. Thus, they directly contribute to the 'diaspora visits' effect as an important economic boost to many local communities (Efendic et al., 2014). These visits usually take place during the European summer months between June and September. Unsurprisingly, since the travel restrictions due to the COVID-19 pandemic were imposed in early 2020, many local communities have suffered economically as well as in terms of their social and cultural exchanges between diaspora and homeland Bosnians.

One of the important and newly emerging development contributions of the Bosnian diaspora relates to the knowledge transfer between Australia and Bosnia (Adams, 2008). Several Bosnian academics and experts from different fields, members of the Australian Bosnian Academic Forum, have been involved in driving and facilitating these exchanges in a number of ways: from taking Australian students and researchers on study tours to Bosnia, to organising and participating in conferences in Bosnia and Australia, to acting as visiting scholars at Bosnian universities, to facilitating exchange agreements between the universities in these two countries, to assisting students from Bosnia to study in Australia. Many of these initiatives have been ongoing and continue to grow, even though they had to be paused or be moved online during the COVID-19 pandemic.

(Trans)local Communities at Global and Transnational Junctures

While the macro-level perspective and different statistics reveal much interesting information about 'Bosnians in Australia', or 'Australian-Bosnians', the complex social realities are better understood if we go below the statistical and collective categories and explore the lives of ordinary 'former' Bosnian refugees and migrants, in the actual places where they live and the settings where they meet their social needs and fulfil their 'Bosnian' identities.

In addition to language (or languages and dialects), as with other diasporic communities, the Bosnian diaspora in Australia has been consolidated around a shared past—especially the most recent past involving war, genocide and forced migration. Their collective narrative and experience have been rooted in both social reality and social imaginary. The different aspects of common socio-cultural characteristics and shared values are manifest in a variety of formal and informal social networks that make up the Bosnian diaspora in Australia. Formal networks are usually constituted around a particular aspect of shared identity such as language, nationality, ethnicity or religion—forms of more abstract or 'imagined' group identities, as Anderson (1983) famously put it. In addition to those 'broader

2 LONG-DISTANCE REFUGEE ACTIVISM: COMMEMORATING, RECREATING... 23

identities' and formal networks, there are also many more informal networks with a strong social 'glue' representing real relationships based on family background, kinship, friendship, dialect and place of origin—such as a particular region, city, village or neighbourhood. These bonds play an important cohesive factor in diaspora as they very often link different individuals and groups to a network of like-minded people representing their collective identity and local particularity within the broader Bosnian diaspora. This phenomenon has been described as translocalism (cf. Appadurai, 1995; Wise & Velayutham, 2008; Halilovich, 2012, 2013), which avoids some of the limitations that the term transnationalism implies.

While some scholars of transnationalism, like Guarnizo and Smith (1998) and Mahler (1998), for instance, recognise the presence and reproduction of 'trans-localities' within the transnational or diaspora process, it is most often the case that transnational process and practices are understood to focus foremost on the production of ethnic and national identities across nation-state borders. Glick Schiller et al. (1999) define transnationalism as 'processes by which immigrants build social fields that link together their country of origin and their country of settlement'; while Vertovec (1999) understands transnationalism as 'multiple ties and interactions linking people or institutions across the borders of nation states'. Similarly, Kearney (1995, p. 548) writes that the 'cultural-political dimension of transnationalism is signalled by its resonance with nationalism as a cultural and political project'. While the concept of transnationalism, as outlined by Glick Schiller et al. (1999), Vertovec (1999) and Kearney (1995, p. 548), seems to be accommodating to various immigrants' identities, it still emphasises states and their formal institutions and underemphasises social factors and identities rooted in a particular locality and specific cultural experiences that often lie beyond—or below—the political supra identities.

The concept of transnationalism, as Al-Ali et al. (2001) argue, is especially limited when it comes to interpreting the complexities of refugee identities and experiences involving forced migration from ancestral homes, and often dramatic separation from spatial practices and identities associated with a particular place. In fact, refugees and the forcibly displaced are very often victims of 'nationalism as a cultural and political project' and would not see themselves as part of its larger, transnational form. Cano (2005, p. 12) goes as far as to claim that 'the use of the term 'transnationalism' has been transformed to a point in which it is practically impossible to sustain the broader sense of the term beyond its generic root'. While not dismissing transnationalism as an explanatory frame in migration studies, this concept has its limitations when exploring the relationship between place, movement, identity and memory in forcefully displaced communities from Bosnia, including those who settled in Australia (Halilovich, 2013, 2019).

Most Bosnian refugees who migrated to Australia under the Refugee and Humanitarian Program during the 1990s and in the early 2000s come from the areas and places such as Srebrenica and Prijedor that were devasted by the war, both in terms of loss of human life and material destruction of *zavičaj*. The concept of *zavičaj*, a barely translatable term, encompasses the wholeness of person-in-place and place-in-person, which in English translates as home, homeland, community, home country, and native place as well as village, county, region, town, and city (Halilovich & Adams, 2013). The sociological concept of *Gemeinschaft* comes close to *zavičaj*'s sense of community, social network and home, a social reality and lived experience for discrete groups, as well as a metaphor for modalities that go beyond conventional state or party-based modes of social organisation. For many people in Bosnia and the former Yugoslavia—especially those who were forcibly displaced—the term *zavičaj* evokes deep feelings of belonging to and nostalgia for a place that is or was the intimate and ultimate home (Halilovich, 2013). The settlement patterns of Bosnian refugees in Australia have been greatly influenced by the local and regional belongings or *zavičaj* from back home, so much so that, for instance, there are whole neighbourhoods where people settled in close proximity to their former neighbours and those with whom they share(d) a common *zavičaj* back in Bosnia.

Such communities can be found in almost every place where Bosnians have settled—such as Melbourne's suburbs of Deer Park, St. Albans, Noble Park, Dandenong and Springvale; Sydney's suburbs of Fairfield, Liverpool, Blacktown, and Hurstville; Brisbane's southern suburbs, including Acacia Ridge, Sunnybank, Runcorn, Kuraby and Eight Mile Plains; and in Perth's suburb of Mirrabooka, Beechboro, Balga and Morley. Similar patterns are clearly identifiable in many other Bosnian diaspora groups in other parts of Australia.

What this suggests is that the Bosnian diaspora communities in Australia and in some 50 other countries, as expressions of collective identities and local particularities, have not been created as a spontaneous reaction to forced displacement, but have involved the active participation of individuals who have made deliberate and informed decisions when choosing destinations for their resettlement. As illustrated in this chapter, in most cases 'local' factors played a decisive role in the migration patterns and social morphology of migrant communities, and translocal factors and patterns of migration are present in the Bosnian diaspora worldwide. The translocal identity and chain migration of Bosnian diaspora communities are in no way unique to Bosnians, nor are they new phenomena. As Sowell (1996, p. 7) points out, some 90 per cent of immigrants to Australia, over a period of half a century, came via the chain migration process. However, in relation to Bosnia, 'chain migration' has created a vibrant global network of translocal communities in both real and cyber space (Halilovich & Kučuk, 2020).

Ethnographies on the role local factors play in migration patterns have been produced by Peleikis (2000), who researched dislocated Lebanese refugees in the Ivory Coast; Capo Zmegac (2007), who completed an ethnographic study on Croatian economic migrants in Germany; Velayutham and Wise (2005), who wrote about a 'trans-local village' made up of South Indians living in Singapore; and Portis-Winner (2002), who conducted a comparative ethnographic study of Slovene villagers and their ethnic relatives in the USA. These case studies in many respects mirror the migration patterns and translocal communities of Bosnians in Australia.

By referring to these translocal networks as communities, I do not imply that they are mainly 'imagined communities', as Anderson (1983) and Appadurai (1995) would argue, nor that they are purely 'concrete communities'. They are rather both increasingly imagined as well as made up of concrete social relations. As described here and in my previous works (cf. Halilovich, 2012, 2013, 2019), these two aspects of communal identities (imagined and concrete) are encapsulated by memory—shared, embodied and performed—creating a sense of 'global intimacy' among members of such re-territorialised groups.

The translocal communities, such as re-territorialised Srebrenica or Prijedor in Melbourne, supersede and give precise and concrete expression to broader identities, and have many 'micro ethnic' qualities of their own—including a recognisable vernacular dialect, cultural enactments and rituals, shared history, and a common feeling of belonging to a specific region, town or village. To borrow Herzfeld's words, translocal communities are like '"interior ethnonyms' ... proactive in promoting a sense of local cultural and moral autonomy and dignity" (1997, p. 16).

These translocal groups within the Bosnian diaspora in Australia are not only concerned with nurturing nostalgia for the home lost and with preservation of their distinct local folklore. There are also economic, charitable and political activities that justify and reinforce their existence. For instance, a number of businesses, predominantly in the building industry, run by members of such communities in Australia are almost exclusively staffed by fellow 'translocals'. Similar trends also exist among the Bosnian diaspora in USA and in Sweden with businesses run by Bosnians who prefer to employ 'their own people' (Halilovich & Efendic, 2019). This reflects social patterns and moral economies from the 'original' home. It is firstly about communal solidarity and trust; but it is also about the status of the individual within the wider network of their translocal community. For instance, information about *Silvertown Construction*, a building company based in Melbourne, and its owner Alen, originally from Srebrenica, has been primarily disseminated by those he employs, fellow locals from the Srebrenica region. Within the wider translocal Srebrenica network, it is known that Alen "has made it over there in Australia" and is a successful and generous employer. Alen's loyalty to his native region (*zavičaj*) is further exemplified by the name he gave to his company, *Silvertown*, being the English translation of his Bosnian hometown of Srebrenica. All this helps Alen maintain his translocal status of respect as an 'elder' in his deterritorialized community made up of several translocal sister communities spread across the globe. The same could be said for Dzeno, a successful Bosnian entrepreneur in Melbourne, who is respected within the Prijedor translocal network for providing support to his native region, for employing his fellow *Prijedorčani* (people from Prijedor), and for generous donations to charitable causes. In terms of what the status mobilises—and also in terms of human and financial capital—these translocal community networks have been pivotal in providing investment and generating employment not only in diaspora—but also in the local communities back in Bosnia, as Efendic et al. (2014), Williams and Efendic (2019) and Halilovich and Efendic (2019) have described.

Diaspora Translocalism in Action

As described earlier in the chapter, charitable and fundraising events for a 'good cause' back home or in the diaspora are the most widespread non-profit activities of translocal groups in Australia. Many charitable actions are intrinsically political and function as performative enactments of identity and memory. Both translocal Srebrenica and Prijedor communities regularly hold fundraising events in places like Melbourne and other cities in Australia. Such events are advertised in the community media, such as 3ZZZ Radio and the SBS Radio Program in Bosnian, as well as through a variety of social media platforms and apps, mobile phones and word-of-mouth. The events, usually hosted by a single translocal group, are not exclusive but open to all members of the Bosnian community as well as to the sympathetic groups and individuals coming from other communities. The events involve a mix of adopted practices from the host society and what is considered to be the traditional Bosnian way of supporting charitable causes. They are commonly organised in either community-based venues or at commercial receptions and involve a prescribed (or expected) level of formality, such as dress code, a live band playing Bosnian and sometimes English music, dancing *kolo*, serving Bosnian-style food such as *ćevapčići* and plenty of both alcoholic and non-alcoholic beverages. The adopted Australian elements include selling raffles and auctioning donated goods and services to the audience. The funds collected from the sold raffle tickets, auctions and donations are then used by the group organising the event to support different causes back in Bosnia.

Such events act as more than performances of long-distance local patriotism. Through mobilising members of the wider Bosnian diaspora in Melbourne for their cause, the members of Srebrenica and Prijedor translocal communities demonstrate the power of their social capital 'over here' which a specific local community 'back home' would benefit from. Similar use of social networks of refugees in exile, employed to advance the interest of the local communities 'back home', have been described by Diaz-Briquets and Perez-Lopez (1997), who explored the social networks and remittances among Cuban and Nicaraguan refugees in the USA, by Van Hear and Cohen (2017), who compared the global Sri Lankan Tamil diaspora and the Russian-speaking minorities in the Soviet successor states, and by Olliff (2018), who discussed Oromo, Palestinian, Iraqi and Karen diaspora communities in Australia. All these different case studies suggest that the causes of displacement of these social groups have a major bearing on how refugee and minority diasporas perceive their relationship with their countries of origin and the communities they come from.

The members of Srebrenica and Prijedor communities use the fundraising occasions to remember their war-torn communities, but also to inspire other members of the Bosnian diaspora in Melbourne to 'remember' Srebrenica and Prijedor, though most of these people might never been in the actual places. Furthermore, these translocal communities demonstrate an ability to influence social change in 'their' old places from far away. On the one hand, rebuilding a destroyed school, mosque or road serves to send a message of defiance—even from a distance—to those who destroyed it: "We haven't forgotten. We are back! You haven't defeated us!" Indeed, these words of defiance were often used in the speeches delivered at several fundraising events that I attended and observed in Melbourne and in other places and countries. On the other hand, the charitable actions demonstrate practical solidarity with the members of their communities, especially with those who actually returned to their shattered villages, neighbourhoods and towns in Bosnia. Despite the fact that the 'former' refugees from Srebrenica and Prijedor, now residing in Melbourne, have been living far from their original communities in Bosnia, they continue to participate in their everyday lives much more than in a purely symbolic way. Some of the individual members might have restored—or possibly even improved—their standing within their old neighbourhood by taking its story to a translocal or global level.

For instance, rebuilding mosques in and around Srebrenica and Prijedor that were systematically targeted and destroyed during the 1992–1995 Bosnian war has been much more than about creating a place for worship for the Muslim survivors of 'ethnic cleansing' and genocide. Very often, those zealously involved in collecting funds and coordinating the building of mosques in post-war Bosnia are not necessarily observant Muslims. Particularly in 'ethnically cleansed' small village communities around Prijedor and Srebrenica, reconstructed mosques serve not only as places of worship but also as monuments to the recent past and shrines to community members who perished in the war. As it was widely described (cf. Riedlmayer, 2002), mosques—as symbols of the collective cultural identity of Bosnian Muslims—were thoroughly obliterated by Serb militias during the war. Therefore, rebuilding the destroyed mosques as important cultural landmarks is regarded by many survivors—both those who returned and those who migrated overseas—as an essential, sometimes as the final, step in a symbolic return and social reconstruction of war-torn communities.

The stories of the translocal communities of Prijedor and Srebrenica in Melbourne, are two examples amongst many that demonstrate how, in Foucauldian terms, the popular memory of ordinary people in diaspora is performed and turned into action—hence power—in (un)making histories from below (Foucault, 1977). What these examples demonstrate is how memory-making and -unmaking processes are defined but not limited by place and displacement.

REMEMBRANCES OF THE SREBRENICA GENOCIDE AND THE PRIJEDOR 'WHITE RIBBON DAY'

The most cohesive narratives and mobilising memories among the members of the Bosnian diaspora in Australia have been those relating to the genocide and atrocities committed during the 1992–1995 war in Srebrenica and Prijedor. Through their formal and informal networks, the translocal communities of Srebrenica and Prijedor have campaigned for the recognition of genocide and crimes against humanity and the right to memorialise the sufferings of their native towns. Members of these translocal communities have organised a number of political events in Australia to raise awareness about what happened in their hometowns and villages in Bosnia. In collaboration with the Bosnian community organisations and local clubs, they have also been involved in organising commemorative events for the Srebrenica genocide victims on 11 July and 'The White Ribbon Day' (*Dan bijelih traka*) on 31 May in memory of the victims of the Prijedor massacres. The 11 July symbolises the 11th of July 1995, when the United Nations Safe Area of Srebrenica was overrun by the Serb troops and subsequently 8372 Bosniak men and boys were rounded up and killed in summary executions (Halilovich, 2017). The International Criminal Tribunal for the Former Yugoslavia (ICTY) found that the massacres at Srebrenica constituted a crime of genocide, the first such crime in Europe since the Holocaust (Nettelfield & Wagner, 2014). *The White Ribbon Day* held on 31 May commemorates the 31st of May 1992, when the Serb nationalists took over the town of Prijedor and ordered all non-Serbs in the Prijedor area to mark their houses with white sheets and to wear white ribbons on their arms. This was the start of the 'ethnic cleansing' of Prijedor, which saw more than 3000 civilians killed and the expulsion of some 50,000 people (Paul, 2021).

A majority of the refugees from Srebrenica and Prijedor who arrived in Australia through the 1990s survived concentration camps, for which Prijedor had become infamous (Vulliamy, 1994; Maass, 1996; Gutman, 1993; Karcic, 2022), or they were war widows with children who lost husbands and fathers in the genocide and massacres that took place during the 1992–1995 war in Bosnia (Halilovich, 2013). One of the first steps these and other newly arrived Bosnian refugees in Australia did was to re-establish their social and cultural life, including places of worship that fulfilled multiple roles—as places to meet the social, cultural and spiritual needs of the community and where the commemorative activities could be performed. Both religious and non-religious types of remembrances and commemorations for the victims of Srebrenica and Prijedor have taken place at these community venues. The events started as grassroots initiatives, with individual community members facilitating *tehvids* (commemorative prayers for the dead). Soon, these events were to include individual members and prominent leaders of other communities, including the mayors of the local councils where the Bosnians had settled and the government representatives.

In 2005, the tenth anniversary of the Srebrenica genocide was marked outside Bosnian community centres and mosques, taking place in the form of two commemorative conferences at the University of Sydney, in Sydney, and Victoria University, in Melbourne. In the chronicles of the Bosnian diaspora in Australia, these events can be regarded as historic and even formative as it was the first time that a gathering of this type and scale, recognising both those who perished in and who survived Srebrenica, Prijedor and other places in Bosnia, took place at public institutions in Australia (Halilovich, 2015).

In fact, the events were ground-breaking in many other ways too. They involved a mix of community-led activism, public mourning, interfaith dialogue and academic lectures. Several survivors provided public testimonies about what they survived and whom they lost in the genocide. During the midday prayer, led by a Bosnian *imam*, the Muslim worshippers prayed on the green grass of the University of Sydney campus. Several community and religious leaders from Muslim, Christian, Jewish and Buddhist faiths participated in the events. Along with them, many prominent Australian academics such as, for instance, Professor Ron Adams, Professor Rob Watts and Professor Paul James, delivered powerful speeches and called for justice for genocide survivors.[2] Both the Sydney and Melbourne events were covered by the Australian mainstream media and broadcast in

---

[2] At the time, many of the masterminds of the genocide—including Radovan Karadzic and Ratko Mladic, who in 2020 and 2021 were convicted of the crimes of genocide and crimes against humanity—were still at large, or their trials at ICTY were not completed.

primetime. What started in 2005, continued every July 11—and since 2012 on May 31—in subsequent years, with commemorations, seminars and other forms of remembrances both online and onsite becoming public events rather than isolated community gatherings of Bosnian diaspora. Thus, it did not come as a surprise when in 2011 the Australian Parliament passed one of the most comprehensive resolutions on the Srebrenica genocide, cited at the beginning of this chapter. This formal act did not only recognise the Bosnian genocide, but it also acknowledged that the tragedy of Srebrenica had become an Australian story too, as it has become the story in many other places across the world where Bosnians had settled.

From the low-key diaspora gatherings in the early 2000s, the Srebrenica and Prijedor commemorations have grown into well-organised and well-attended public events, increasingly attracting a wide spectrum of people—from human rights activists, academics and students, to artists and politicians. The commemorations have strengthened the bonds between members of the Bosnian diaspora and their host communities as well as reinforced connections with their fellow compatriots in other countries and in Bosnia. Thanks to such activities and their ability to mobilise not only the members of the Bosnian diaspora but also political leaders and the government representatives in Australia, the power, sophistication and the full potential of the diaspora has also been increasingly recognised back in Bosnia. As a result, a growing number of prominent personalities, human-rights activists and political representatives from Bosnia have responded to the invitations to take part at such events held by the Bosnian diaspora in Australia. Moreover, the commemorative activities have become a regular feature in the Bosnian and international mainstream media.

The remembrances of Srebrenica and Prijedor in Australia continue to serve multiple roles by: bringing members of the Bosnian diaspora together through fostering communal solidarity among themselves and in the process creating new homes based on the idea of old home (Karabegovic, 2014); creating 'a safe' space for public mourning and sharing individual and communal experiences of survivors; sending an explicit message of support to their fellow compatriots living in Bosnia and other countries; positioning themselves in relation to their new places by sharing their stories of suffering and survival with the host communities and societies they settled in, and in that way inscribing their own memories in the new socio-cultural and political landscape in Australia (Halilovich, 2015). The Srebrenica and Prijedor remembrance events in diaspora are getting increasingly synchronised and coordinated between the Bosnians living in different countries, and thanks to the information and communication technology and the time difference between Australia, Europe and the USA, it is possible to have a series of 'simultaneous' commemorations taking place several hours apart so that remembering Srebrenica and Prijedor both online and onsite literally moves across the world, in both time and space.

Conclusion

While genocide, politically motivated violence and forced displacement were the primary reasons for massive migration from Bosnia and the emergence of the Bosnian diaspora in Australia, Bosnian refugees and migrants who settled in Australia have continued to maintain active support for their original homeland and their local communities—economically, politically and symbolically. Over the last three decades, Srebrenica and Prijedor narratives have had an important formative role in shaping the collective identity among the displaced Bosnians and have become inseparable from the narrative of the Bosnian diaspora in Australia. In that regard, Srebrenica and Prijedor remembrances in diaspora also represent an act of defiance and a demonstration of resilience, reaffirming the identity of the decimated communities and their destroyed places that will continue to exist as long as they will be remembered and longed for. Moreover, the described examples of diaspora activism and public commemorations demonstrate that the very idea of the Bosnian diaspora, as a distinct de-territorialised transnational community, revolves around the shared memory of genocidal violence in Bosnia in which Srebrenica and Prijedor remembrances serve as performative enactment of such memory, communal solidarity and identity. These activities are matched by the diaspora's direct involvement in development initiatives back in Bosnia and their economic, social and cultural contribution to Australian society. At the same time, Australia's Parliament resolution on Srebrenica demonstrates both the Bosnian diaspora's influence over Australian understandings of genocide and Australia's commitment to acknowledging and defending human rights outside Australia.

REFERENCES

Adams, R. (2008). Capacity-Building in Bosnia-Herzegovina: The Challenge for Universities. *Cesa Review, 35*, 45–56.

Al-Ali, N., Black, R., & Koser, K. (2001). Refugees and Transnationalism: The Experience of Bosnians and Eritreans in Europe. *Journal of Ethnic and Migration Studies, 27*(4), 615–634.

Anderson, B. (1983). *Imagined Communities: Reflections on the Origin and Spread of Nationalism.* Verso.

Appadurai, A. (1995). The Production of Locality. In R. Fardon (Ed.), *Counterworks: Managing the Diversity of Knowledge* (1st ed., pp. 204–225). Routledge.

Australian Bureau of Statistics. (2006/2011/2016). *Census of Population.* Australian Government. Retrieved December 25, 2020, from http://www.abs.gov.au/

Bleby, M. (2017, November 20). Perth-Based Pro9 Global Wants Sydney Factory to Boost Existing Bosnian Capacity. *Australian Financial Review.* Retrieved March 15, 2021, from http://www.afr.com/business/construction/perth-based-pro9-global-wants-sydney-factory-to-boost-existing-bosnian-capacity-20171120-gzp9j1#ixzz52TAI8I2m

Cano, G. (2005, April 7–10). *The Mexico-North Report on Transnationalism* [Conference presentation abstract]. The 63rd Annual Conference of the Midwest Political Science Association, Chicago, IL, United States.

Capo Zmegac, J. (2007). *Strangers Either Way: The Lives of Croatian Refugees in Their New Home.* Berghahn Books.

Colic-Peisker, V. (2003). Bosnian Refugees in Australia: Identity, Community and Labour Market Integration [Working Paper 97]. *New Issues in Refugee Research.* Retrieved March 10, 2021, from https://www.unhcr.org/research/working/3fb4f8a64/bosnian-refugees-australia-identity-community-labour-market-integration.html

Colic-Peisker, V. (2005). At Least You're the Right Colour: Identity and Social Inclusion of Bosnian Refugees in Australia. *Journal of Ethnic and Migration Studies, 31*(4), 615–638.

Day, W. (2017). *Migration to Australia: Refugees.* Redback Publishing.

Department of Home Affairs. (2016). *Bosnia and Herzegovina-Born: Community Information Summary.* Australian Government. https://www.homeaffairs.gov.au/mca/files/2016-cis-bosnia-and-herzegovina.PDF

Diaz-Briquets, S., & Perez-Lopez, J. (1997). Refugee Remittances: Conceptual Issues and the Cuban and Nicaraguan Experiences. *International Migration Review, 31*(2), 411–437.

Efendic, A., Babic, B., & Rebmann, A. (2014). *Diaspora and Development – Bosnia and Herzegovina.* Embassy of Switzerland in Sarajevo.

Foucault, M. (1977). Counter-Memory: The Philosophy of the Difference. In F. D. Bouchard (Ed.), *Language, Counter-Memory, Practice: Selected Essays and Interviews by Michel Foucault* (1st ed., pp. 113–165). Cornell University Press.

Gilroy, P. (1995). Roots and Routes: Black Identity as an Outernational Project. In H.W. Harris, H.C. Blue &E.H. Griffith (Eds.), *Racial and Ethnic Identity: Psychological Development and Creative Expression* (pp. 15–30). Routledge.

Glick Schiller, N., Basch, L., & Szanton-Blanc, C. (1999). Trans-Nationalism: A New Analytic Framework for Understanding Migration. In S. Vertovec & R. Cohen (Eds.), *Migration, Diasporas and Trans-Nationalism* (pp. 26–50). Edward Elgar Publishing.

Guarnizo, L. E., & Smith, M. P. (1998). The Locations of Transnationalism. In L. E. Guarnizo & M. P. Smith (Eds.), *Transnationalism from Below* (pp. 3–34). Transaction Publisher.

Gutman, R. (1993). *Witness to Genocide*. Macmillan.

Halilovich, H. (2012). Trans-Local Communities in the Age of Transnationalism: Bosnians in Diaspora. *International Migration, 50*(1), 162–178.

Halilovich, H. (2013). *Places of Pain: Forced Displacement, Popular Memory and Trans-Local Identities in Bosnian War-Torn Communities*. Berghahn Books.

Halilovich, H. (2015). Long-Distance Mourning and Synchronised Memories in a Global Context: Commemorating Srebrenica in Diaspora. *Journal of Muslim Minority Affairs, 35*(3), 410–422.

Halilovich, H. (2017). *Kako opisati Srebrenicu / Writing After Srebrenica*. Buybook.

Halilovich, H. (2019). The Everlasting Presence of the Disappeared in Genocide: War Widows and Fatherless Families in the Bosnian Diaspora. *Migration and Ethnic Themes, 35*(3), 277–295.

Halilovich, H., & Adams, R. (2013). People in Place—Place in People: The Global Contextualization of Local Traditions as Modalities for Reconciliation. In S. Pavlovic & M. Zivkovic (Eds.), *Transcending Fratricide: Political Mythologies, Reconciliations, and the Uncertain Future in the Former Yugoslavia* (1st ed., pp. 149–164). NOMOS.

Halilovich, H., & Efendic, N. (2019). From Refugees to Trans-Local Entrepreneurs: Crossing the Borders Between Formal Institutions and Informal Practices in Bosnia and Herzegovina. *Journal of Refugee Studies, 34*(1), 663–680.

Halilovich, H., Hasić, J., Karabegović, D., Karamehić-Muratović, A., & Oruč, N. (2018). *Mapping the Bosnian-Herzegovinian Diaspora (BiH Migrants in Australia, Austria, Denmark, Germany, Italy, Netherlands, Slovenia, Sweden, Switzerland, and the United States of America). Utilizing the Socio-Economic Potential of the Diaspora for Development of B&H*. International Organization for Migration, Ministry of Human Rights and Refugees B&H.

Halilovich, H., & Kučuk, I. (2020). Refuge(e)s in Digital Diaspora: Reimagining and Recreating "Ethnically Cleansed" Villages as "Cyber Villages". *Etnološka Tribina: Journal of Croatian Ethnological Society, 50*(43), 182–196.

Haveric, D. (2009). *History of the Bosnian Muslim community in Australia: Settlement Experience in Victoria* [Unpublished doctoral dissertation]. Victoria University.

Herzfeld, M. (1997). *Cultural Intimacy: Social Poetics in the Nation-State.* Routledge.

Jupp, J. (2011). Religion and Integration in a Multifaith Society. In M. Clyne & J. Jupp (Eds.), *Multiculturalism and Integration: A Harmonious Relationship* (1st ed., pp. 135–150). ANU ePress.

Karabegovic, D. (2014). "Što Te Nema?" Transnational Cultural Production in the Diaspora in Response to the Srebrenica Genocide. *Nationalism and Ethnic Politics, 20*, 455–475.

Karcic, H. (2022). *Torture, Humiliate, Kill: Inside the Bosnian Serb Camp System.* University of Michigan Press.

Kearney, M. (1995). The Local and the Global: The Anthropology of Globalisation and Transnationalism. *Annual Review of Anthropology, 25*, 547–565.

Maass, P. (1996). *Love Thy Neighbor: A Story of War.* Random House.

Mahler, S. J. (1998). Theoretical and Empirical Contributions Towards a Research Agenda for Transnationalism. In L. E. Guarnizo & M. P. Smith (Eds.), *Transnationalism from Below* (pp. 64–100). Transaction Publisher.

Markovic, M., & Manderson, L. (2002). Crossing National Boundaries: Social Identity Formation Among Recent Immigrant Women in Australia from Former Yugoslavia. *Identity: An International Journal of Theory and Research, 2*(4), 303–316.

Nettelfield, L. J., & Wagner, S. E. (2014). *Srebrenica in the Aftermath of Genocide.* Cambridge University Press.

Olliff, L. (2018). From Resettled Refugees to Humanitarian Actors: Refugee Diaspora Organizations and Everyday Humanitarianism. *New Political Science, 40*(4), 658–674.

Parliament of Australia. (2011, November 21). Srebrenica Remembrance. *House of Representatives Official Hansard* 18. Retrieved June 10, 2021, from https://parlinfo.aph.gov.au/parlInfo/search/display/display.w3p;db=CHAMBER;id=chamber/hansardr/e3438d90-354a-4802-8540-6d3a85164a3a/0225;query=Id:%22chamber/hansardr/e3438d90-354a-4802-8540-6d3a85164a3a/0229%22

Paul, J. (2021). White Armband Day: From Global Social Media Campaign to Transnational Commemoration Day. *Memory Studies, 14*(4), 1–17. https://doi.org/10.1177/1750698021995991

Peleikis, A. (2000). The Emergence of a Translocal Community: The Case of a South Lebanese Village and Its Migrant Connections to Ivory Coast. *Cahiers d'Études sur la Méditerranée Orientale et le Monde Turco-Iranien, 30*(1), 297–317.

Portis-Winner, I. (2002). *Semiotics of Peasants in Transition: Slovene Villagers and Their Ethnic Relatives in America.* Duke University Press.

Riedlmayer, A. J. (2002). *Destruction of Cultural Heritage in Bosnia-Herzegovina: A Post-War Survey of Selected Municipalities.* Harvard University Press.

Sowell, T. (1996). *Migrations and Cultures: A World View.* Basic Books.

Valenta, M., Jakobsen, J., Župarić-Iljić, D., & Halilovich, H. (2020). Syrian Refugee Migration, Transitions in Migrant Statuses and Future Scenarios of Syrian Mobility. *Refugee Survey Quarterly, 39*(2), 153–176.

Valenta, M., & Ramet, P. S. (2011). Bosnian Migrants: An Introduction. In M. Valenta & P. S. Ramet (Eds.), *The Bosnian Diaspora: Integration of Transnational Communities* (pp. 1–23). Ashgate.

Valenta, M., & Strabac, Z. (2013). The Dynamics of Bosnian Refugee Migrations in the 1990s. *Refugee Survey Quarterly, 32*(3), 1–22.

Van Hear, N., & Cohen, R. (2017). Diasporas and Conflict: Distance, Contiguity and Spheres of Engagement. *Oxford Development Studies, 45*(2), 171–184.

Velayutham, S., & Wise, A. (2005). Moral Economies of a Translocal Village: Obligation and Shame Among South Indian Transnational Migrants. *Global Networks, 5*(1), 27–47.

Vertovec, S. (1999). Conceiving and Researching Transnationalism. *Ethnic and Racial Studies, 22*(2), 447–462.

Voloder, L. (2017). *A Muslim Diaspora in Australia: Bosnian Migration and Questions of Identity.* I.B. Tauris.

Vujcich, D. (2007). Faith, Flight and Foreign Policy: Effects of War and Migration on Western Australian Bosnian Muslims. *The Australian Journal of Social Issues, 42*(1), 71–86.

Vulliamy, E. (1994). *Seasons in Hell: Understanding Bosnia's War.* Simon and Schuster.

Waxman, P. (1999). The Residential Location of Recently Arrived Bosnian, Afghan and Iraqi Refugees and Humanitarian Entrants in Sydney, Australia. *Urban Policy and Research, 17*(4), 287–299.

Williams, N., & Efendic, A. (2019). Internal Displacement and External Migration in a Post-Conflict Economy: Perceptions of Institutions Among Migrant Entrepreneurs. *Journal of International Entrepreneurship, 17*(1), 558–585.

Wilson, L. (2010, September 28). New MP is First in Australia to be Sworn in with Koran. *The Australian.* http://www.theaustralian.com.au/news/nation/new-mp-is-first-in-australia-to-be-sworn-in-with-koran/story-e6frg6nf-1225930365789

Wise, A., & Velayutham, S. (2008). Second-Generation Tamils and Cross-Cultural Marriage: Managing the Translocal Village in a Moment of Cultural Rupture. *Journal of Ethnic and Migration Studies, 34*(1), 113–131.

York, B. (1998). *Maltese in Australia: Wandering Through the Maltese-Australian Story from Convict Times to the Present.* Victoria University of Technology.

CHAPTER 3

The Co-Construction of the Myanmar Diaspora in Australia

Susan Banki

Introduction

Following a coup in Myanmar in February 2021, strong resistance emerged within the country in the form of creative demonstrations, citizen journalism, and a widespread civil disobedience campaign. These activities have been well documented in the popular press (for example, Beech, 2021). But Myanmar's diaspora communities—based in countries both near Myanmar and further away—have also been active. In Australia, diaspora actors engaged in a number of activities that fall into the category of 'homeland activism' or 'homeland politics'—that is, protest, activism, or advocacy that seeks to engender change in the home country. A hefty literature examines the variables that explain homeland activism by diaspora actors (Betts & Jones, 2016). And there is an increasing acknowledgement that the relationships between diasporas and home governments require a further understanding of how they are mediated by host government relations, and the institutions that govern these relationships

---

S. Banki (✉)
University of Sydney, Sydney, NSW, Australia
e-mail: susan.banki@sydney.edu.au

© The Author(s), under exclusive license to Springer Nature
Switzerland AG 2022
M. Phillips, L. Olliff (eds.), *Understanding Diaspora Development*,
https://doi.org/10.1007/978-3-030-97866-2_3

37

(Gamlen, 2019; Koinova, 2021). There has been a less systematic examination, however, of how diaspora actors are constructed as agents and knowledge bearers by host countries.

I begin this chapter by reviewing the literatures that demonstrate that diaspora actors are most commonly constructed as victims, celebrities, or troublemakers. Drawing on three examples of activism carried out by Australia's Myanmar diaspora, I suggest a fourth overlooked possibility: that of emplaced expert. Further, I show, the case of Australia demonstrates that diaspora actors can be co-constructed as experts. I conclude by noting the utility of the expert construction.

Diasporas and Transnationalism

Diasporas as agents of homeland activism are not a new phenomenon, and the literature that examines these transnational practices is abundant and growing. Research examines both the factors that facilitate it (Betts & Jones, 2016; Ostergaard-Nielsen, 2003) and the elements that hinder it (Adamson, 2020; Chaudhary & Moss, 2019). It is shaped by a range of factors that are elucidated by Maria Koinova, whose exhaustive work on Palestinian, Albanian, and Armenian diasporas navigating the contested states from which they come suggests that diasporas' relationships with their host country are complicated by the host country's physical, political and social relationship with the home country. This 'sociospatial' factor, coined by Koinova, supports a recognition that diaspora mobilisers play niche roles in their activism that is dependent on place (Koinova, 2021).

These works do a fine job mapping out the interconnections between sites, as well as the uniqueness of specific site activity, but they tell us less about how diaspora mobilisers are constructed as actors. That is, while diasporas may be comfortably embedded in host societies, they are still, ontologically speaking, acting for or identifying with a place of difference, whether that be a home country, or, as understood by some diaspora scholars, an exiled identity (Clifford, 1994). A window into how the host (a country or dominating identity) constructs the diaspora will be useful in gaining a fuller understanding of diaspora roles vis-à-vis the homeland. I identify three such types of construction: victim construction, celebrity construction, and troublemaker construction.

Victim Construction

An understanding of diaspora as victims first and foremost comes from an often well-intentioned position of considering the history that rendered particular groups as diasporas in the first place. That is, diasporas are viewed through the lens of the victimised status that forced them to leave their original homeland. This imposition of the victim identity is not unique to diasporas. A common critique levelled at humanitarian actors, victim construction foregrounds the experiences of what is 'done' to individuals. In the telling of victims' stories, from discrimination (Bumiller, 1992), to violence done to domestic partners (Chung, 2002; Donovan & Hester, 2010) to torture and genocide (Eisenman et al., 2000; Straus, 2001), victim construction tends to view those who experience it as sufferers; in need of support and assistance, surely, but also passive and without voice.

The refugee literature is replete with discussions of refugees as victims, and for almost as long, there have been critiques of that view. Generations of scholars have diligently cited the work of Barbara Harrell-Bond (1986) and Liisa Malkki (1995) who examined how the nexus of humanitarian aid, host state policies, and refugee emplacement elevated the 'victim' identity for Ugandan refugees in South Sudan and Hutu refugees in Tanzania, respectively. Since then, a version of the 'refugees are not just passive victims' trope has usefully become a standard part of a significant number of refugee-related anthropological or sociological texts, whether examining refugees in Asia (Saltsman, 2014) or Latin America (Guerrero & Tinkler, 2010), whether in countries of proximate refuge (Brooten et al., 2015) or in resettlement contexts (Ghorashi, 2005).

The well-trodden yet important critique suggests that, in positioning refugees as victims, refugees are deprived of their autonomy. This is the case even though such a narrative is often necessary for refugees to substantiate their claims for asylum in order to secure protection. For example, Gambian female asylum seekers in London wear the mantle of victims in decrying the backward practices of their homeland, simplifying complex relationships and positioning the Global North as saviour (Kea & Roberts-Holmes, 2013). Much literature has bemoaned the impacts of victim construction: refugees are not accorded the appropriate tools to respond to their situations effectively (Pupavac, 2008); refugees lose livelihood opportunities because they are not viewed as capable (Giles, 2010); and refugee stories are manipulated not for their own benefit but for the benefit of humanitarian actors, who rely on such narratives to survive and

40   S. BANKI

thrive in a context of donor power and necessary fundraising (Morris, 2019; Wroe, 2018). This literature is often described, falsely, in a linear fashion: refugees used to be viewed as victims but we have learned our lesson. In fact, while there has been a welcome and rising call—from refugees—for refugees to be in charge of their own narratives,[1] victim constructions remain salient.[2]

It is not a large leap to see how refugee constructions are easily transposed to diasporas more broadly. Thus, a victim identity moves all too easily from the refugee identity to the diaspora identity, retaining the narrative of 'persecuted in homeland' even when diaspora populations are firmly embedded in their host countries, and even when they explicitly challenge being turned into victims (Arhin, 2016; Cohen, 1996; Young & Park, 2009).

Celebrity Construction

At the other end of the spectrum, diaspora histories can be elevated and glorified to produce diaspora actors who gain celebrity status. Celebrity is, of course, all about construction: the way the media and fans produce and reproduce tropes that they love or hate. Celebrities also construct themselves. Writings on the sociology of celebrity status explore the way (global, media, public) attention is accumulated by the celebrity as a form of capital whose commodification relies on ever-increasing markets comprised of viewers and audiences (Van Krieken, 2012). These commodified spaces—what Franck has called a 'vanity fair'—demand inflationary modes of attention, with elite celebrities bestowing attention capital on one another, in a process that mirrors financial capital accumulation by the elite (Franck, 2019).[3]

---

[1] Refugee participation is a widespread theme at workshops and conferences that focus on refugees. Examples include: the Democratizing Displacement workshop held at Oxford in 2019, numerous panels over the years at conferences organised by the International Association for the Study of Forced Migration (IASFM), the Refugee Alternatives conference organised by the Refugee Council of Australia, and thematic sessions about refugee participation at the annual Asia-Pacific Conference on Refugee Rights (APCRR).

[2] There has also been a push to reject binary representations of refugees as passive/active and victims/heroes (Doná, 2007; Fiddian-Qasmiyeh, 2009).

[3] Franck, in fact, argues that celebrity proximity begets further celebrity. The power of proximity as a means for raising attention capital is something I cover in a separate work on the importance of borders. There is no scope for this exploration in this chapter, but it is worth noting that the notion of proximity is under-explored in literatures that examine power relationships.

The performative aspects of celebrity are closely linked to the importance of generating attention. These performances, it has been argued, require certain types of literacy to concretise the celebrity identity (Robinson, 2007). These range from appropriate generational linguistic codes, to cognitively consonant imagery (through appearances and other iconic communications), to skills reliant on 'sociotechnical labour' that are particularly relevant in the context of mass social media (Tse et al., 2018). Relevant to this chapter, the literature on celebrity also points out that generating attention may have a humanitarian or advocacy intent, two separate but interlinked possibilities (Kapoor, 2012; Richey & Brockington, 2020). In this curious phenomenon, people who are skilled at acting or making music, for example, are constructed as sufficiently knowledgeable to have credibility when they make calls for policy reform or pressure governments to impose sanctions on authoritarian regimes (De Waal, 2008; Mostafanezhad, 2013, 2017). At the same time, celebrities can invoke 'theatrical dynamics of pity' (Chouliaraki, 2012) that turn symbolic humanitarian capital into spectacle. The imperialist tone of such expressions notwithstanding, they point to the prevalence of constructing celebrities as both humanitarians and advocates (Biccum, 2016).

The performance of celebrity calls to a mind a dialectic engagement. On the one hand, it is argued, the 'real' person behind the celebrity lies in tension with the constructed one (Marshall, 2010). As projected on the screen, the magazine cover, and now the Twitter/TikTok sphere, the public-facing celebrity identity simplifies, and perhaps even replaces 'multiple, perhaps incongruent, "true selves"' (Tse et al., 2018, p. 142). On the other hand, the literature suggests that celebrities' power to deploy their symbolic capital gives them agency (Hearn, 2008). That they are treated as idols catapults them to the status of gods of a para-religion, and while fans map their own desires and identities on to such figures, this elevated status gives them potency (Ward, 2019, as cited in Stoddard, 2013).

While information overflows on the internet have produced—empirically and conceptually—myriad transnational celebrities (Tsaliki et al., 2014), these are generally identified as celebrities whose *fame*, rather than the people themselves, has crossed borders. But we know that celebrity diaspora individuals exist, across time and space: Albert Einstein was part of a German Jewish diaspora in the United States. Kim Kardashian makes no secret of being part of the Armenian diaspora. Behrouz Boochani is a widely celebrated Kurdish-Iranian author whose portrait won the People's Choice award in the 2020 Archibald Prize. Despite their empirical presence, scholars have had less to say on the intersection of celebrity and diasporas, and how the latter are viewed partially through the lens of being rendered famous by their experiences of migration, displacement and changing nationality.[4]

The nature of celebrity—and the charisma that accompanies it (Weber, 2006)—might suggest that diaspora actors who attain celebrity status would rarely be linked to their home country because of their association with that broader group, but rather because of their individual characteristics and relationships. But the crafted narratives that are served up for celebrity consumption often incorporate a homeland story. Behrouz Boochani regularly incorporates reference to his Kurdish homeland, even when he is writing about his experiences in detention (Boochani, 2018). The Dalai Lama's celebrity status comes not only from the patronage he developed from other celebrities, but also from his ability to construct an image of his religion and its place in a mystical homeland (Cusack, 2011). Even when celebrities studiously embrace their new citizenships, the diaspora identity sticks. For example, the Korean-born, New Zealand resident golf sensation, Lydia Ko, is constructed as a celebrity not just for her exceptional golf prowess, but for the relationship between her golfing and the practices of other Korean golfers (Chang et al., 2019). It is not that such individuals are *only* famous for their or their ancestors' experiences of migration, but that these experiences often become part of the celebrity story.

Troublemaker Construction

The connection of diasporas with the homeland has generated a third type of construction, well-known to sociologists, in which those who flee their homeland retain sentimental and steadfast nationalism that only grows with time. The oft-quoted reference to the 'long-distance nationalist' (Anderson, 1998) has produced a hefty scholarship on diaspora populations who are seen through the eyes of various stakeholders as troublemakers for their unwavering (or so it is claimed) support for a particular vision of the homeland (Demmers, 2002).

From the perspective of host states that clearly want to set the terms of their interaction with the home state—whether this interaction is conflictual or amicable—transnational actors who promote their own homeland-oriented agendas may be viewed as troublemakers. Of course, depending

---

[4] Some exceptions include Giardina (2002) and Chang et al. (2019).

on what type of trouble one wants to stir up, this trouble may be considered an advantage or a detriment. In either instance, diaspora actors with this set of (assumed) priorities are viewed through a rather monolithic lens. This is so despite evidence to the contrary that diaspora political organisers vary their practices and goals considerably, depending on different 'sites of resistance' (Beatty, 2009).

Recently, a sub-literature has emerged that examines the ways in which home governments influence and corral their diasporas through institution building (Gamlen, 2019). This increasingly noted phenomenon occurs for a range of economic, social and political reasons that can be mutually beneficial for home states and for diaspora actors themselves. In these instances, fealty to a homeland, mediated through diaspora institutions, is positively regarded at home but viewed with wariness in host countries. In other cases, the presence of institutions in the host country can support diaspora groups to counter host government narratives, fronting resources (Betts & Jones, 2016) and/or mitigating precarity (Banki, 2015).

The image of diaspora actors as long-distance nationalists has become a trope with powerful symbolic value, and it is therefore manipulated variously by: governments that seek to simplify diaspora identity; humanitarian actors that want access to gatekeepers in the home country; diaspora actors themselves that may benefit from the attention of said humanitarian actors; and, to be completely fair, researchers of transnational politics who are enriched (through publications and promotions) by its study. In sum, the troublemaker construction may be hard to shed because it benefits a great many stakeholders, even if a more nuanced picture would better represent the diaspora.[5]

MYANMAR'S TURBULENT HISTORY

Myanmar's turbulent history could be described as a poisonous mix of a colonial legacy, a deeply entrenched military, geopolitical and regional power dynamics that keep outside actors from intervening, myriad ethnic struggles, and associated border-periphery governance issues related to

---

[5] It is worth noting that for refugees who remain in situations of precarity—for example, Syrians in Lebanon—these same constructions are also present. An excellent article in *OpenDemocracy* notes that this population is generally framed, problematically, either as victims or troublemakers. https://www.opendemocracy.net/en/north-africa-west-asia/why-its-important-to-see-displaced-people-as-more-than-just-refugees/.

mining and drug production. In the most problematic way possible, it is a country that 'has it all' (Banki, 2020).

While motions in the direction of democracy in the early 2010s relaxed many restrictions, opened up the country to international money, and eventually ushered in a new government—in the form of the former opposition leader, Aung San Suu Kyi—much commentary sounded a cautionary note, with good reason. Following a humiliating defeat in elections in 2020, the Myanmar military—the Tatmadaw—proved itself unwilling to give in to a true democracy, and in February 2021, overthrew the democratically elected government and imprisoned those it considered threats to its power, including Aung San Suu Kyi, many incumbent representatives, and even a well-known Australian academic who had been serving as an economic aide to Ms. Suu Kyi, Professor Sean Turnell.[6]

The response within Myanmar to the coup—passionate, popular, and longstanding—may have taken the generals by surprise. Risking arrest and attacks by the police and military, people have marched in protest, photographed police/military violence, and engaged in a civil disobedience campaign that is believed to number hundreds of thousands of civil servants refusing to work under the current government. A shadow government has also formed in the form of two related groups: the Committee Representing Pyidaungsu Hluttaw (CRPH) and the National Unity Government (NUG), which, together, are releasing statements, trying to set policy (with no way to carry it out at this point, it must be said), and raising funds to help the civil disobedience movement to continue.

Protests have had a significant international dimension as well, coming, in one form or another, from every corner of the globe. Some of these responses have come from well-established advocacy organisations whose bread and butter is raising awareness, documentation, and lobbying, such as the International Campaign for the Rohingya and Human Rights Watch. Other organisations are led by diaspora actors from Myanmar, both further afield, like the Burmese Rohingya Organisation UK, or closer to Myanmar, across porous borders, such as Progressive Voice in Thailand. In Australia, as in other Global North locations, Myanmar's diaspora has engaged in its own activities. I focus on three events to examine diaspora construction of homeland mobilisation.

---

[6] As of this writing, Sean Turnell remains in prison in Myanmar. Calls for his release have until now gone unheeded.

Australia's Myanmarese Diaspora

Myanmar's diaspora population of about 32,000 in Australia is represented by a range of ethnicities: 43% Burman, 14% Chin, 14% Karen, and the remainder a smattering of other ethnicities, including a small number of Rohingya.[7] Just as in Myanmar itself, the diaspora is represented by a range of interests and religions. Questions about exactly *what* ideal post-coup governance would look like remains salient, with groups such as the Karen, the Rohingya, and Burmese at odds on responses.[8] But there have been, at the very least, loud and emphatic responses from many corners of Australia in the wake of the coup. The following sections examine three moments that demonstrate that neither victim, nor celebrity, nor trouble-maker constructions do justice to describing Myanmar's diaspora. A fourth possibility emerges here, which I term 'emplaced expert'. I use the term to refer to expert knowledge that draws not only on normatively accepted evidence and facts, but also on knowledge drawn from one's localised history related to a certain place. It is important to note that this is not about a person's experiences, traumatic or otherwise, but often about deeply embedded knowledges that come from longstanding personal connections, family lore, and local knowledge. It is the weaving together of the former and latter, I argue, that produces 'emplaced experts'. In the coming pages, I show how diaspora knowledge—which is expert to be sure—is deployed by weaving together sophisticated understandings of points of international leverage with diaspora members' own emplaced experiences. Diasporas who act as emplaced experts are perceived this way by Australian stakeholders interested in Myanmar, and are therefore co-constructed.

'Junta Children': Australia's Version of Social Punishment

While there is widespread aversion to the coup, there have been precious few cracks within the regime and within the Tatmadaw. This is because the members of the military are in many ways isolated from the rest of the population, living in separate housing and spending time only with other

---

[7] https://www.homeaffairs.gov.au/mca/files/2016-cis-myanmar.PDF.

[8] A brief survey of the websites of these respective organisations demonstrates that they are promoting different visions of a future Myanmar, with little agreement on future leaders and future priorities. These perspectives, while interesting, are outside the scope of this paper.

members of junta society. They are further socialised to see protest as chaos (Selth, 2021). Even for those who want to defect, the pressure to remain loyal is enormous; defectors and their families lose their livelihoods, their housing, and the support systems to which they have grown accustomed.[9] Aware of this dynamic, anti-coup actors, both within Myanmar and outside, seek to raise the cost of consorting with the junta. In one version of social punishment, people within the country that even nominally support the current government are shamed through social media. In another version, family members of those in the military or government are outed and ostracised.

In Australia, this version of social punishment takes on a particular hue as members of the Myanmarese diaspora call out other expatriates with ties to the current regime, not just to shame them in Myanmarese circles, but also to publicise their connections widely and try to wreak far heavier consequences. For example, anti-coup Myanmarese diaspora members protest openly at sites where 'junta children' work. In one example covered by Reuters, a doctor whose mother is the junta's attorney general found himself the subject of a shaming campaign, when a compatriot travelled 1500 kilometres to stand outside the hospital where he works and call him out for not speaking out against the coup (Lamb, 2021).

Other members of the diaspora want to raise the cost of consorting much higher: to have relatives of the junta expelled from Australia. In 2007, more than 400 high-level officers from Myanmar were sanctioned by the Australian Government and the court eventually ruled in favour of deporting the Australian resident daughter of one brigadier-general (Doherty et al., 2021; The Irrawaddy, 2010). Similarly, post-coup, there are calls for the investigation and cancelling of visas of children of high-level military figures. Drawing on their intimate and specialised knowledge of family relationships within Myanmar, anti-coup diaspora actors have submitted lists of known family members of the junta to the Department of Foreign Affairs and Trade. Multiple individuals throughout the country are working on this project, and they have a clear message, which links those in Australia to the riches of their junta relatives and then suggests that, as financial beneficiaries of the junta's violence, they not be permitted to live comfortably here in Australia. As Nang Si Si Win, a founder of

---

[9] See, however, Bertil Lintner's August 2021 analysis in the *Irrawaddy* that suggests that cracks may be on the horizon: https://www.irrawaddy.com/opinion/guest-column/what-has-happened-to-myanmars-tatmadaw.html.

Democracy 4 Burma told the *Sydney Morning Herald*, 'We need to get those who are here, sanction them, at least then they will know their grandchildren or children are affected and it will make them think twice' (Galloway & McKenzie, 2021).

This is a uniquely Australian means of trying to place pressure on the regime, because as one Australian-Myanmar lawyer noted, Australia is 'the destination of choice for families and children of senior members of the military regime' (Melinda Tu, *Committee Hansard*, 2021, p. 20). It is important to note that anti-coup actors are not united in this approach. Some family members who are being targeted have spoken out against the regime. Some claim to have rejected their family back home, and some have been active on social media promoting the civil disobedience movement (Doherty et al., 2021). But part of the logic of targeting these family members and preparing a list of them in Australia, is to differentiate them from anti-coup Myanmarese whose visas are soon to expire and who are worried about being sent back in the post-coup environment. These temporary visa holders, about 3400 in number, are also the target of advocacy but, in this instance, the idea is that they be permitted to stay in Australia past the expiry of their visas. The identification of junta-connected families (and the singling them out for possible deportation) clearly differentiates them from those who might continue to deserve the protection of Australia.

It is easy to see how a campaign to implicate the relationships between the junta, the resources they gained from power, and the lives of their relatives living in Australia would require specific and unique types of knowledge that emerge from place-based experience. To put a fine point on it, it would be difficult for an Australian bureaucrat, no matter how well trained in the political and social history of Myanmar, to locate junta relatives as effectively and quickly as can the Myanmar diaspora. This localised knowledge—which can only be deployed by emplaced actors—takes on a transnational flavour when overlaid with advocacy and migration policy. Anti-coup diaspora actors thus construct themselves as knowledgeable and worthy of attention—in other words, as experts. That the media heeds this call (through coverage in the *Sydney Morning Herald* (Galloway & McKenzie, 2021), *Guardian* (Doherty et al., 2021), and *Reuters* (Lamb, 2021)) indicates that this representation has been effective, thereby permitting a co-constructed expert identity. A discussion about the advisability of ostracising junta families has also made its way into government discourse through public hearings, the topic of the next section.

TESTIMONY IN PARLIAMENT

Two-and-a-half months after the coup, Australia's Myanmar diaspora self-represented at a public hearing held by the Foreign Affairs and Aid Subcommittee of the Joint Standing Committee of Foreign Affairs, Defence and Trade. This public hearing, held on 13 April 2021, gathered submissions from more than 60 individuals and organisations, including contributions from academics, advocates (from Amnesty International and Human Rights Watch, e.g.), and from Australian stakeholders, such as Chris Sidoti (former Australian Human Rights Commissioner and member of the Independent International Fact Finding Mission on Myanmar) and members of the Australian Trade and Investment Commission. Also present—the subjects of this examination—were 12 members of the Myanmarese diaspora from various advocacy and community-based organisations who represent both ethnic minorities (specifically the Karen and the Chin) and broader democracy-based groups. Their interventions—and their treatment by the Chair—offer an indication of how this diaspora group has been constructed.

From the outset, the twelve diaspora actors—called 'witnesses' in proper parlance—were viewed as valuable contributors at the hearing. This is to be expected, as the Joint Standing Committee chooses to invite people that they deem important on any topic. Yet there was also an understanding of the precarious position in which some anti-coup actors find themselves, but without victimising tendencies. For example, the meeting opened with an acknowledgment that 'there are individuals who wish to offer their expertise to the committee but do not wish to speak publicly' (*Committee Hansard*, 2021, p. 1). Here, the word 'expertise' is telling, and a foreshadowing of the way such witnesses and their contributions would be incorporated into the proceedings.

The Chair of public hearings in Parliament generally requests short introductions from invited witnesses before longer discussion. At the 13 April hearing, the Myanmar diaspora witnesses used the introduction as an opportunity to foreground a number of salient issues: the terrifying abduction of activists from their homes; reference to international institutions that could serve as points of leverage (like the International Criminal Court); the need for sanctions against the military; China's interests; and the fraught nature of Aung San Suu Kyi's government for ethnic minorities—specifically here, the Karen and the Chin. This last point suggests that Myanmarese diaspora actors were not simply valued for one-sided testimony, but for their ability to provide nuanced, and even diverging, thoughts on what a post-coup democracy would look like.

Following introductions, diaspora actors had the opportunity to make longer interventions, and from these interventions and the questions asked by other members of the Committee, it was clear that diaspora actors projected a sophisticated understanding of Myanmar's local and geopolitical context and possible responses. This was not a testimony in which diaspora actors were asked to reflect on their personal experiences of persecution—although these were certainly people who had histories of victimisation—but on complex dynamics that touched on international initiatives, such as the Responsibility to Protect and urging for the recognition of the CRPH and NUG. The statement of Melinda Tun, an Australian-Myanmar lawyer, was emblematic of this complexity. Beginning with the words, 'This is not a time for quiet diplomacy', Ms. Tun's statement then went on to urge the Australian Government to take strong action (*Committee Hansard*, 2021, pp. 20–21). In the edited extract below, one gets a feel for this remarkable piece of political theatre:

First, Australia has unique leverage that few other countries have… Many [children of senior members of the military regime] are living and studying here funded by the proceeds of their parents' military connections and involvement in military enterprises. Their presence in this country is fundamentally contrary to our foreign policy interests…. This is not the time for quiet diplomacy.

There is also evidence of Australian citizens doing business with military family members, including those on the US sanctions list…. We must stop people who are aiding and abetting the Myanmar military in their crimes, including their family members, from enjoying the proceeds of their abuses right here on the shores of this country. Second, on the issue of sanctions, we are trying to reverse an incomplete coup …. The last time sanctions were imposed on the military in the 1990s and 2000s it was to remove a regime that had been in power for decades and was extremely isolated. But 2021 is a different story. The military, their associates and their families now have extensive international business ties, built in the last 10 years after the transition to democracy. This time strong, effective sanctions and visa bans can hurt but we must do it now. This is not the time for quiet diplomacy.

…At present, the military does not have effective control over the population or the state apparatus to be recognised as the government of the sovereign state of Myanmar. Ordinary people in Myanmar are showing extraordinary courage to ensure their state, their country, does not fall under military rule. Democracies like Australia cannot stand idly by issuing statements while the military removes an elected government at gunpoint and commits atrocities on 54 million civilians. Committee members, if, as you say, Australia is serious about protecting the human rights of people around the world, we must act now, not six months or one year down the track when the military has consolidated power and gained the upper hand. I repeat: this is not the time for quiet diplomacy.

… Myanmar represents one of the most serious regional crises in South-East Asia in decades. If this continues there will be significant regional instability, large outflows of refugees and armed conflict in the heart of Asia for years. If Australia wants to be taken seriously as a regional player and a middle power we must master the political will to act rather than sitting on the sidelines and issuing statements…. I repeat: this is not the time for quiet diplomacy.

The clear references in this intervention to international norms and geopolitical elements—and the space given for such interventions—positioned diaspora members as actors with expert status. Further, the sense of Myanmar history drawn out by Melinda Tu—who compared the imposition of sanctions from the 1990s and 2000s to today, for example, and referred to this coup as 'incomplete'—gave her testimony an emplaced feel—the credibility of a witness who understands and communicates effectively a ground-upwards view of contemporary dynamics in Myanmar.

LINKING INSIDE AND OUT: ART AS A FORM OF PROTEST

The rich literature on art as a form of protest (McQuiston, 2019) explores the numerous ways that structural violence and human rights violations can be communicated through creative visual representations, both as useful tools for advocacy (Lenette, 2019) and problematically by Global North appropriators (Brooten et al., 2015). In Myanmar, following the coup, artists turned their attention to social justice and human rights: iconography of the three-finger salute; photography of violent responses to the protests; and posters of hipsters holding signs inscribed with the words 'You Messed with the Wrong Generation'. As this underground scene grew increasingly precarious, the possibility of exhibiting art outside Myanmar emerged. In Sydney, two art galleries—The Art Syndicate in Surry Hills and 16Albermarle in Newtown—showcased art from artists inside Myanmar who had sent prints of their work electronically. Both gallery managers promised to send the proceeds from all sales back to the artists who painted them, thereby supporting the civil disobedience movement, at least indirectly.

Both galleries used their art space to hold awareness-raising events. The gallery 16Albermarle organised a closing reception (the opening reception was cancelled because of COVID) in conjunction with the Sydney Southeast Asia Centre (SSEAC) of the University of Sydney in an exhibit entitled 'Fighting Fear: #WhatsHappeningInMyanmar', with guest speakers, Burmese food, and free small prints of some of the exhibit's most recognisable taglines. The Art Syndicate used their space as a backdrop for a series of podcasts organised by the Australian-organised Democracy For Burma campaign. Crucially, both galleries involved diaspora actors in these events, and their respective contributions demonstrated that they were positioned as experts in the process, rather than victims, celebrities or troublemakers.

For example, at 16Albermarle, the reception included remarks by two diaspora actors who were valued for their intellectual contributions rather than for their personal histories.[10] Manny Maung, a Myanmarese researcher from Human Rights Watch, spoke about the efforts of international advocacy organisations to place pressure on the Australian Government. Sophia Sarkis, a Burmese community activist, highlighted the importance of keeping the military, and their families, accountable. While she did mention her personal experience as a child during the 1988 protests and subsequent crackdown, this was not the focus of her talk. Discussions about the leverage that stakeholders can and should exert were highlighted above personal stories of woe. Similarly, the podcasts that were recorded at the Art Syndicate involved diaspora actors as expert commentators. One episode, for example, 'Australia's Role in Burma: Past, Present and Future', featured Dr. Tun Aung Shwe who spoke as a representative of the New South Wales chapter of the CRPH/NUG support group. With attention to evidence and contextual history, he spoke authoritatively about the lesser-discussed, but highly relevant issue of Myanmar's thriving illegal drug production and Australia's mistargeted role in trying to stem it by funding Myanmar's law enforcement. With incisive references to Australia's drug eradication budget, and to China's central role in providing raw materials for meta-amphetamines, Dr. Shwe crafted a sophisticated and convincing argument as to why Australia should review its foreign policy

---

[10] The author was one of the other speakers at the 16Albermarle event.

52   S. BANKI

and development assistance to Myanmar.[11] This line of argument was supported and reinforced by the podcast episode's moderator and other speakers, who clearly valued Dr. Shwe for his analysis.

The showcasing of Myanmar art in Australia and the associated talks by diaspora actors highlighted, once again, the relevance of expert *and* local knowledge. Many pieces in the art exhibits had specific cultural references that were best understood and explained by Myanmar actors themselves, suggesting the value of their territorialised histories. They were also given space to speak authoritatively about the Australia-Myanmar relationship, and subsequently offered insightful analysis on the sources of, paths to, and outcomes emerging from, Australian intervention in Myanmar.

CONCLUSION

In this chapter, I examined three moments carried out by the Myanmarese diaspora in Australia in the wake of the February coup. First, I unpacked the debate around Australia's version of the social punishment campaign, in which the family members of the junta currently residing in Australia were outed, ostracised, and made objects of a campaign (undertaken by Myanmar's diaspora) to have them removed from Australia. Second, I explored the testimony of Myanmar diaspora actors at a Parliament session of the Joint Standing Committee on Foreign Affairs, Defence and Trade. Third, I reflected on the political inflections of an art exhibit showcasing Myanmar artists. Each of these 'moments', which included a range of diaspora actors, demonstrated that neither victim, nor celebrity, nor troublemaker constructions do justice to describing Myanmar's diaspora. Instead, they might best be understood as 'emplaced experts'—acknowledged not *just* for their place of origin, but certainly incorporating understandings of it. Further, they were constructed, and *co*-constructed, as actors with local, domestic and international background knowledge. Without having to use the language of academics, Myanmar diaspora actors actively constructed themselves as experts, a welcome change to prior tropes that fail to see them in this light.

Constructing diaspora agents as experts is important for a number of reasons. First, the host countries that see them in this light stand to benefit from their emplaced expertise. This chapter has demonstrated that at least some Australian stakeholders have already participated in their

[11] https://democracyforburma.com.au/.

3 THE CO-CONSTRUCTION OF THE MYANMAR DIASPORA IN AUSTRALIA 53

co-construction, and therefore genuinely welcomed their expert views. The fact that much of their advice has not been heeded has less to do with how diaspora members are constructed than with the unwillingness of nation states to do anything against Myanmar's Tatmadaw more broadly. In other words, *no one* who has called for a strong response to the coup has been listened to, no matter how much of an expert they are considered to be.

Second, the construction of diaspora actors as experts gives credence to related actors, such as refugees and asylum seekers. It is well known that refugees' own voices are often subsumed when governments seek substantiation for claims of refugee protection because of a 'widespread and pervasive culture of disbelief' (Sigona, 2014, p. 374). A greater acceptance of diaspora actors as experts could, over time, give them a greater role in providing background information for refugee determination processes, a role that is now more often accorded to academic researchers, who may or may not have emplaced knowledge. This is one example of the way that expert construction could benefit diasporas themselves, but it speaks to the broader power dynamics that such construction could bring.

Finally, the epistemic community would benefit from widening its membership to actors—diaspora, refugees, and other liminal subjects—whose emplaced experiences push us to think about what legitimate expertise means. There is already a conversation in media channels along these lines. An article in *OpenDemocracy* tells the personal story of a Syrian PhD researcher and candidate at the University of Sydney whose expert opinion on air strikes was edited out of a news interview, only to highlight his trauma.

> This humiliating experience taught me that despite my background as a citizen journalist and an academic, for some I will forever be a traumatised Syrian refugee whose primary role is to evoke sympathy and tears.[12]

A Twitter post encapsulates this problem in two clever lines:

> Ethnic person: we're indigenous to this land, we've been here for generations
> Colonizer "academic": eummm source?[13]

---

[12] https://www.opendemocracy.net/en/refugee-stories-could-do-more-harm-good/?fbc
lid=IwAR2IRv6DFxpjnDa0VQH0wIFibIk1rIH2JX0qPKJ0U_6nOpXd4wZBVrScJ2U.
[13] https://twitter.com/howisthatspelt/status/1425296790106955777?s=20. I note that even including this Twitter post as an example of decolonised dialogue is part of a decolonising project; the publishers of this volume advise in their publishing material that we should

For those of us trained to assess academic credibility through exclusionary lenses, resetting our norms around the construction of diaspora communities will make for a richer base of knowledge going forward. Identifying and presenting diaspora agents as experts, rather than victims, celebrities, or troublemakers, is part of a broader project of decolonising knowledge.

REFERENCES

Adamson, F. B. (2020). Non-state Authoritarianism and Diaspora Politics. *Global Networks, 20*(1), 150–169.

Anderson, B. (1998). *The Spectre of Comparisons: Nationalism, Southeast Asia, and the World*. Verso.

Arhin, A. (2016). A Diaspora Approach to Understanding Human Trafficking for Labor Exploitation. *Journal of Human Trafficking, 2*(1), 78–98.

Banki, S. (2015). Transnational Activism as Practised by Activists from Burma: Negotiating Precarity, Mobility and Resistance. In R. Egreteau & F. Robinne (Eds.), *Metamorphosis: Studies in Social and Political Change in Myanmar* (pp. 234–259). NUS Press.

Banki, S. (2020). Myanmar: The Country that 'Has it All'. *Journal of Southeast Asian Human Rights (JSEAHR), 4*(1), 128–139. https://doi.org/10.19184/jseahr.v4i1.17922

Beatty, L. M. (2009). Democracy Activism and Assistance in Burma. *International Journal, 65*, 619–636.

Beech, H. (2021, February 17). Paint, Poems and Protest Anthems: Myanmar's Coup Inspires the Art of Defiance. *New York Times.* https://www.nytimes.com/2021/02/17/world/asia/myanmar-coup-protest-art.html

Betts, A., & Jones, W. (2016). *Mobilising the Diaspora: How Refugees Challenge Authoritarianism*. Cambridge University Press.

Biccum, A. R. (2016). What Might Celebrity Humanitarianism have to do with Empire? *Third World Quarterly, 37*(6), 998–1015.

Boochani, B. (2018). *No Friend but the Mountains: Writing from Manus Prison*. Picador Australia.

Brooten, L., Ashraf, S. I., & Akinro, N. A. (2015). Traumatized Victims and Mutilated Bodies: Human Rights and the 'Politics of Immediation' in the Rohingya Crisis of Burma/Myanmar. *International Communication Gazette, 77*(8), 717–734.

---

not 'not link to user-generated content and other "unprofessional" websites, for which it is unlikely that the content has undergone adequate rights checks.' https://resource-cms.springernature.com/springer-cms/rest/v1/content/990/data/Manuscript+guidelines+for+English+books.

3 THE CO-CONSTRUCTION OF THE MYANMAR DIASPORA IN AUSTRALIA 55

Bumiller, K. (1992). *The Civil Rights Society: The Social Construction of Victims.* JHU Press.

Chang, I. Y., Jackson, S., & Tak, M. (2019). Globalization, Migration, Citizenship, and Sport Celebrity: Locating Lydia Ko between and beyond New Zealand and South Korea. *The International Journal of the History of Sport, 36*(7–8), 643–659.

Chaudhary, A. R., & Moss, D. M. (2019). Suppressing Transnationalism: Bringing Constraints into the Study of Transnational Political Action. *Comparative Migration Studies, 7*(1), 9.

Chouliaraki, L. (2012). The Theatricality of Humanitarianism: A Critique of Celebrity Advocacy. *Communication and Critical/Cultural Studies, 9*(1), 1–21.

Chung, D. (2002). Questioning Domestic Violence Orthodoxies: Challenging the Social Construction of Women as Victims and as Being Responsible for Stopping Male Violence. *Women Against Violence: An Australian Feminist Journal, 11,* 7.

Clifford, J. (1994). Diasporas. *Cultural Anthropology, 9*(3), 302–338.

Cohen, R. (1996). Diasporas and the Nation-State: From Victims to Challengers. *International Affairs, 72*(3), 507–520.

Committee Hansard. (2021, April 13). Annual Report 2019–20, Myanmar Department of Foreign Affairs and Trade, Department of Foreign Affairs.

Cusack, C. M. (2011). The Western Reception of Buddhism: Celebrity and Popular Cultural Media as Agents of Familiarisation. *Australian Religion Studies Review, 24*(3), 297–316.

De Waal, A. (2008). The Humanitarian Carnival: A Celebrity Vogue. *World Affairs, 171*(2), 43–55.

Demmers, J. (2002). Diaspora and Conflict: Locality, Long-distance Nationalism, and Delocalisation of Conflict Dynamics. *The Public-Javnost, 9*(1), 85–96.

Doherty, B., Bucci, N., & Butler, B. (2021, May 8). Children of the Junta: The Relatives of Myanmar's Military Regime Living in Australia. *The Guardian.* https://www.theguardian.com/australia-news/2021/may/08/children-of-the-junta-the-relatives-of-myanmars-military-regime-living-in-australia

Doná, G. (2007). The Microphysics of Participation in Refugee Research. *Journal of Refugee Studies, 20*(2), 210–229.

Donovan, C., & Hester, M. (2010). 'I Hate the Word "Victim"': An Exploration of Recognition of Domestic Violence in Same Sex Relationships. *Social Policy and Society, 9*(2), 279.

Eisenman, D. P., Bergner, S., & Cohen, I. (2000). An Ideal Victim: Idealizing Trauma Victims Causes Traumatic Stress in Human Rights Workers. *Human Rights Review, 1*(4), 106–114.

Fiddian-Qasmiyeh, E. (2009). Representing Sahrawi Refugees' 'Educational Displacement' to Cuba: Self-sufficient Agents or Manipulated Victims in Conflict? *Journal of Refugee Studies, 22*(3), 323–350.

Franck, G. (2019). The Economy of Attention. *Journal of Sociology, 55*(1), 8–19.

Galloway, A., & McKenzie, N. (2021, May 5). Home Affairs Investigating Relatives of Myanmar Military in Australia. *Sydney Morning Herald*. https://www.smh.com.au/politics/federal/home-affairs-investigating-relatives-of-myanmar-military-in-australia-20210504-p57ood.html

Gamlen, A. (2019). *Human Geopolitics: States, Emigrants and the Rise of Diaspora Institutions*. Oxford University Press.

Ghorashi, H. (2005). Agents of Change or Passive Victims: The Impact of Welfare States (The Case of the Netherlands) on Refugees. *Journal of Refugee Studies, 18*(2), 181–198.

Giardina, M. D. (2002). Global Hingis: Flexible Citizenship and the Transnational Celebrity. In *Sport Stars* (pp. 211–227). Routledge.

Giles, W. (2010). Livelihood and Afghan Refugee Workers in Iran. In *Class, Contention, and a World in Motion* (pp. 23–40). Berghahn Press.

Guerrero, A. L., & Tinkler, T. (2010). Refugee and Displaced Youth Negotiating Imagined and Lived Identities in a Photography-based Educational Project in the United States and Colombia. *Anthropology & Education Quarterly, 41*(1), 55–74.

Harrell-Bond, B. (1986). *Imposing Aid: Emergency Assistance to Refugees*. Oxford University Press.

Hearn, A. (2008). Meat, Mask, Burden: Probing the Contours of the Branded Self. *Journal of Consumer Culture, 8*(2), 197–217.

Kapoor, I. (2012). *Celebrity Humanitarianism: The Ideology of Global Charity*. Routledge.

Kea, P. J., & Roberts-Holmes, G. (2013). Producing Victim Identities: Female Genital Mutilation and the Politics of Asylum Claims in the United Kingdom. *Identities, 20*(1), 96–113.

Koinova, M. (2021). *Diaspora Entrepreneurs and Contested States*. Oxford University Press.

Lamb, K. (2021, March 19). Outed by Online Campaign, Children of Myanmar Junta Hounded Abroad. *Reuters*. https://www.reuters.com/article/uk-myanmar-politics-punishment-feature-idUKKBN2BB0E2

Lenette, C. (2019). *Arts-based Methods in Refugee Research: Creating Sanctuary*. Springer.

Malkki, L. H. (1995). *Purity and Exile: Violence, Memory, and National Cosmology Among Hutu Refugees in Tanzania*. University of Chicago Press.

Marshall, P. D. (2010). The Promotion and Presentation of the Self: Celebrity as Marker of Presentational Media. *Celebrity Studies, 1*(1), 35–48.

McQuiston, L. (2019). *Protest!: A History of Social and Political Protest Graphics*. White Lion Publishing.

Morris, J. C. (2019). Violence and Extraction of a Human Commodity: From Phosphate to Refugees in the Republic of Nauru. *The Extractive Industries and Society, 6*(4), 1122–1133.

Mostafanezhad, M. (2013). 'Getting in Touch with Your Inner Angelina': Celebrity Humanitarianism and the Cultural Politics of Gendered Generosity in Volunteer Tourism. *Third World Quarterly, 34*(3), 485–499.

Mostafanezhad, M. (2017). Celebrity Humanitarianism and the Popular Geopolitics of Hope along the Thai-Burma Border. *Political Geography, 58*, 67–76.

Ostergaard-Nielsen, E. (2003). The Politics of Migrants' Transnational Political Practices. *International Migration Review, 37*(3), 760–786.

Pupavac, V. (2008). Refugee Advocacy, Traumatic Representations and Political Disenchantment. *Government and Opposition, 43*(2), 270–292.

Richey, L. A., & Brockington, D. (2020). Celebrity Humanitarianism: Using Tropes of Engagement to Understand North/South Relations. *Perspectives on Politics, 18*(1), 43–59.

Robinson, L. (2007). The Cyberself: The Self-ing Project Goes Online, Symbolic Interaction in the Digital Age. *New Media & Society, 9*(1), 93–110.

Saltsman, A. (2014). Beyond the Law: Power, Discretion, and Bureaucracy in the Management of Asylum Space in Thailand. *Journal of Refugee Studies, 27*(3), 457–476.

Selth, A. (2021, June 15). Myanmar, Terrorism and the Demands of International Politics. *Lowy Interpreter.* https://www.lowyinstitute.org/the-interpreter/myanmar-terrorism-and-demands-international-politics

Sigona, N. (2014). The Politics of Refugee Voices: Representations. In *The Oxford Handbook of Refugee and Forced Migration Studies* (pp. 369–382). Oxford University Press.

Stoddard, B. (2013). Gods Behaving Badly: Media, Religion, and Celebrity Culture. *Journal of Religion and Popular Culture, 25*(2), 312–313.

Straus, S. (2001). Contested Meanings and Conflicting Imperatives: A Conceptual Analysis of Genocide. *Journal of Genocide Research, 3*(3), 349–375. https://doi.org/10.1080/14623520120097189

The Irrawaddy. (2010, June 10). Burmese General's Daughter Forced to Leave Australia. *The Irrawaddy.* https://www2.irrawaddy.com/article.php?art_id=18840

Tsaliki, L., Frangonikolopoulos, C. A., & Huliaras, A. (2014). *Transnational Celebrity Activism in Global Politics: Changing the World?* Intellect Books.

Tse, T., Leung, V., Cheng, K., & Chan, J. (2018). A Clown, a Political Messiah or a Punching Bag? Rethinking the Performative Identity Construction of Celebrity through Social Media. *Global Media and China, 3*(3), 141–157.

Van Krieken, R. (2012). *Celebrity Society.* Routledge.

Ward, P. (2019). *Celebrity Worship.* Routledge.

Weber, M. (2006). The Sociology of Charismatic Authority: The Nature of Charismatic Authority and its Routinization. In P. Marshall (Ed.), *The Celebrity Culture Reader* (pp. 55–71). Routledge.

Wroe, L. E. (2018). 'It Really is about Telling People Who Asylum Seekers Really Are, Because We Are Human like Anybody Else': Negotiating Victimhood in Refugee Advocacy Work. *Discourse & Society, 29*(3), 324–343.

Young, L. A., & Park, R. (2009). Engaging Diasporas in Truth Commissions: Lessons from the Liberia Truth and Reconciliation Commission Diaspora Project. *International Journal of Transitional Justice, 3*(3), 341–361.

PART II

Transnational Belongings

CHAPTER 4

Transnational Economic Engagements: The Africa-Australia Nexus

Farida Fozdar, David Mickler, Sarah Prout Quicke, Mary B. Setrana, Muhammad Dan Suleiman, and Dominic N. Dagbanja

This chapter reports data from an innovative modified Delphi study of the African-Australian diaspora's ongoing transnational connections to countries of origin. After considering the meaning and value of the term 'diaspora' and its relationship to transnationalism, we outline existing research focussing on the economic engagements of diasporas while acknowledging their interrelationships with social, cultural, and political dimensions. The chapter then describes the Delphi technique as employed and presents the key forms of economic transnational interaction identified by the Delphi participants. Some of the material has a focus on the Ghanaian and,

F. Fozdar (✉)
Department of Social Sciences, Curtin University, Perth, WA, Australia

D. Mickler • M. D. Suleiman
Africa Research & Engagement Centre (AfREC), The University of Western Australia, Crawley, WA, Australia
e-mail: david.mickler@uwa.edu.au; muhammad.suleiman@uwa.edu.au

© The Author(s), under exclusive license to Springer Nature Switzerland AG 2022
M. Phillips, L. Olliff (eds.), *Understanding Diaspora Development*,
https://doi.org/10.1007/978-3-030-97866-2_4

61

to a lesser extent, Kenyan diasporas in Australia, offering some specificity to the general points participants made. We also consider participants' recommendations for leveraging the rich and grounded resources that the diaspora offers.

INTRODUCTION

In 2003, the African Union (AU) amended its Constitution to include explicit reference to the "African diaspora" as an important core in building the African Union and its development agenda (African Union, 2003). Adding to the five geopolitical regions of the African continent (Northern, Southern, Eastern, Western and Central), the AU pronounced the global African diaspora of around 170 million people, the "sixth region of Africa" (Mwagiru, 2012, p. 77; Kamei, 2011, pp. 60–61). It defined this diaspora as "peoples of African origin living outside the continent, irrespective of their citizenship and nationality and who are willing to contribute to the development of the continent and the building of the African Union" (African Union, 2006).

This move exemplifies the growing interest in Africans outside their countries of origin as a potential developmental resource as well as a source of diasporic consciousness. Indeed, pan-Africanism, with its roots in black consciousness movements, its significance for national liberation struggles on the continent, and its contemporary transnational dimensions (Ndlovu-Gatsheni, 2015), is an important political, economic, and social phenomenon (Mickler & Sturman, 2021). It is, in many ways, an instance of the contemporary growth in diaspora consciousness—new forms of transnational identity, governance, affective connection and citizenship (Gamlen, 2014, 2019). These moves are part of a wider reconfiguration of world politics: state-led or

---

S. P. Quicke
Department of Geography, The University of Western Australia, Perth, WA, Australia
e-mail: sarah.proutquicke@uwa.edu.au

M. B. Setrana
Centre for Migration Studies, University of Ghana, Legon, Accra, Ghana

D. N. Dagbanja
Department of Law, The University of Western Australia Law School, Crawley, WA, Australia
e-mail: dominic.dagbanja@uwa.edu.au

region-led transnationalisms that recognise the ongoing relationships migrants have with regions of origin and their consequent development implications.

The turn to diaspora studies builds on transnationalism, which challenges the unidirectional and unidimensional approach of earlier migration studies by emphasising the non-linear, evolving, and dynamic processes through which diasporas are constructed and reproduced through both agential and structural forces. Transnationalism can be defined as the "regular and sustained" cross-border activities of individuals (Portes et al., 1999), a condition where "transmigrants ... maintain, build, and reinforce multiple linkages with their countries of origin" (Glick-Schiller et al., 1995, p. 52). These linkages may take a range of forms, resulting in what Levitt has called the transnational social field, where transnational practices of individuals ground the field across a range of dimensions (Levitt, 2001), including social, cultural, political and economic. Contrary to the usual celebratory accounts of transnationalism, Waldinger and Fitzgerald (2004) note that transnationalism may represent both a threat and an opportunity for sending and receiving countries, taking benign or malign forms which may help or hinder development and have a range of other consequences. Migration is now generally seen as a boon for origin country development, with diasporic communities conceiving, financing, and leading programmes targeted at improving their homelands and the sending countries developing policies to recruit their diasporas to support development initiatives. Such approaches are embraced by the international development community as positive, promoting 'diaspora-centred development'. However Boyle and Kitchin (2014, p. 28) argue that there are a range of problems associated with this fundamentally neo-liberal approach, to which we will return in the conclusion.

McIntyre and Gamlen (2019, p. 36) define diasporas as "dispersed migrant populations that retain a shared group identity and orientation towards a distant homeland", recognising that the connection is relational and emotional. Diasporas have "transformative potential" (Phillips, 2013, p. 178) to mobilise people around a shared identity. There are also socio-economic and political imperatives behind diaspora formation which are either internally defined or externally championed (Esman, 1986). Origin country governments may develop 'diaspora strategies' to harness the economic value of their transnational populations, and these are often pursued by poor and middle-income countries, including some African nations (Boyle & Kitchin, 2014). Origin-state diaspora institutions encourage the continuing identification and engagement of migrants with their homelands (Gamlen, 2014, 2019). Such institutions are found in over half the world's countries, being used by origin states in a form of "human geopolitics", to "tap" migrants for resources, "embrace" them for identity projects, and as leverage to "govern" them, with the latter function now dominating (Gamlen, 2019).

The reconfiguring impact of transnationalism on world politics is also evident in approaches taken to diaspora communities by host countries. In the Australian context, the Australian Government appears to have replaced the phrase 'migrant communities' with the term diasporas, thus recognising these ongoing transnational ties and their potential value. Diaspora communities are seen as valuable to processes of settlement, international relations, economic development, and investment (see Commonwealth of Australia, 2017). Indeed, the 2021 Senate Foreign Affairs Defence and Trade References Committee Report (2021, p. xi) goes so far as to recommend the active participation of diasporas in intergovernmental dialogues and debates.

While significant research exists on the African-Australian refugee diaspora (particularly the South Sudanese; see Fozdar, 2021, for a review), little work to date has focussed on the application of the concept of diaspora more broadly to the highly diverse African-Australian population (however, see Hiruy & Hutton, 2020; Fozdar et al., 2022) and to their continuing and developing transnational political, economic, social and cultural relationships, and their impacts on development. This chapter describes the findings of a methodologically innovative project that sought to begin to address this gap. It focusses on one element of that study: the economic transnational engagements of Africans in Australia.[1]

Background: African Diaspora Economic Engagement

The wider literature identifies a range of ways in which the African diaspora globally maintains economic engagements with countries of origin. These overlap to some extent with political connections. For example, dozens of African countries offer dual citizenship for citizens abroad, and diaspora communities lobby home countries for political and electoral participation (Adebayo, 2011; Whitaker, 2011); similarly political party

---

[1] We use the term 'Africans in Australia' rather than African-Australians or some other option, as it encompasses both those in Australia permanently with citizenship, those in Australia permanently but without citizenship, and those in Australia temporarily.

branches in the diaspora and hometown associations support political and economic engagement from afar, and communication technologies enhance these connections (Kyei & Setrana, 2017). Such transnational political connections feed into economic engagement opportunities by maintaining ties that support economic activity and enabling the transfer of resources and investment, and through allowing influence to facilitate such transactions. In other political activities, post-conflict societies' diasporas may actively support peacebuilding through lobbying, supporting legal institutions, and providing financial support for moderate political parties (Antwi-Boateng, 2011). It has also been suggested that diasporic engagement with countries of origin may help to de-politicise development and enable the application of critical perspectives to development choices (Marabello, 2013). Engagement with homelands through participation in traditional institutions, such as the "Return Chiefs" initiative (Kleist, 2011; Bob-Milliar, 2009), may spur local development and modernise chieftaincy institutions.

Diaspora organisations within host countries have been shown to strengthen transnational connections through sharing knowledge and assisting local civil society groups, while also supporting political systems in countries of origin and contributing to national development and policy (Norglo et al., 2016; Baggio, 2014; Bodomo, 2013). Such activities may positively impact peace, security, economic development, and integration. However, Waldinger and Fitzgerald (2004) make the point that such organisations may seek to remain a-political, even anti-political, in order to adequately represent their very diverse constituents. So their activities may be less political, and more economic, cultural and social. 'Geo-ethnic' diaspora organisations may be useful during crises such as Ebola (Gamlen, 2019; Pailey, 2017; Phillips, 2013; Lampert, 2012), through mobilising awareness and material support. However, some authors argue the influence of diasporas may be exaggerated (Bekoe & Burchard, 2016), with the actual effect of those living elsewhere limited by distance, both physical and in terms of knowledge capital. Country of origin governments also may be careful to balance attracting investment against attached political influence (Mohan, 2008).

In terms of African diaspora economic engagement, research has highlighted the benefits of circulating (including return) labour, technology transfer, and business ties via transnational diaspora communities (e.g. Setrana & Tonah, 2016). However, unidirectional financial remittances are the focus of much of the literature on diaspora and development impacts, and are the subject of considerable scholarly debate (see Boyle & Kitchin, 2014). On the one hand, remittances are seen by some as a critical alternative to African countries' reliance on foreign aid (Bodomo, 2013; Ratha & Mohapatra, 2011; Mohan & Zack-Williams, 2002). Unlike foreign aid, which risks being misappropriated at the governmental and non-governmental levels, the remittances go directly to the people (Bodomo, 2013) or are channelled through collectives such as hometown associations. According to Ratha and Mohapatra (2011), the potential annual savings of the African diaspora globally is about US$53 billion. Of this figure, about US$30.5 billion is attributable to the diaspora of Sub-Saharan African countries, which of course includes the large expatriate South African community (Bodomo, 2013; Ratha & Mohapatra, 2011; Mohan & Zack-Williams, 2002). This money is vital for impoverished states (Mohan, 2008). Remittances are also found to be psychologically beneficial at an individual level—migrant and return migrant households have better wellbeing than non-migrant households do (Kuschminder et al., 2018). The diaspora also contributes to tourism, generating related economic benefits (Addo, 2011). According to Cliggett (2003), money continues to have symbolic value for those involved in remittances to Africa, with it being a foundation for alliance building.

On the other hand, household remittance dependence and the high cost of remitting services have been identified as detrimental to household and community wellbeing in receiving countries in Africa (Nanziri & Gbahabo, 2020). There is also some debate within the literature about the extent to which remitting activities actually stimulate local markets, and whether they may exacerbate inequalities in communities of origin and foster migrant precarity in the host nation (e.g. de Haas, 2010). The diasporic community may become estranged from local customs and realities over time and distance (Kleist, 2011); and returned migrants may have difficulty re-establishing themselves in jobs, accommodation and networks, and also adjusting to poor infrastructure and the expectations of extended family members (Setrana & Tonah, 2016). Additionally, 'liberalisation from below', which emphasises local ownership of development processes and projects in home countries, may complicate the role of the African diaspora as development agents (Davies, 2012).

A range of structural, theoretical and policy challenges regarding African diasporic economic engagement with home countries also exists. Some diasporic communities may be antagonistic towards home governments and therefore also towards the idea of contributing to the development agenda of home countries, while home governments may lack the political will to implement policies that incorporate diasporic communities into national development (Crush & Chikanda, 2017). Relatedly, engagements through embassies may be politically difficult (Plaza, 2009). Balancing domestic interests (remittances from migration) and international interests (reducing migration) is also a challenge (Altrogge & Zanker, 2019).

The focus on financial remittances by both governments and researchers has been criticised, while other forms of values, knowledge, and skills remitted to support investment and other economic development benefits in origin countries remain under-researched. However, scholars of transnational migration are gradually shifting their attention to recognise that diaspora economic engagements are about more than just money (Setrana & Arhin-Sam, 2021). Diaspora engagements include sharing and transfer of information, values, ideas, and other non-monetary transfers (Levitt, 1998). Diasporas promote transnational ties, and act as bridges or as mediators between their home and host societies (Shain & Barth, 2003, pp. 449–50). On the latter, diasporas are well placed "to manipulate international images and thus to focus attention on the issue of (home) identity [and] this dynamic can be used to influence foreign policy decision making" of, and towards, home countries (Shain & Barth, 2003, p. 451). This can have economic impacts. They may transmit entrepreneurial spirit and skills that home countries may lack (Shain & Barth, 2003, pp. 449–50). Apart from remittances, African diasporas also contribute with other forms of tangible and intangible capital which Plaza & Ratha (2011, p. 33) refer to as the "5Cs" of "Intellectual capital, Financial capital, Political capital, Cultural capital and Social capital".

In the Australian context, there is little literature on transnational economic contributions to Africa. From the Australian perspective, the African diaspora is assumed to be useful but under-utilised in supporting Australia's foreign policy agenda for the continent, with people-to-people links particularly important in developing positive foreign policy and development agendas (Phillips, 2013). Organisations such as the African Think Tank and a range of South Sudanese organisations, among others, have supported a renewed foreign policy and development focus on Africa (Phillips, 2013). Beyond these observations however, scholars have identified a paucity of research addressing the economic dimensions of diasporic activity between Africa and Australia (Ndhlovu, 2014; Forrest et al., 2013). Indeed, the national dialogue about Africans in Australia tends to focus on humanitarian entrants who are commonly considered a drain on the Australian economy. The current study sought to push national dialogues beyond these flat stereotypes and begin to build a deeper and more nuanced understanding of the transnational political economy of African migrants in Australia.

Approach

The findings presented below are derived from a 2019–2020 pilot study of the transnational political, economic, social, and cultural engagements of Africans in Australia with their region of origin, using a modified Delphi technique. The Delphi method, established in the 1950s as a decision making and forecasting technique, is a structured method to assist the development of deep, respectful relationships through applied research (Sekayi & Kennedy, 2017). Experts offer feedback about a problem/question/issue based on research, policy, and experience. The facilitator generates a report, which is fed back to the expert group in an iterative manner over several rounds until a consensus is reached. The use of this technique builds a shared knowledge base, while removing interpersonal effects common in face-to-face research, such as social desirability and hierarchy deference effects (Davies & Hughes, 2014). It also builds trust between researcher and expert participants, through its iterative structure and encourages empowerment and ownership of the results (Keeney et al., 2011). It is particularly useful when (a) knowledge about a problem is nascent and future directions are unclear (e.g. when exploring new research frontiers), and (b) when working with experts who are not well known to each other and/or may be geographically dispersed (Charlton, 2004; Ziglio, 1996; Dalkey, 1967). This approach is appropriate for the current research, which explores a new question about a relatively new population, and where existing research is limited but experts with lived experience, as well as research and policy expertise, are available. It is a useful method where there are issues of distance and communication. The Delphi normally utilises quantitative mechanisms wherein the expert panel members rank or rate items developed as part of the first round (Sekayi & Kennedy, 2017). The modified Delphi often uses a prompt to generate responses, and qualitative approaches simply invite responses to a set of general questions, often based on background material provided.

For the current research, the first round of the modified qualitative Delphi used a short four-page literature review outlining existing research on political, economic, and socio-cultural engagements of the African diaspora as background. Participants were invited to respond to specific questions generated from this literature review and inductively by the researchers. These included open-ended questions about the drivers of migration; types of political, economic, and socio-cultural engagements; benefits and challenges of these engagements; and about how they might be enhanced or minimised respectively. We had a particular interest in the Kenya and Ghana diasporas, as a function of the research partners and grant conditions. The participants had varied backgrounds with a range of knowledge and experiences of diaspora-related engagements. The researchers were seeking insights into particular issues the literature had identified and the questions it had prompted, as well as inviting further contributions from participants.

An abductive approach to data analysis from Round 1 was taken (Timmermans & Tavory, 2012), with initial responses influenced by the literature review and prompt questions. Common themes were identified and summarised, with a number of direct quotes extracted for illustrative purposes. Outliers were also examined to signal contrasting opinions. These themes were then organised into a summary document according to whether they focussed on political, economic, or socio-cultural evidence of transnational diasporic engagement.

For Round 2, participants were sent the Round 1 summary document, with instructions that the goal was to develop consensus and identify any missing observations. Participants were invited to comment on, or provide specific examples of, any of the points included in the summary of themes, as well as to respond to the list of recommendations that had been generated. While a third round is common, due to the significant attrition rate (see below) and apparent consensus, the Delphi was suspended at this point. Given the fundamentally exploratory nature of this particular research question and the types and range of responses received, no attempt to seek ranking of responses or quantified endorsement was undertaken. Instead, the stability of the responses, and lack of further engagement, was taken as consensus (Scheibe et al., 1975).

The main limitation of the approach was the difficulty of recruiting and sustaining active participants. Our sample was drawn from existing research and professional networks, searches of publicly available contact details through organisational websites, and snowballing, and with criteria for participation including research or professional experience and expertise on the themes involved, and/or being a member of the African diaspora in Australia. 131 potential participants were invited to respond to the Delphi using this method, drawn from across government, intergovernmental and non-governmental migration, development, and business sectors in Australia and partner African countries (Kenya and Ghana), as well as from among diaspora communities living in Western Australia (where most of the research team are located). From these invitations, 38 experts agreed to participate. Of these, 21 sent responses for Round 1 (12 based in Australia, 7 in Ghana, 1 in USA and 1 in South Africa), and ultimately less than 20% of these completed Round 2. There is a range of possible reasons for the attrition rate, including time pressures, the COVID-19 environment, the assumption that silence indicates agreement, and lack of familiarity with the process. As a result, findings are somewhat limited, particularly due to the low numbers of Kenyan respondents. However, the first round is equivalent to a single interview, which is the basis of much of the existing research on the African diaspora in Australia. The abductive approach also allows plausible conclusions to be drawn based on the best available evidence without claiming comprehensive positive verification.

EMERGENT THEMES REGARDING THE TRANSNATIONAL POLITICAL ECONOMY

While the research findings presented here focus in particular on the economic dimensions of African-Australian diasporic engagement, these can never be completely disentangled from some of the other dimensions examined in the study. For example, political issues such as the right to dual citizenship and the ability to vote and contribute politically in home countries affected opportunities for economic engagement and ongoing affective connection, investment and retirement plans. On the other hand, the establishment of political mechanisms such as Diaspora Affairs Offices in origin countries, or initiatives such as the 'Year of Return' in Ghana, are seen as facilitating development activities and economic investment.

Among the Delphi participants, there was a consensus that a general lack of interest by African governments in the Australian diaspora, due to a combination of its size, distance from parts of Africa (in comparison, for example, with Europe) and strategic priority, meant that potential economic opportunities were missed. Many Delphi participants within the African diaspora in Australia were also somewhat suspicious of the Australian Government's sporadic efforts to engage the diaspora, seeing it as self-interested and limited. In terms of African Union efforts, the Pan-African Australasian Diaspora Network (PAADN), whose purpose is to contribute towards and advance the AU's Agenda 2063, was seen as helping to link the diaspora to political institutions in Africa (e.g. the African Union) and Australia (e.g. the Commonwealth Government), by representing the African diaspora in Australasia in the AU's political, economic and education dialogues, and potentially being useful for supporting diaspora involvement in development. Involvement in business and investment in Africa (including through partnerships with businesses in the host country) was seen as potentially important in promoting economic and jobs growth in the face of political instability in some African countries, with the diaspora potentially serving "as agents of transformation." Another function of the diaspora was seen as lobbying the host government to support countries of origin in their development agendas (politically and financially).

Below we outline the main economic themes, which focussed on remittances, brain drain/gain, and a range of other factors including investment and informal exchanges and support.

Remittances

While remittance flows from Australia to Africa were described as lower in volume than they are from the diaspora in other countries such as the UK and USA, the overwhelming focus of our Delphi responses to questions about diaspora economic engagement centred on remittances. In alignment with the international literature on remittances to Africa, diverse views were expressed regarding their impact. On the one hand, a number of participants outlined positive impacts: remittances are used to invest in housing and this has spin-off effects on a large number of businesses in home countries. People also spend remittances on starting businesses, which in turn reduces unemployment. Remittances are also spent on consumption more generally, and on living expenses (education, hospital bills, marriage ceremonies, funerals, and migration costs were mentioned). Some remittances sent by hometown associations and individual migrants are used to finance community development projects, and some diasporic engagement occurs through philanthropic and charity activities. For example, the *One Dollar Project* in Kenya established by members of the Kenyan diaspora in Perth in 2010 offers charitable support based on a dollar a week donations, and aims to be self-sustaining, spending nothing on administrative costs. Other participants drew attention to some of the potentially negative impacts of remitting practices. Two participants, for example, noted that remittance flows can enhance inequalities in recipient communities; and two others suggested that remittances can become a form of passive welfare for recipients, breeding, in their words, 'laziness'.

Challenges were also highlighted with respect to the infrastructure in place to support the process of remitting. Four participants described high ('predatory') transaction fees, duties, and taxes on remittances. While these fee structures enable African governments to access foreign currency to cushion exchange rates and hence improve development agendas, they also cause many people to try to transfer remittances through informal channels, such as friends and relatives, and to self-carry when visiting home. Some hide money in letters being posted (and often this gets lost). Remittances sent through official channels also create challenges for recipients in the home country. For example, in Ghana, many rural dwellers do not have bank accounts. They have to queue at financial institutions and adhere to personal identification processes that make such channels inaccessible for some. However, some African countries, it was noted, have a well-developed architecture for diaspora engagement and managing the flow of remittances. For example, Kenya is one of Africa's top remittance-receiving countries and has reduced the cost of remitting money through "multiple channels including digital applications [which have boosted] the number and volume of transfers". It was suggested that these countries could be 'best practice' case studies in understanding processes of remittances.

Participants also highlighted challenges for remitters in Australia. The sense of obligation for migrants to provide for their family members in Africa can place significant stress on migrants, particularly if they did not come to Australia through the skilled migration stream:

> Through working with people from refugee backgrounds, I am aware that there is a strong sense of obligation felt by people to send money back to family in the home country (or a third country, or refugee camp, wherever family members might be). This is very understandable as often family members are in very dire situations. ... I am aware that the sending of money back to the home country can also cause tensions within the family in Australia partly because of the financial stress it causes and partly because the family members of one partner (the husband or wife) may be favoured over

the family of the other partner, causing resentment. (Migrant settlement service manager, Perth)

Friends and family rely on African-Australians for support of livelihoods back home. This is central to family life and, in fact, the 'social security' for most families in the absence of a state sponsored social security system. That brings high expectations and sometimes puts unnecessary pressure on them. (Ghanaian UN adviser)

The practice of 'reverse remitting' was also identified by participants, indicating just how precarious the socio-economic circumstances of some African migrants in Australia can be and/or the lack of availability in Australia of certain goods and services:

Quite a few people I know have sent enough for their relatives to live comfortably in Kenya. On the other hand, I believe that the flow may be the other way where parents or other relatives are funding some of the expenses of those who are on student visas or who have not found a strong financial footing in Australia. (Asian Kenyan Australian migrant, researcher)

There are also reverse remittances that are sent from Ghana, for example, to the diaspora. Most of these reverse remittances include but are not limited to local concoctions, food items and African print wear. (Representative, Ghana Immigration Service)

They feel an ongoing connection to the African continent through what is called in the literature as reverse remittances where family members back home send them items like local foods, cloths, traditional medicines … Also some of them with specialised skills are invited or called upon to contribute to our developmental programmes as and when they are needed. (Representative, Ghana Refugee Board)

Although the subject of reverse remittances is hardly mentioned in the literature (see Mazzucato, 2011), our evidence suggests that remittances are not unidirectional but that those in the origin countries also remit to families living in Australia.

Brain Drain/Gain?

There were very divergent perspectives amongst first round participants regarding the extent to which African migration to Australia could be conceptualised as a process of 'brain drain', posed in this framing as a negative phenomenon in terms of development on the African continent. To indicate this diversity, we note that five participants broadly agreed, six broadly disagreed, and seven described it as a highly complex situation that did not neatly fit into a 'yes' or 'no' response category. Many highlighted the importance of temporal dimensions in answering this question: initially, emigration creates a brain drain, but after some time, migrants remit and become involved in improving the situation in their country of origin through advocacy, business, lobbying and return migration. For example, one noted that the new national cathedral in Accra has been designed, and will be constructed, by a member of the diaspora. So, for many, it was felt that there was a balance between loss and gain of human and economic capital through migration.

Those that agreed with the brain drain thesis pointed to the fact that the skilled migrants that have left Africa, after being trained locally, are needed back home to develop the continent. Emigration of medical and academic professionals was viewed as particularly problematic for countries of origin:

> I think the impact on missing skills is clear. In the health sector alone the continent loses USD 2 billion annually. Many countries have invested in training medical professionals only for them to leave. Similar outcomes have been calculated for public service, education and construction. Skilled labour is an important aspect of sustainable development in Africa and it is well established that brain drain impacts this negatively. (Senior migration consultant, Institute for Security Studies, Africa)

Some of those who disagreed argued that there are thousands of Africans graduating from universities on the continent each year who cannot find jobs. They viewed emigration as a failure of source country government leadership to maintain and utilise these human resources. Others included this context as one component of a complex set of circumstances driving emigration:

> Many Africans who choose to migrate to Australia are highly skilled and this is part of an overall movement of skilled people from developing countries

into developed countries where there may be more opportunities and better salaries. However, it is also true that highly educated professionals in their African country of origin are often unemployed or under-employed so their skills are not being utilised in the country of origin anyway. I think the idea of "brain drain" is problematic. It assumes a simplistic analysis of people getting qualifications and then leaving their country to get a better (i.e. better paid) job elsewhere instead of staying and contributing their skills to their country. I believe the situation is more complex than that. There may be no opportunities in the home country for a range of reasons including very weak economies, non-existent IT sectors, limited manufacturing sector, no investment in research and development and lack of development in their professional sectors. There may be systemic issues such as corruption or ethnic divisions which create barriers for some to get jobs in their fields. Additionally, if there is political instability, persecution or conflict, people with skills have a greater chance of being able to migrate (rather than take the long and often futile route of becoming a refugee) than those without skills. Ultimately, the way to circumventing or reducing loss of skilled people from their country of origin is for that country to be able to provide opportunities, a reasonable standard of living and a sense of security for its citizens. (Migrant settlement service manager, Perth)

However, the most common response regarding the extent to which emigration represented a brain drain was an acknowledgement that it is predominantly skilled workers who are leaving the continent for countries like Australia; this could be compensated for through specific strategies to engage the diaspora in development initiatives in their country of origin. Strategies suggested include support for remittances and investment, shared research collaborations and skills transfer (i.e. brain circulation), and creation of an architecture to harness the potential of return migrants to contribute to home country development and then aggressively incentivise their return:

It has already been established that it is students and the mostly highly skilled or semi-skilled who migrate to Australia the most. This means a drain on a developing country like Ghana, but with a well-managed migration and good diaspora policy these persons can contribute positively to the origin country … In this era of migration and development the diaspora is seen as a brain gain and a source of rich experiences and both human and financial capital that can be tapped for development. (Representative, Ghana Immigration Service)

A number of participants spoke of the importance of returning migrants who bring capital, help to establish businesses, fill home country vacancies, and provide their expertise for the development of the continent. Others invest in housing, transportation and the education sectors. African-based organisations are also involved in business engagements by creating networks and business advisory and advocacy groups in Australia to help promote and facilitate business between Australia and Africa. For example, the Ghana-Alumni Association is made up of people who received their education in Australia and have returned home, contributing their skills to the development of Ghana through discussion of Ghana-Australia issues with the Australian High Commission in Ghana and in activities such as the organisation of educational fairs (like trade fairs, but for education) in collaboration with Australian universities.

Three participants noted that returnees from Australia to Ghana bring many benefits (including new skills and knowledge critical for nation building):

> Most of those who studied in Australia are now working in government institutions, such as the Immigration Service, and some are government appointees. Others are lecturing in the universities and some are in the private sector particularly mining ... The diaspora also serve as agents of transformation as well as economic diplomats, linking the country to Australia and vice versa. In this regard, they have become ambassadors, not only for Ghana but also for Australia, selling the countries to his/her peers. (Representative, Ghana Immigration Service)

Some governments have been proactive in encouraging return migration and economic investment of diaspora members. For instance, participants noted the Ghanaian government has introduced a range of measures to try to harness the diaspora for national developmental purposes (refer to Box 4.1 for more details of such investments).

Other Economic Engagements

While, comparatively speaking, there has been limited economic engagement between Australia and Africa, there is a growing range of economic connections between the continents. Some are micro-connections sustained through the committed labour of diaspora groups. These include the work of churches and migrant associations that support new migrants

> **Box 4.1:** Ghanaian Government Programmes to Engage the Diaspora (as identified by participants)
>
> - establishing diaspora desk offices within diplomatic missions to assist diaspora members to engage in opportunities back home;
> - creating a Diaspora Affairs Unit under the Office of the President, enabling matters relating to the diaspora to be directly dealt with;
> - generating partnerships with the International Organisation for Migration and the European Union to engage expatriates in key projects;
> - securing land for those willing to return to assist with development initiatives;
> - introducing the 'Year of Return' (2019) initiative, which saw more members of the diaspora visiting;
> - rolling out a 'Beyond the Return' agenda to encourage diaspora investment; and
> - introducing incentive packages in key sectors (e.g. health, education) to attract return migrants.

to find jobs, assist newly arrived students to settle, and organise activities to educate the diaspora about Australian employment and education systems, as well as providing English language training. They also support the promotion of national and continental landmark events, such as Africa Day, and identify opportunities to engage in remittance practices and humanitarian programmes, as well as international trade and investment schemes.

> Much of the effort in this area … is being picked up by community organisations and passionate individuals who do not have the resources or the reach to make a sustained impact in terms of people being given the support to move upward financially. (Asian Kenyan Australian migrant, Researcher)

Other economic exchanges identified are more formalised. These include:

- trade and economic agreements between governments (which have increased in recent years);

- business establishment and investment that generates employment in both countries;
- the importation of goods (e.g. fabrics, arts and crafts, food) from Africa to Australia;
- Foreign Direct Investment (FDI);
- diasporic and consular services for welfare, trade and tourism promotion and investment forums; and
- international business collaborations (particularly in the mining sector), which generate diasporic connections as African employees are transferred to Australia and Australian companies operating in Africa hire African-Australians for cultural and logistical reasons.

Another important area of economic engagement identified between Africa and Australia is the promotion of diaspora bonds and investments by African governments to their diasporic communities in Australia. These bonds provide states with capital needed for development. Some African governments hold seminars and 'road shows' to publicise these initiatives among diaspora communities.

In general, participants noted that these engagements had produced benefits in the form of increased employment in both home and host countries, a boost in trade, investment and tourism activities, and skills and knowledge transfers through educational scholarships and exchange opportunities, together with research collaborations. One participant also noted that diasporic communities in Australia play a critical role in holding Australian businesses to account when they exploit African partners and government trusts.

The assessment of economic exchange between the continents was not, however, wholly positive. Participants described blockages to enhanced economic exchanges, from cumbersome clearance procedures at ports, to a dearth of professional integration structures and the high costs associated with trade fairs and exhibitions in Australia. They also described a lack of credit facilities, business investment opportunities, and tourism infrastructure in African home countries as stalling greater economic exchange between the continents. Corruption was also mentioned as a barrier to meaningful economic exchange.

Conclusion

The African diaspora globally has a significant influence on the continent's development trajectory and this influence will likely increase as population growth outpaces other regions of the world, suggesting increased pressure for extra-continental migration and concomitant opportunities for transnational economic engagements and development. The AU, in acknowledging this trajectory, has sought to harness this influence. Similarly, host country governments are beginning to appreciate the importance, and potential power, of large diaspora communities. While the African diaspora in Australia is relatively small when compared to other regions of the world, it is growing as a significant presence in Australia.

This chapter has outlined some findings from a Delphi study of engagements between Africans in Australia and their home region, particularly economic transnational engagements and their implications for development. Many of the issues identified align with the existing literature and confirm that patterns and issues raised in other national and regional contexts are also relevant in Australia. The sorts of development initiatives identified by Boyle and Kitchin (2014, p. 19), for example, "hometown associations to agricultural cooperatives, from charities to advocacy groups, from churches and religions to learned medical and scientific academies, ... from political parties to national arts and cultural institutions, from electoral systems to citizenship laws, ... from satellite TV media to social networking sites, and from university alumni projects to technology transfer" are found among the Delphi responses, influencing their homelands, and host country, in a range of ways. Key is the identification of diaspora members as agents of development in the countries of origin; but in addition, there exists the more nuanced and complex relationship between diaspora and development, making it problematic to conclude diaspora impact as solely positive or negative. Again, the nexus between diaspora engagement and development is not only in financial contributions but also includes other forms of economic engagements, such as skills transfer and community development. The Delphi approach provided an opportunity for specific local examples and experiences to be shared as illustrations of wider trends in transnational economic engagement. In particular, it identified a range of important areas for future research: from more nuanced understandings of the actual remitting practices of African migrants, to the possibilities for wider political influence that may impact development trajectories in countries of origin. Such work is critical for moving national dialogues about Africans in Australia beyond simplistic narratives of humanitarianism that fail to capture the multitude of ways in which agency is exercised in the shaping of development trajectories of both host and origin localities.

However, a word of caution is appropriate. Boyle and Kitchin (2014, p. 28) identify a range of problems associated with the "diaspora for development" approach including "the neglected intellectual bases of the agenda, the degree to which an unhelpful cottage industry has surfaced around it, the extent to which the concept of the diaspora is being mobilised wittingly or unwittingly to include and exclude certain communities, the failure to think through how citizenship rules might affect and be affected by diaspora-centred development, the extent to which the multiple stakeholders involved in diaspora strategies are being aligned, and, finally, the question of who development benefits, where, how, and why." There is no space to engage with each of these in any depth, but it is worth noting them and considering the ways in which the Delphi participants have bought into or resisted these narratives. The lived experience and observations of the Delphi experts identify both positive and negative impacts of the transnational economic interactions they describe, including uneven impacts, exclusions of some sections of the community, issues around citizenship, and conflicts between the interests of different stakeholders. Another feature of Australia-Africa economic engagement, one that is not discussed here given our specific focus on diaspora relationships, but which is important to mention given its negative impact, is that of mainstream Australian business interests in Africa. Of particular concern is the potentially exploitative, extractive nature of the expanding Australian mining initiatives in Africa. This is an area the African diaspora in Australia is vocal about and which, with sufficient political influence, it may have the potential to influence, to secure better development outcomes for Africa.

There were a number of recommendations from the project. Participants felt African governments should explore the value of developing, resourcing and implementing comprehensive diaspora engagement plans, including reducing bureaucratic red tape and building trust to facilitate diaspora contributions. The creation of a Migration and Diaspora Office and closer work with embassies was suggested to facilitate engagement. Improving remittance infrastructure was also seen as urgent and vital. There was also a desire for leadership by home countries to encourage diaspora members to advocate national unity and national development goals over narrower political ends. Finally, there was an identified need for home governments to support reintegration of returned diaspora members, where appropriate.

Participants also felt that the Australian Government could improve diaspora participation through setting in place better structures for identifying and engaging Africans in Australia. Developing infrastructure to enumerate this population and assess settlement outcomes was seen as a prerequisite to positively working together for the benefit of both home and host countries. The Government was encouraged to engage with the African Union and non-traditional African country potential trading partners, and to deepen Australia-Africa international relationships to enable social and cultural engagements to be developed and strengthened. Reconsideration of visa requirements to enable greater interaction was also suggested.

Overall, the flourishing of dynamic and meaningful transnational development-focused relationships across the Indian Ocean between the African diaspora in Australia and the African continent requires a long-term strategy involving the establishment of relevant institutions and socialisation practices, perhaps similar to those that have been successfully developed between several Asian countries and Australia over the last four decades. Such a strategy could facilitate positive two-way economic relationships that would benefit both regions.

Acknowledgements The authors would like to acknowledge the support of a UWA Research Collaboration Award that funded the research.

REFERENCES

Altrogge, J., & Zanker, F. (2019). *The Political Economy of Migration Governance in the Gambia.* Arnold Bergstraesser Institute. Retrieved May 18, 2021, from https://www.arnold-bergstraesser.de/sites/default/files/field/pub-download/medam_gambia_report_altrogge_zanker.pdf

Adebayo, A. (2011). The New African Diaspora: Engaging the Question of Brain Drain-Brain Gain. *Journal of Global Initiatives: Policy, Pedagogy, Perspective, 6*(1), 61–89.

Addo, E. (2011). European Heritage and Cultural Diversity: The Bricks and Mortar of Ghana's Tourism Industry. *Journal of Contemporary African Studies, 29*(4), 405–425.

African Union. (2006). *Decision on the Definition of the African Diaspora.* Retrieved May 10, 2021, from https://archives.au.int/handle/123456789/4589

African Union. (2003). *Protocol on Amendments to the Constitutive Act of the African Union*. Retrieved May 10, 2021, from https://archives.au.int/handle/123456789/6435

Antwi-Boateng, O. (2011). The Political Participation of the US-based Liberian Diaspora and Its Implication for Peacebuilding. *Africa Today, 58*(1), 3–26.

Baggio, F. (2014). *Africans on the Move: Human Mobility in Ghana, Nigeria, Angola and South Africa*. Scalabrini Institute for Human Mobility in Africa-SIHMA.

Bekoe, D., & Burchard, S. (2016). The Kenyan Diaspora in the United States and the 2013 Elections: When Money Does Not Equal Power. *Diaspora Studies, 9*(2), 128–140.

Bob-Milliar, G. (2009). Chieftaincy, Diaspora, and Development: The Institution of Nkosuohene in Ghana. *African Affairs, 108*(433), 541–558.

Bodomo, A. (2013). African Diaspora Remittances Are Better Than Foreign Aid Funds. *World Economics, 14*(4), 21–29.

Boyle, M., & Kitchin, R. (2014). Diaspora-centred Development: Current Practice, Critical Commentaries, and Research Priorities. In S. Sahoo (Ed.), *Global Diasporas and Development* (pp. 17–37). Springer.

Charlton, J. (2004). Delphi Technique. In M. Lewis-Beck, A. Bryman, & T. Liao (Eds.), *The SAGE Encyclopedia of Social Science Research Methods* (p. 245). SAGE Publications.

Cliggett, L. (2003). Gift Remitting and Alliance Building in Zambian Modernity: Old Answers to Modern Problems. *American Anthropologist, 105*(3), 543–552.

Commonwealth of Australia. (2017). *2017 Foreign Policy White Paper: Opportunity, Security, Strength*. Commonwealth of Australia.

Crush, J., & Chikanda, A. (2017). Mutual Antagonisms: Why the South African Diaspora and the South African Government Do Not Engage. In J. Mangala (Ed.), *Africa and Its Global Diaspora* (pp. 331–357). Palgrave Macmillan.

Dalkey, N. (1967). *Delphi*. Rand Corporation.

Davies, M., & Hughes, N. (2014). *Doing a Successful Research Project: Using Qualitative or Quantitative Methods*. Palgrave Macmillan.

Davies, R. (2012). African Diasporas, Development and the Politics of Context. *Third World Quarterly, 33*(1), 91–108.

de Haas, H. (2010). Migration and Development: A Theoretical Perspective. *International Migration Review, 44*(1), 227–264.

Esman, M. (1986). The Chinese Diaspora in Southeast Asia. In G. Sheffer (Ed.), *Modern Diasporas in International Politics* (pp. 130–163). Croom Helm.

Forrest, J., Johnston, R., & Poulsen, M. (2013). Middle-Class Diaspora: Recent Immigration to Australia from South Africa and Zimbabwe. *South African Geographical Journal, 95*(1), 50–69.

Fozdar, F. (2021). Belonging in the Land Down Under: Black Africans in Australia. *International Migration*. https://doi.org/10.1111/imig.12862

Fozdar, F., Quicke, S. P., & Mickler, D. (2022). Are Africans in Australia a Diaspora?. *Diaspora Studies, 15*(1), 87–117.

Gamlen, A. (2019). *Human Geopolitics: States, Emigrants, and the Rise of Diaspora Institutions.* Oxford University Press.

Gamlen, A. (2014). Diaspora Institutions and Diaspora Governance. *International Migration Review, 48,* S180–S217.

Glick-Schiller, N., Basch, L., & Blanc, C. (1995). From Immigrant to Transmigrant: Theorizing Transnational Migration. *Anthropological Quarterly, 68*(1), 48–63.

Hiruy, K., & Hutton, R. (2020). Towards a Re-imagination of the New African Diaspora in Australia: Superdiversity, Interconnectedness and Cultural Brokerage. *African Diaspora, 12*(1–2), 153–179.

Kamei, S. (2011). Diaspora as the 'Sixth Region of Africa': An Assessment of the African Union Initiative, 2002–10. *Diaspora Studies, 4*(1), 59–76.

Keeney, S., Hasson, F., & McKenna, H. (2011). *The Delphi Technique in Nursing and Health Research.* Wiley-Blackwell.

Kleist, N. (2011). Modern Chiefs: Tradition, Development and Return among Traditional Authorities in Ghana. *African Affairs, 110*(441), 629–647.

Kyei, O., & Setrana, B. (2017). Political Participation Beyond National Borders: The Case of Ghanaian Political Party Branches in the Netherlands. In S. Tonah, B. Setrana, & J. Arthur (Eds.), *Migration and Development in Africa: Trends, Challenges, and Policy Implications* (pp. 41–55). Lexington Books.

Kuschminder, K., Andersson, L., & Seigel, M. (2018). Migration and Multidimensional Well-Being in Ethiopia: Investigating the Role of Migrants Destinations. *Migration and Development, 7*(3), 321–340.

Lampert, B. (2012). Diaspora and Development? London-based Nigerian Organisations and the Transnational Politics of Socio-Economic Status and Gender. *Development Policy Review, 30*(2), 149–167.

Levitt, P. (2001). *The Transnational Villagers.* University of California Press.

Levitt, P. (1998). Social Remittances: Migration Driven Local-Level Forms of Cultural Diffusion. *The International Migration Review, 32*(4), 926–948.

Marabello, S. (2013). Translating and Acting Diaspora: Looking Through the Lens of a Co-development Project between Italy and Ghana. *African Studies, 72*(2), 207–227.

Mazzucato, V. (2011). Reverse Remittances in the Migration-Development Nexus: Two-Way Flows between Ghana and the Netherlands. *Population Space and Place, 17*(5), 454–468.

McIntyre, C., & Gamlen, A. (2019). States of Belonging: How Conceptions of National Membership Guide State Diaspora Engagement. *Geoforum, 103,* 36–46.

Mickler, D., & Sturman, K. (2021). Pan-Africanism, Participation and Legitimation in the African Governance Architecture. *Journal of Common Market Studies, 59*(2), 446–458.

Mohan, G. (2008). Making Neoliberal States of Development: The Ghanaian Diaspora and the Politics of Homelands. *Environment and Planning D: Society and Space, 26*(3), 464–479.

Mohan, G., & Zack-Williams, A. (2002). Globalisation from Below: Conceptualising the Role of the African Diasporas in Africa's Development. *Review of African Political Economy, 29*(92), 211–236.

Mwagiru, M. (2012). The African Union's Diplomacy of the Diaspora: Context, Challenges and Prospects. *African Journal on Conflict Resolution, 12*(2), 73–85.

Nanziri, L., & Gbahabo, P. (2020). Remittance Prices and Welfare: Evidence from Sub-Saharan Africa. In M. Konte & L. Mbaye (Eds.), *Migration, Remittance and Sustainable Development in Africa* (pp. 82–96). Taylor and Francis.

Ndhlovu, F. (2014). *Becoming an African Diaspora in Australia: Language, Culture, Identity.* Springer.

Ndlovu-Gatsheni, S. (2015). Decoloniality in Africa: A Continuing Search for a New World Order. *Australasian Review of African Studies, 36*(2), 22–50.

Norglo, B., Goris, M., Lie, R., & Ong'ayo, A. (2016). The African Diaspora's Public Participation in Policy-making Concerning Africa. *Diaspora Studies, 9*(2), 83–99.

Pailey, R. (2017). Liberia, Ebola and the Pitfalls of State-Building: Reimagining Domestic and Diasporic Public Authority. *African Affairs, 116*(465), 648–670.

Phillips, M. (2013). Migration and Australian Foreign Policy towards Africa: The Place of Australia's African Transnational Communities. In D. Mickler & T. Lyons (Eds.), *New Engagement: Contemporary Australian Foreign Policy Towards Africa* (pp. 176–192). Melbourne University Press.

Plaza, S. (2009). Promoting Diaspora Linkages: The Role of Embassies. Conference on *Diaspora and Development*, July 14, 2009. World Bank, Washington, DC.

Plaza, S., & Ratha, D. (2011). Harnessing Diaspora Resources for Africa. In D. Ratha & S. Plaza (Eds.), *Diaspora for Development in Africa* (pp. 1–54). World Bank.

Portes, A., Guarnizo, L., & Landolt, P. (1999). The Study of Transnationalism: Pitfalls and Promise of an Emergent Research Field. *Ethnic and Racial Studies, 22*(2), 217–237.

Ratha, D., & Mohapatra, S. (2011). *Preliminary Estimates of Diaspora Savings.* Migration and Development, Brief 14. World Bank: Washington, DC.

Scheibe, M., Skutsch, M., & Schofer, J. (1975). Experiments in Delphi Methodology. In H. Linstone & M. Turoff (Eds.), *The Delphi Method: Techniques and Applications* (pp. 262–287). Addison-Wesley Publishing Company.

Sekayi, D., & Kennedy, A. (2017). Qualitative Delphi Method: A Four Round Process with a Worked Example. *The Qualitative Report, 22*(10), 2755–2763.

Senate Foreign Affairs Defence and Trade References Committee. (2021). *Issues Facing Diaspora Communities in Australia*. Retrieved May 12, 2021, from https://parlinfo.aph.gov.au/parlInfo/download/committees/reportsen/024485/toc_pdf/IssuesfacingdiasporacommunitiesinAustralia.pdf; fileType=application%2Fpdf

Setrana, M., & Arhin-Sam, K. (2021). Harnessing Social and Political Remittances for Africa's Development: The Case of Skilled Returnees and Skilled Return Migrant Groups in Ghana. In M. Konte & L. Mbaye (Eds.), *Migration, Remittances, and Sustainable Development in Africa* (pp. 138–156). Routledge.

Setrana, M., & Tonah, S. (2016). Do Transnational Links Matter After Return? Labour Market Participation among Ghanaian Return Migrants. *The Journal of Development Studies, 52*(4), 549–560.

Shain, Y., & Barth, A. (2003). Diasporas and International Relations Theory. *International Organization, 57*(3), 449–479.

Timmermans, S., & Tavory, I. (2012). Theory Construction in Qualitative Research: From Grounded Theory to Abductive Analysis. *Sociological Theory, 30*(3), 167–186.

Waldinger, R., & Fitzgerald, D. (2004). Transnationalism in Question. *American Journal of Sociology, 109*(5), 1177–1195.

Whitaker, B. (2011). The Politics of Home: Dual Citizenship and the African Diaspora. *The International Migration Review, 45*(4), 755–783.

Ziglio, E. (1996). The Delphi Method and Its Contribution to Decision-making. In M. Adler & E. Ziglio (Eds.), *Gazing into the Oracle: The Delphi Method and Its Application to Social Policy and Public Health* (pp. 3–26). Jessica Kingsley Publishers.

CHAPTER 5

From Resettled Refugees to Humanitarian Actors: The Transformation of Transnational Social Networks of Care

Louise Olliff

In June 2021, a short video was shown at a high-level meeting of governments, non-governmental organisations (NGOs) and UN agencies involved in the resettlement of refugees.[1] The video featured a young woman from Central African Republic who had been living as a refugee in Cameroon since 2014. The woman, Marie, tells the story of her life before and after becoming a refugee.[2] It is a story that is full of violence, loss, displacement, and struggle; her parents were killed in front of her, and Marie struggled to find somewhere safe to live as a young woman on her own. But the story Marie narrates ends on a hopeful note, for she has been

---

[1] The video was shown at the Annual Tripartite Consultations on Resettlement (ATCR) where the author was present as a representative of the Refugee Council of Australia.

[2] Pseudonym.

L. Olliff (✉)
School of Regulation and Global Governance, Australian National University, Canberra, ACT, Australia
e-mail: louise.olliff@anu.edu.au

© The Author(s), under exclusive license to Springer Nature Switzerland AG 2022
M. Phillips, L. Olliff (eds.), *Understanding Diaspora Development*, https://doi.org/10.1007/978-3-030-97866-2_5

granted a permanent visa to resettle in Australia. She says (translated), "When they told me I was among those chosen to go and live in Australia, I was so happy! ...My life will change in so many ways; I can say in every way." At the end of the video, Marie's manner visibly shifts. From sitting back and speaking with a soft voice and arms crossed as she tells of her past and present, Marie then leans towards the camera and speaks with conviction about her imagined future in Australia. She says:

> I know if I leave Cameroon I must continue my education and after, I must find work, and I must look back and help others who are suffering like me. Orphans, widows, I have to help them, because I am one of them. And if I can become someone, there is no way I can forget others. I cannot stand by and watch refugees suffer. That's impossible. It's impossible.

The idea of former refugees living in countries like Australia 'looking back' and acting to help forcibly displaced people in other parts of the world is one that has received scant attention from researchers, policymakers and practitioners. This chapter focuses on how the resettlement of refugees like Marie in 'third countries' provides fertile ground for processes of diasporisation—the uncertain, indeterminate process of coming together as 'a people' (Tölölyan, 2007)—and collective action, as new arrivals who identify both with a homeland *and* with experiences of forced displacement come together for a variety of purposes. More specifically, this chapter explores the question of how resettlement and the formation of refugee diaspora organisations (RDOs) transforms transnational social networks of care, with significance for refugees and people seeking asylum living in very difficult circumstances elsewhere in the world. While much has been written about diaspora transnationalism and development from a binary of home- and host-lands, this chapter focuses on diaspora engagement in sites of displacement, drawing our attention to diaspora interventions in humanitarian contexts.

This chapter begins by conceptualising refugee diasporas and diaspora transnationalism before turning to how experiences of dispersal (third country resettlement) and the Australian context structure diaspora transnational social networks and practices. I describe the characteristics of diaspora organisations commonly set up by resettled refugees to help 'their people' living in displacement contexts in other parts of the world, what they do, and the implications of diaspora humanitarianism for people of concern to the international refugee regime. I conclude with a

5 FROM RESETTLED REFUGEES TO HUMANITARIAN ACTORS...   89

discussion of how countries like Australia might reimagine resettlement beyond the immediate protection it affords small numbers of refugees, but as a contribution to building more robust transnational networks of support and care through a more considered engagement with refugee diaspora communities.

Conceptualising 'Refugee Diasporas'

The term 'refugee diasporas' broadly denotes groups of people who connect in diasporic ways and are, have been, or have connections to persons of concern to the international refugee regime. This regime itself can be understood as 'the principles, norms, rules and decision-making procedures that influence the treatment of refugees by actors in the international system, including states, international organizations, and NGOs' (Betts et al., 2012, p. 125). 'Refugee diasporas' should be seen as an analytical construct and not one that is claimed or widely used by groups who may be conceptualised in this way. Indeed, there are many who could be considered within this sub-set for research purposes who are unfamiliar with either the 'diaspora' term and/or do not necessarily associate or group themselves with other communities within this sub-set. Instead, people tend to self-identify as a diaspora community first and foremost by affiliation to ethnic, religious, country or region of origin identities (e.g. Hazara, Assyrian, Lebanese or Oromo communities). Grouping different diasporas together as a sub-set by this dispersal experience (i.e. refugee displacement), I argue, has utility more for exploring the implications of diaspora networks on humanitarian responses to forced displacement than for comparative purposes, such as comparing refugee diaspora to other 'types' of diaspora. In this, it is assumed that what brings this sub-set together is lived experience or engagement with the international refugee regime, and presumably knowledge and networks that have implications for this regime and those who are its central objects.

There are other scholars who have also found utility in the refugee diaspora concept, notably the important work of Nicholas Van Hear (1998, 2006, 2009) who has long argued that "if displacement persists and people consolidate themselves in their territories of refuge, complex relations will develop among these different domains of what we may call the 'refugee diaspora': that is, among those at home, those in neighbouring territories, and those spread further afield" (Van Hear, 2006, p. 9). As in my own research, Van Hear focuses on the implications of refugee diaspora

90   L. OLLIFF

transnationalism—on the interrelationships between groups of people who are dispersed—rather than on the effects of diasporic identity on local lives and communities. What Van Hear suggests is that interrelationships between different groups of refugee diaspora have effect; they *do* things (see also Monsutti, 2004).

In terms of conceptualising refugee diaspora transnational networks, Van Hear notes that there are important differences within these networks that can be understood both spatially and structurally, with the 'near diaspora' being those in neighbouring territories and the 'wider diaspora' being those further from the homeland, mostly in more affluent countries such as Canada, the United States, parts of Europe and Australia. Van Hear (2006, p. 11) suggests that at least three sets of relations emerge from this understanding of refugee diaspora: between the 'homeland' or territory of origin and the neighbouring country of first asylum; between the neighbouring country of first asylum and the wider diaspora; and between the 'homeland' and the wider diaspora. For example, for those in the near diaspora, the precarity of lives lived in countries of first asylum (Agier, 2008) and geographical proximity to a homeland where one has fled violence and persecution shapes the possibilities for connection both to those 'back home' and to those in the wider diaspora who are often perceived as the 'lucky ones' with an obligation to support those they left behind. For the purposes of this chapter, I focus specifically on the inter-relationships between the wider diaspora (refugees resettled in Australia) and near diaspora (refugees and others displaced from the homeland, most of whom reside in neighbouring countries).

Refugee Diaspora Transnationalism

As to what exactly refugee diasporas do, there is a significant and growing body of literature since the 1990s on political, economic and socio-cultural dimensions of diaspora transnationalism, and on the relationships between diasporas and homelands in particular (cf. Brinkerhoff, 2012; Collier, 2000; Fullilove, 2008; Nyberg-Sørensen, 2007; Sharma et al., 2011; Zinterer, 2005). Collier (2000), for example, focuses on the role of diasporas in financing and exacerbating conflicts in their homelands, emphasising the 'romanticised attachments to their group of origin' and their propensity to 'nurse grievances as a form of asserting continued belonging' (p. 14). More recent studies of (refugee) diaspora transnationalism provide a more discerning view, suggesting that 'the influence of diasporas is rarely consistent across whole groups and often shifts over time' (Van Hear & Cohen, 2017, p. 172). Van Hear and Cohen (2017) develop a useful schema for understanding these multiple and shifting transnational engagements, arguing that there is value in distinguishing three spheres of diaspora engagement:

> The largely private and personal sphere of the household and the extended family; the more public sphere of the 'known community', by which is meant collectivities of people who know one another or know of one another; and the largely public sphere of the 'imagined community', which includes the transnational political field, among other arenas. (pp. 172–173)

While this chapter is focused on this second sphere of engagement—on how groups in the wider diaspora help people in refugee situations who are 'known' to them—it is useful to situate these actions within different spheres and sites of diaspora transnationalism. As Van Hear and Cohen (2017) usefully suggest, those in the diaspora are often pulled in multiple directions by a portfolio of obligations. Understanding the plurality of spheres and sites of transnational engagements also helps to avoid generalising statements about the effects of refugee diasporas. For example, the effects of remittance-sending practices between households and extended families has received considerable attention (see Hansen, 2004; Horst, 2008; Lum et al., 2013; Monsutti, 2004; Poole, 2013; Shandy, 2006), as has political activism within 'imagined communities' (see Betts & Jones, 2016; Danforth, 1995; Koinova, 2011; Missbach, 2013; Mojab & Gorman, 2007), with varying conclusions drawn. For those interested in imagined communities and long-distance politics, diasporas have been cast either as the makers or as breakers of peace. For those interested in household survival, those in the diaspora are vital lifelines for conflict-affected communities. Yet these engagements happen simultaneously and often involve the same people. Those in the wider refugee diaspora can be sending money to families displaced by conflict at the same time as they are lobbying or otherwise supporting parties to a conflict. (Olliff, 2022).

Structurisation, Dispersal and Dwelling

Before turning to the findings of research on one sphere of diaspora transnationalism (refugee diaspora humanitarianism), I first want to establish how experiences of dispersal (i.e. migration pathways) and dwelling (the

92 L. OLLIFF

context in which one resides) structure refugee diaspora transnationalism. How does refugee resettlement as a process and system, and integration in the Australian context, lead to observable and predictable patterns of people associating collectively to try to help 'their people' elsewhere in the world?

Dispersal: Refugee Resettlement

Third country resettlement has long been held as one of three main 'solutions' to forced displacement, sitting alongside voluntary repatriation and local integration in the international refugee regime's 'durable solutions framework' (UNHCR, 2004). According to the UN Refugee Agency, resettlement is 'the transfer of refugees from an asylum country to another State that has agreed to admit them and ultimately grant them permanent settlement' (UNHCR, n.d.-a). People considered for resettlement are those who have been recognised as refugees in another country and are considered particularly vulnerable due to being survivors of torture and/ or violence, or being women and girls at risk, or children or adolescents at risk. Resettled refugees also include those who have protection (legal and/ or physical), medical or family reunification needs, or those for whom there is a lack of any foreseeable alternative durable solutions. Since the resettlement of 170,000 Hungarian refugees in the aftermath of the 1956 Hungarian Revolution, well over a million refugees have found a new life through third country resettlement programmes (UNHCR, 2019). While there have been 46 countries involved in resettlement processes to date, in reality the vast majority of resettled refugees have ended up in one of three countries: the United States, Canada or Australia (ibid.).

Resettlement has sat uneasily in the international refugee regime in both practice and effect (Bessa, 2010; Olliff, 2019). On a practical level, resettlement has only ever provided a modest contribution to resolving the longer-term status and protection needs of refugees and others of concern to the international refugee regime (i.e. stateless, internally displaced, and asylum seekers). The number of global resettlement places available each year has rarely exceeded 100,000 and, in 2019, only 63,726 refugees were resettled through referral by the UN Refugee Agency (UNHCR, n.d.-b).[3] At the same time, the number of people identified by UNHCR

---

[3] In 2020, only 22,770 people were resettled through UNHCR processes (UNHCR, n.d.-b). This was due to both a massive reduction in the US resettlement programme as well as

as in need of resettlement has steadily grown. In 2020, an estimated 1.44 million of the world's 26 million refugees were identified as in need of third country resettlement (ibid.). Based on 2019 resettlement numbers, this means that fewer than 1 in 25 refugees who need access to resettlement are likely to get this opportunity.

In the context of the chasm between resettlement needs and available places, resettlement processes are less than ideal. It can take years, even decades, for a person to go through the multitude of bureaucratic hurdles to reach a resettlement country. It is possible that, even for the very vulnerable, resettlement quotas and priorities that are determined by States will in effect mean they have little chance of ever being resettled. Concerns have also been raised periodically about the prioritisation criteria for resettlement places decided by States, with some countries being accused of selecting people based not on vulnerability and need, but on problematic ideas such as 'integration potential' (Long & Olsen, 2007), or excluding admission to entire groups of refugees based on their country of origin (Aldana, 2018). Some States, including Australia, have used resettlement programmes as justification for limiting the protection afforded to those who seek asylum in their territory (Bessa, 2010). Aside from limiting the practices of protection by resettlement states, there have been other reservations aired, including how the promise of resettlement in a wealthy country may have (unintended) consequences for how refugees in host countries consider their options, and how vulnerabilities and deficiencies rather than strengths are amplified or distorted in a system that (nominally) prioritises these things (De Montclos, 2008; Garnier et al., 2018; Horst, 2006; Sandvik, 2009).

This brief outline of the scarcity and problematics of refugee resettlement is necessary for understanding the structuring effects of this experience of dispersal on processes of diasporisation and transnationalism. Firstly, almost all resettled refugees will have spent time in a country that is not their homeland before arriving in Australia, hence it being called *third* country resettlement. Secondly, due to the long timeframes and scarcity of resettlement places, some resettled refugees will have spent many years or even decades in a host (second) country before arriving in Australia, significantly shaping the nature of their social networks. For example, a young person who grew up as a refugee may have much stronger and more active social connections with other refugees or with people

the wide-spread closure of borders due to the COVID-19 pandemic.

from the local (host) community than with a (homeland) community they may have no memory of. Thirdly, the scarcity of resettlement places and the precarious existence in which many of the world's refugees live is deeply and personally understood by those who have spent time as a refugee and negotiated resettlement processes to get to Australia. For some, this can amplify a sense of survivor guilt and mingle with other animating forces (e.g. obligation, faith, individual and family values), providing powerful animating forces to help those 'left behind' (Olliff, 2018). Finally, the fact that over 537,000 people have arrived in Australia on humanitarian visas since 1977[4] means that there are sizeable groups of people living in the Australian context who have shared this experience of dispersal—in other words, the makings of diaspora community networks.

Dwelling: Refugee Diasporas in Australia

In terms of the Australian context of dwelling, Fig. 5.1 provides a visual representation of how we might understand who the refugee diasporas in Australia are. Although an over-simplification, the larger group of 'ethnic minorities' could be considered anyone who migrated or is the descendent of a migrant. In Australia, this would mean almost the entire population,[5] although if we focus on more recent migrant experience (first and second generation), this equates to roughly half the total population.[6] The circle of 'refugee and humanitarian entrants' is anyone who arrived through Australia's Refugee and Humanitarian Program. This is a discrete group defined by migration experience and identifiable by visa category. As Australia has maintained a fairly consistent offshore resettlement programme since the 1970s, with an average of nearly 14,000 refugee and humanitarian entrants per annum granted permanent visas since the

---

[4] Source: Australian Government. 1977–2012: www.refugeecouncil.org.au/getfacts/statistics/aust/australias-refugee-humanitarian-program-visa-grants-stream-1977-78-2011-12/; 2012–2016: www.border.gov.au/about/reports-publications/reports/annual (accessed 3/10/17). 2016–2020: https://www.homeaffairs.gov.au/research-and-stats/files/australia-offshore-humanitarian-program-2019-20.pdf (accessed 22/2/21).

[5] Apart from the 2.8% of the Australian population who identify as Indigenous, all other Australians are migrants or the descendants of migrants. Even the largest self-identified ethnic group—Anglo Australians—can be considered an 'ethnic minority' (36.1% in 2016). In the question about ancestry in the 2016 population census, only 33.5% of respondents self-identified as 'Australian' (Australian Bureau of Statistics, 2017).

[6] The 2016 Australian Population Census indicated that one-third of the population was born outside Australia (33.3%) and nearly half the population (49% of stated responses) had one or both parents born overseas (Australian Bureau of Statistics, 2017).

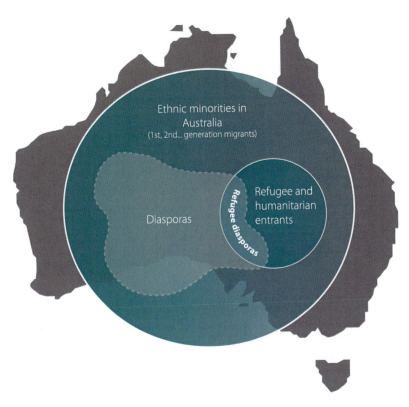

Fig. 5.1 Refugee diasporas in Australia

programme was established, there would be over half a million people in this group. The shape depicting 'diasporas' would more accurately be drawn and redrawn as constantly moving, acknowledging as Tölölyan's (2007) has done, that diasporas are not discrete groups, but a process whereby people identify collectively in different ways and at different points of time.

While it is important to note that not all refugee and humanitarian entrants will identify or relate to each other in diasporic ways, there are characteristics of the Australian context which lend themselves to the mobilisation of diaspora identities and networks. Firstly, multiculturalism has been an official government policy in Australia since the 1970s. Although what 'multiculturalism' means in practice and effect is highly debatable (see Hage, 2012), at a legal and policy level there is an articulation of 'the rights of all to celebrate, practise and maintain their cultural traditions within the law and free from discrimination' (Commonwealth of Australia, 2011). Different tiers of government support multiculturalism through initiatives such as the establishment of multicultural advisory councils, anti-racism strategies and legislation, policy and programme commitments to access and equity to government services, and providing funding for multicultural arts, festivals and sports. Multicultural policies have enabled, to some extent, the expression of language, culture, and associational forms of people who have settled in Australia. There are, for example, ethnic communities' councils across all states and territories of Australia (see FECCA, n.d.).

Australia's approach to multiculturalism and migrant integration is significant for understanding why resettled refugees form organisations, and why they do so as clearly identifiable ethnic, cultural or religious associations. Not only is there official endorsement of people celebrating, practising and maintaining cultural traditions, but there are also laws and policies that govern and support the establishment of community-based and voluntary organisations (e.g. incorporated associations) and allow groups to establish themselves as legal entities. Moreover, there is a long history in Australia of ethno-specific or migrant support organisations being established by different waves of settlers and playing an important role in people's lives as sources of support, advice, advocacy and belonging (Jakubowicz, 2002). It is unsurprising, then, that newer arrivals draw on the experiences of earlier migrants and establish organisations based on diasporic identities, utilising systems that have been built around supporting (and in many ways managing and controlling) the establishment and regularisation of community-based civil society organisations in Australia.[7] Indeed, there are a range of networks and supports targeting 'new and emerging' communities, such as the New and Emerging Communities working group within the Federation of Ethnic Communities' Councils of Australia, which normalise the formation and consolidation of diaspora associational forms (FECCA, 2019).

---

[7] It is not within the scope of this chapter to comment on the limitations of these structures for diaspora communities working transnationally. This has been discussed elsewhere (Olliff, 2022, chapter on Governance) and points to the problematics of formal governance requirements for incorporated associations in Australia that are volunteer-run, have fluid mandates and informal governance structures, and are focused on philanthropy in refugee or conflict situations overseas.

5 FROM RESETTLED REFUGEES TO HUMANITARIAN ACTORS... 97

At the same time, official government policy, funding and support for ethno-specific associations only goes so far in explaining the formation and practices of diaspora communities in Australia. Government engagement with these communities has, for the most part, been about facilitating the integration of groups of migrants into a socially cohesive but diverse Australian society and has tended to ignore the many and varied ways in which these same communities are engaged, identify and act *transnationally*. Moreover, the spheres of diaspora transnationalism where there has been more visibility and institutional engagement have tended towards seeing the utility of diaspora networks in economic terms (e.g. facilitating business and trade linkages with countries of origin) or as potential security threats (e.g. links with terrorism, a source of foreign fighters and potential avenues for foreign government interference), with only passing interest in diasporas as development actors, let alone as humanitarians responding to displacement crises in other parts of the world. As such, diaspora humanitarianism happens in a context of little institutional recognition or support.

REFUGEE DIASPORA HUMANITARIANISM

The following section turns to the findings of ethnographic research that sought to understand how refugee diaspora communities in Australia come together to undertake collective acts of helping forcibly displaced people elsewhere in the world. Building from this understanding of refugee resettlement as a structuring experience and the Australian context providing fertile ground for the establishment of diaspora organisations, the following describes the characteristics, actions, and implications of refugee diaspora humanitarianism as a sphere of diaspora transnational engagement.

Methods

This section draws on findings from a multi-sited and mobile ethnographic study involving participant-observation over an 18-month period and interviews with representatives from 26 refugee diaspora organisations or groups[8] (RDOs) formed in Australia. By focusing on organisations, this

---

[8] Recruitment information used the phrase 'organisations and groups' in anticipation that some collective action was being undertaken by more informal groups that may not identify

research complements other research focused at diaspora transnationalism at an individual or household level (see Monsutti, 2004; Maher et al. in this book). Fieldwork was conducted in Australia, Switzerland, Thailand, Indonesia, in transit and online. It involved participating in and/or observing the day-to-day operations and activities of RDOs (e.g. fundraising events, planning meetings, community awareness-raising activities, online discussion forums and social media groups, and annual general meetings). Fieldwork included travelling with members of an Oromo RDO to Indonesia to join their efforts in trying to help a group of Oromo asylum seekers, visiting a site on the Thai-Burma border where a Karenni RDO had been actively engaged, and undertaking fieldwork in Geneva at and around the annual UNHCR NGO Consultations, where more than 500 delegates from over 200 NGOs and 91 countries working in refugee protection were in attendance. This fieldwork was enabled by the author's role as both a doctoral researcher and as an employee of the Refugee Council of Australia. Participation in the Australian NGO delegation to Geneva allowed for the observation of interactions between refugee diaspora advocates and other humanitarian actors and for engagement in formal and informal discussions.

The 26 RDOs that participated in this research were selected because they satisfied two main criteria: (1) they were formed and led by people who identified as being from the same community as the population targeted by their actions; and (2) they were involved in helping people who were forcibly displaced overseas. Figure 5.2 provides a summary of key characteristics of participating RDOs and to where and whom their activities were targeted. All were working outside their self-defined homeland. While some were working with internally displaced people in their country of origin, most were operating in refugee camp or urban settings. This distinction is significant, as diaspora-led development is often discussed in a homeland-hostland binary, rather than involving transnational actors who are engaged wherever 'their people' reside. For refugee diasporas, this often means sites of displacement where refugees have limited rights or legal status.

---

as an 'organisation' or may be wary of calling themselves an organisation if they had not been legally incorporated in Australia. This proved to be the case.

RDO	Country of origin	Community (self-identified)	Country where RDO is working	Characteristics of humanitarian context						Target beneficiaries
				Internally displaced	Refugee - camp	Refugee - urban	PRS [25]	Complex emergency[26]	Other [27]	
1	Afghanistan	Hazara	Afghanistan	■					■	Afghan (including Hazara)
2	Afghanistan	Hazara	Indonesia			■			■	Any (majority Hazara)
3	Afghanistan	Hazara	Pakistan			■	■			Hazara
4	Afghanistan	Hazara	Pakistan			■	■			Hazara
5	Afghanistan	Hazara women	Pakistan / Iran			■	■		■	Hazara women
6	Bhutan	Lhotsampa	Nepal		■	■			■	Lhotsampa / Nepalese
7	Ethiopia	Ogaden	Kenya		■		■			Ogaden
8	Ethiopia	Oromo	Indonesia			■	■			Oromo
9	Ethiopia	Oromo	Global			■	■			Oromo
10	Ethiopia	Oromo	Yemen / Horn of Africa			■	■			Oromo
11	Eritrea	Eritrean	Sudan				■			Eritrean
12	Eritrea	Eritrean	Sudan				■			Eritrean
13	Eritrea	Eritrean	Yemen / Egypt / Horn of Africa						■	Eritrean
14	Iran	Baha'i	Iran						■	Iranian (majority Baha'i) women
15	Iraq	Chaldean	Iraq	■						Iraqi Christians
16	Iraq	Iraqi	Iraq	■						Iraqi (any)
17	Iraq	Mandaean	Iraq / Syria / Jordan	■		■				Mandaean
18	Iraq / Syria	Assyrian	Iraq			■				Assyrian
19	Iraq / Syria / Lebanon	Eastern Orthodox	Syria / Lebanon			■	■			Iraqi / Syrian Christians
20	Myanmar	Karen	Thailand	■			■			Karen
21	Myanmar	Karen	Thailand / Burma	■	■					Karen
22	Myanmar	Karenni	Thailand / Burma	■	■					Karenni
23	Myanmar	Rohingya	Global			■			■	Rohingya
24	Myanmar	Zo	Malaysia			■				Zo
25	Palestine	Palestinian	Lebanon / Iraq		■		■			Palestinian
26	South Sudan	South Sudanese	South Sudan	■						South Sudanese
Total				10	12	15	15	8	9	

Fig. 5.2 RDO characteristics

What RDOs Do to Help

In terms of what refugee diasporas do to help in displacement contexts, the activities of RDOs are not easily characterised. As the Europe-based Diaspora Emergency Action and Coordination (DEMAC) initiative well describes, 'diaspora organisations can be considered as multi-mandate organisations that couple relief and recovery with political, economic and social reform, linking relief, rehabilitation and development and thereby challenging the typical notions associated with humanitarian aid'

(DEMAC, 2016, p. 6). In other words, RDOs are often involved in a range of activities that may not fit easily in dominant humanitarian or development intervention frameworks. When talking to diaspora humanitarians about how they identified needs and responses, it was evident that RDO activities are very much shaped by the skills, networks and capacities of the people involved in these organisations, rather than through applying broader decision-making frameworks or undertaking holistic needs assessments. If the RDO in Australia is led by health professionals, for example, it is more likely that the RDO will focus on health-related projects, drawing on the resources, interests, and skills of those most heavily involved.

In general, the type of activities RDOs participating in this research were most commonly involved in were advocacy[9] (n = 13), education projects (n = 12), material aid (n = 10), emergency relief (n = 10) and migration support[10] (n = 9), along with health, infrastructure, livelihoods and women's empowerment initiatives. Some RDOs were involved in a wide range of activities simultaneously, or as opportunities arose.

It should be noted that capturing RDO activities in the above way tends to privilege certain understandings of what constitutes helping—those that can be easily named and measured. For example, the activities that were spoken about when I asked interviewees, 'What does your organisation do to help?' tended to draw on dominant humanitarian and development discourses. Yet it was apparent through fieldwork that there are many, less measurable things that RDOs do to help, which speak more of what Barnett (2011) writes when he laments the professionalisation and bureaucratisation of international humanitarian practice:

> The desire to measure places a premium on numbers—for instance, lives lost and saved, people fed, children inoculated—to the neglect of non-quantifiable goals such as witnessing, being present, conferring dignity, and demonstrating solidarity. Is it possible to quantify, for instance, the reuniting

---

[9] RDOs predominantly targeted their advocacy at the Australian Government, UNHCR, the UN Human Rights Council, and international NGOs, and focused their advocacy on raising the profile or attention given to their target population to enhance protection.

[10] Migration support included filling in visa application forms and sponsoring individuals or groups of people for resettlement in Australia. Note: decisions about who to support and how to support their migration were made on a collective rather than a family or individual basis. For example, many RDOs worked with existing community structures or community-based organisations overseas to identify cases in priority need of resettlement.

5 FROM RESETTLED REFUGEES TO HUMANITARIAN ACTORS... 101

of families, the providing of burial shrouds, or the reducing of fear and anxiety in individuals who are in desperate situations? (p. 216)

Indeed, it is the non-quantifiable acts of caring—of standing in solidarity, bearing witness or amplifying the voices of the displaced—that refugee diaspora humanitarianism seems to offer much. There is no accounting, for instance, for what a small group of Oromo Australians achieved by travelling to Indonesia in 2016 to meet with a group of asylum seekers there (see Olliff, 2022). This act was as much a demonstration of solidarity and a process of community-building as it was about the transfer of modest resources to a small number of people trying to survive in extremely difficult circumstances. As Rosanna, an Iranian Australian woman I interviewed, described, 'It is not always (about) sending the money. You also have to send the message.' As to what the message is that refugee diaspora humanitarians and their organisations send, perhaps it is that displaced people have not been forgotten, that they have a voice, and that there is a larger community that can be called on in times of need. Importantly, refugee diaspora humanitarians who identify with an affected population perceive and recognise the suffering of displacement in its collective form; not only through a lens of individual suffering, but through the lens of suffering felt by 'a people' or 'community' that is brought about by the rupturing of social fabric. RDO activities, then, should also be seen in terms of the non-quantifiable and complex process of reconfiguring, recreating, and supporting social networks of care in situations of displacement.

To provide an illustration of what RDOs do, Akademos Society provides a useful case study of both the quantifiable and non-quantifiable effects of refugee diaspora humanitarianism. Akademos Society was established in 2013 by a small group of early career professionals (Hazara Australians) who 'felt a moral and social obligation to help talented yet disadvantaged students of our besieged community' (Akademos Society, 2021). The committee behind Akademos Society is involved in a voluntary capacity in overseeing projects, fostering collaborative partnerships with local community-based organisations in the places where they are active, and raising funds to support disadvantaged students in Pakistan and Afghanistan. Since 2013, Akademos Society has provided annual scholarships to cover the costs of college-level education for Hazara students in Pakistan, and since 2017 has funded a supplementary learning class and a 'Kids off the Street' programme that provides financial assistance to child labourers in Afghanistan to enable them to access educational opportunities. In 2021, Akademos Society collaborated with a local community-based organisation to establish a computer lab in Afghanistan's Daikundi province that could 'connect students with the outside world' (ibid.). The organisation's annual budget of around AUD $30,000 (in 2019–2020) is mostly raised from within the Hazara community in Australia through personal and community networks and online fundraising via social media.

Like most of the RDOs in this study, Akademos Society operates at a very small and (trans)localised level across multiple countries (Australia, Afghanistan, Pakistan, and with involvement from diaspora members in other parts of the world) and draws extensively on the social networks, expertise and interests of those most heavily involved. Echoing the rationale of other RDOs that focus on education, Akademos Society emphasise the collective ('the community') in their vision, stating:

> Akademos Society believes that in the struggle for peace no medium is mightier than education. We believe educating the youth is one of the most effective ways of providing a sustainable and prosperous future *for the community*. (ibid., emphasis added)

While there are undoubtedly benefits for the small number of individuals who receive scholarships, access to classes or computers, the intention of this small RDO is to contribute through education to strengthening 'a people' who have suffered great violence, injustices and displacement, weaving ongoing connections between those in the wider diaspora and those from the 'known' community who face ongoing existential threats in Afghanistan and Pakistan.

RESETTLEMENT AND THE TRANSFORMATION OF TRANSNATIONAL SOCIAL NETWORKS OF CARE

This chapter has argued that refugee resettlement in Australia is a structuring experience that transforms transnational social networks and provides fertile ground for processes of diasporisation, including the formation of collective associations—RDOs—that act to help those 'left behind'. In other words, the movement (dispersal) of groups of people from situations of persecution and precarity (forced displacement contexts) to one of permanent residency or citizenship in a wealthy country like Australia, leads to somewhat predictable patterns of diaspora mobilisation and transnationalism.

What, then, does this tell us more broadly about diasporas as humanitarian (or development) actors? Firstly, there is a tendency in scholarship either to emphasise the deterritorialised nature of diaspora as fluid political networks or 'imagined communities' that transcend the state, or to hone in on the implications for development of diaspora relationships with their host- and home-lands first and foremost. This research on refugee diaspora humanitarianism suggests that we instead need to understand diasporas both as territorialised actors (i.e. shaped by the sociopolitical, historical and economic contexts in which they dwell) as well as 'decentralized, distributed patterns of human organization' (Ghorashi & Boersma, 2009, p. 670), or rhizomatic networks (Deleuze & Guttari, 1987) that have implications beyond diaspora homelands. Furthermore, these rhizomatic networks are not neutral phenomena, but involve people with differential power, resources and social capital. As Ghorashi and Boersma (2009) write:

> Social capital is the sum of resources, actual or virtual, that increases if an individual becomes connected to networks of more or less institutionalized (durable) relationships.... In this way, social capital is linked to one's identity, not so much in terms of one's roots but in terms of one's rhizomatic, networked connections. (p. 670)

Resettled refugees in Australia who mobilise to help 'their people' elsewhere in the world add to the social capital of those with whom they are networked, as they move within these transnational social networks from situations of precarity (a refugee context) to one in which permanent residency or citizenship in a wealthy state in the global North (Australia) opens up new possibilities for action.

Secondly, and linked to this first point, is that diaspora transnational networks have implications for the international refugee regime and the quality of protection that is afforded to refugees and others forcibly displaced. Diaspora transnational networks care for 'their people' wherever they are located, and they should be seen as development (or humanitarian) actors and not only in relation to their self-defined homelands. This is significant because most refugees today live in countries in the global South with limited rights, security, access to resources or power to effect change (Agier, 2008). Refugees who are resettled from these spaces of marginality act alongside other humanitarians to provide education, healthcare, emergency relief and solace to forcibly displaced people with whom they maintain connections. Often these acts are invisible to other institutional actors. While individual or household remittance-sending practices are more readily understood as part of humanitarian ecosystems, collective remittances through RDOs are given much less attention and are rarely factored into coordinated system responses. While these small and often informal activities of RDOs in no way represent a panacea to the shortcomings of the international humanitarian system, they are still part of the tapestry of care that individuals, families and communities draw on in times of need. In the context of the widely acknowledged failings of both the international refugee regime and the humanitarian system to ensure the effective protection of refugees, the contribution of refugee diaspora networks and organisations should not be so readily overlooked. Transnational social networks are a vital source of support for many refugees and their impact in displacement contexts is still poorly understood.

To date, the main actors involved in refugee protection (UNHCR, NGOs and host states), as well as resettlement states such as Australia, have not engaged in any substantive way with the transnational social support networks of refugees. Instead, refugees who are resettled are no longer considered in the picture of the international refugee regime; there is a sense that they should just get on with their lives in Australia, the US or Canada, now that they are no longer in need of international protection. While it is understandable that there are concerns about the weight of obligation to help people elsewhere in the world for recent arrivals struggling to find their feet in a new country, it is also unrealistic to expect that those who have been told they are 'the lucky ones' and who have intimate knowledge and connection with people living in very difficult displacement contexts, will simply forget and move on as soon as they arrive in a wealthy and safe country. For refugee diaspora humanitarianism to be more fully realised and impactful, state and non-state actors would do well to engage more meaningfully with refugee diasporas as transnational actors to understand, amplify and strengthen the webs of engagement that emanate from refugee diaspora communities. In this way, Australia's Humanitarian Program should not be seen just as a programme to assist a small number of refugees to find a durable solution to displacement each year, but as a programme that has implications for the much greater number of refugees who are *not* resettled, through the transformation of diaspora transnational networks of care.

To end this chapter, I want to return to the point where it started, with the young woman from Central African Republic (CAR) waiting in Cameroon to be able to resettle in Australia. Although we do not know whether Marie will realise her desire to 'look back and help others', this and other research on refugee diaspora humanitarianism (see also DEMAC, 2016; Sweis, 2019) suggests there is a very good reason to believe that she will try. Following in the path of resettled refugees who have come before, we may well predict the coming together of newcomers from CAR as a diaspora in Australia, perhaps establishing their own organisation/s to link those in Australia with those back home or in exile. If Marie drives this organisation, perhaps it will focus on refugee women and orphans in Cameroon, drawing on her lived experience, transnational social networks, and knowledge of this particular local context. I only hope, in this imagined future, there is stronger recognition and support available to amplify the impact of refugee diaspora humanitarians who mobilise to care for those who are forcibly displaced.

References

Agier, M. (2008). *On the Margins of the World: The Refugee Experience Today*. Polity.

Akademos Society. (2021). *About Us; What We Do*. Retrieved July 28, 2021, from https://akademossociety.org/

Aldana, R. (2018, July 11). The Travel Ban in Numbers: Why Families and Refugees Lose Big. *The Conversation*. Retrieved July 11, 2021, from https://theconversation.com/the-travel-ban-in-numbers-why-families-and-refugees-lose-big-99064

Australian Bureau of Statistics (2017). *2016 Census of Population and Housing*, Retrieved April 23, 2022, from https://www.abs.gov.au/websitedbs/censushome.nsf/home/2016

Barnett, M. (2011). *Empire of Humanity: A History of Humanitarianism*. Cornell University Press.

Bessa, T. (2010). From Political Instrument to Protection Tool? Resettlement of Refugees and North-South Relations. *Refuge, 26*(1), 90–100.

Betts, A., & Jones, W. (2016). *Mobilising the Diaspora: How Refugees Challenge Authoritarianism*. Cambridge University Press.

Betts, A., Loescher, G., & Milner, J. (2012). *The United Nations High Commissioner for Refugees (UNHCR): The Politics and Practice of Refugee Protection*. Routledge.

Brinkerhoff, J. M. (2012). Creating an Enabling Environment for Diasporas' Participation in Homeland Development. *International Migration, 50*(1), 75–95.

Collier, P. (2000). *Economic Causes of Civil Conflict and Their Implications for Policy*. World Bank Group.

Commonwealth of Australia. (2011). *The People of Australia: Australia's Multicultural Policy*.

Danforth, L. (1995). *The Macedonian Conflict: Ethnic Nationalism in a Transnational World*. Princeton University Press.

De Montclos, M.-A. P. (2008). Humanitarian Aid, War, Exodus, and Reconstruction of Identities: A Case Study of Somali "Minority Refugees" in Kenya. *Nationalism & Ethnic Politics, 14*(2), 289–321.

Deleuze, G., & Guttari, F. (1987). *A Thousand Plateaus: Capitalism and Schizophrenia*. University of Minnesota Press.

DEMAC. (2016). *Diaspora Humanitarianism: Transnational Ways of Working*. Copenhagen: Diaspora Emergency Action and Coordination (DEMAC).

FECCA. (2019). *New and Emerging Communities in Australia: Enhancing Capacity for Advocacy*. Canberra: Federation of Ethnic Communities' Councils of Australia.

FECCA. (n.d.). Federation of Ethnic Communities' Councils of Australia: Who We Are. Retrieved July 28, 2021, from https://fecca.org.au/about/who-we-are/

Fullilove, M. (2008). *World Wide Webs: Diasporas and the International System*. Lowy Institute for International Policy.

Garnier, A., Jubilut, L. L., & Sandvik, K. B. (Eds.). (2018). *Refugee Resettlement: Power, Politics, and Humanitarian Governance*. Berghahn.

Ghorashi, H., & Boersma, K. (2009). The "Iranian Diaspora" and the New Media: From Political Action to Humanitarian Help. *Development & Change, 40*(4), 667–691.

Hage, G. (2012). *White Nation: Fantasies of White Supremacy in a Multicultural Society*. Taylor & Francis.

Hansen, P. (2004). *Migrant Remittances as a Development Tool: The Case of Somaliland*. Migration Policy Research. IOM.

Horst, C. (2006). Buufis amongst Somalis in Dadaab: the Transnational and Historical Logics behind Resettlement Dreams. *Journal of Refugee Studies, 19*(2), 143–157.

Horst, C. (2008). The Transnational Political Engagements of Refugees: Remittance Sending Practices amongst Somalis in Norway. *Conflict, Security & Development, 8*(3), 317–339.

Jakubowicz, A. (2002). Living as a Diaspora: The Politics of Exclusion in Relation to Refugees and Disabled People. *ISAA Review, 2*(3), 6–12.

Koinova, M. (2011). Diasporas and Secessionist Conflicts: The Mobilization of the Armenian, Albanian and Chechen Diasporas. *Ethnic and Racial Studies, 34*(2), 333–356.

Long, K., & Olsen. (2007). *A Comparative Study of Integration Potential as an Additional Selection Criterion for the Resettlement of Refugees.* UDI.

Lum, B., Nikolko, M., Samy, Y., et al. (2013). Diasporas, Remittances and State Fragility: Assessing the Linkages. *Ethnopolitics, 12*(2), 201–219.

Missbach, A. (2013). The Waxing and Waning of the Acehnese Diaspora's Long-distance Politics. *Modern Asian Studies, 47*(3), 1055–1082.

Mojab, S., & Gorman, R. (2007). Dispersed Nationalism: War, Diaspora and Kurdish Women's Organizing. *Journal of Middle East Women's Studies, 3*(1), 58–85.

Monsutti, A. (2004). Cooperation, Remittances, and Kinship among the Hazaras. *Iranian Studies, 37*(2), 219–240.

Nyberg-Sørensen, N. (2007). *Living Across Worlds: Diaspora, Development and Transnational Engagement.* International Organization for Migration.

Olliff, L. (2018). From Resettled Refugees to Humanitarian Actors: Refugee Diaspora Organizations and Everyday Humanitarianism. *New Political Science, 40*(4), 658–674.

Olliff, L. (2019). Time to Reimagine Resettlement? *Asylum Insight.* Retrieved May 12, 2021, from https://www.asyluminsight.com/c-louise-olliff#.YJtOz2YzaL8

Olliff, L. (2022). *Helping Familiar Strangers: Refugee Diaspora Organizations and Humanitarianism.* Indiana University Press.

Poole, A. (2013). Ransoms, Remittances, and Refugees: The Gatekeeper State in Eritrea. *Africa Today, 60*(2), 67–82.

Sandvik, K. B. (2009). The Physicality of Legal Consciousness: Suffering and the Production of Credibility in Refugee Resettlement. In R. A. Wilson & R. D. Brown (Eds.), *Humanitarianism and Suffering: The Mobilization of Empathy* (pp. 223–244). Cambridge University Press.

Shandy, D. J. (2006). Global Transactions: Sudanese Refugees Sending Money Home. *Refuge, 23*(2), 28–35.

Sharma, K., Kashyap, A., & Ladd, P. R. (Eds.). (2011). *Realizing the Development Potential of Diasporas.* United Nations University Press.

Sweis, R. K. (2019). Doctors with Borders: Hierarchies of Humanitarians and the Syrian Civil War. *International Journal of Middle Eastern Studies, 51*(4), 587–601.

Tölölyan, K. (2007). The Contemporary Discourse of Diaspora Studies. *Comparative Studies of South Asia, Africa, & the Middle East, 27*, 647–655.

UNHCR. (2004). Framework for Durable Solutions for Refugees and Persons of Concern. *Refugee Survey Quarterly, 23*(1), 179–200.

UNHCR. (2019). *The History of Resettlement: Celebrating 25 Years of the ATCR*. Geneva: UNHCR.

UNHCR. (n.d.-a). *Resettlement*. Retrieved April 5, 2021, from https://www.unhcr.org/resettlement.html

UNHCR. (n.d.-b). *Resettlement Data Finder*. Retrieved April 5, 2021, from https://rsq.unhcr.org/

Van Hear, N. (1998). *New Diasporas: The Mass Exodus, Dispersal and Regrouping of Migrant Communities*. UCL Press.

Van Hear, N. (2006). Refugees in Diaspora: From Durable Solutions to Transnational Relations. *Refuge, 23*(1), 9–15.

Van Hear, N. (2009). The Rise of Refugee Diasporas. *Current History, 108*(717), 180–185.

Van Hear, N., & Cohen, R. (2017). Diasporas and Conflict: Distance, Contiguity and Spheres of Engagement. *Oxford Development Studies, 45*(2), 171–184.

Zinterer, T. (2005). Diaspora Networks as High Risk or High Potential: The Transnational Turn in National Policy Discourses on Migrants. *Conference Papers—International Studies Association*, 1–19.

PART III

Responding to War, Conflict and Disaster

CHAPTER 6

Pacific Diaspora Humanitarianism: Diasporic Perspectives

Jeevika Vivekananthan and Phil Connors

Diaspora communities respond to war, conflict and disaster in their self-identified homelands. They provide support to their people in homelands, neighbouring countries and wider diaspora in difficult times. Their responses vary from sending money and relief materials to sharing life-saving information. However, there is a limited understanding among academia, the formal humanitarian community and policymakers about why and how diaspora communities respond in a crisis. The dearth of knowledge about diaspora actors and their actions in a crisis causes misunderstanding, scrutiny, lack of support and absence of coordination mechanisms by other actors in crisis response (DEMAC, 2016, 2018).

The characteristics of a particular diaspora are unique, dynamic, multifaceted and contextual. The complexity in forming and maintaining group identity and relationships between the members of a group requires a comprehensive understanding across time and space. Diaspora humanitarianism is being understood and compared within the cognitive, normative and regulative measures of a Westernised, institutionalised and

---

J. Vivekananthan (✉) • P. Connors
Deakin University, Burwood, NSW, Australia
e-mail: jeevika@deakin.edu.au

© The Author(s), under exclusive license to Springer Nature
Switzerland AG 2022
M. Phillips, L. Olliff (eds.), *Understanding Diaspora Development*,
https://doi.org/10.1007/978-3-030-97866-2_6

111

internationalised humanitarian system (Horst et al., 2016). Such understanding poses a risk to the originality, versatility and diversity of diaspora humanitarianism. Our chapter provides insights into why and how the Pacific diaspora in Australia respond to disasters in Pacific Island Countries (PICs). We propose 'understanding diaspora humanitarianism from a diasporic perspective' as a decolonial mechanism to study the originality, versatility and diversity of diaspora humanitarianism. We use constructivist and neo-institutionalist approaches to place 'diasporic perspectives' in a broader discourse of humanitarianism.

THE HUMANITARIAN SYSTEM, HUMANITY AND HUMANITARIANISMS

Acts of humanity are an essential part of being human and are generally understood and acknowledged as demonstrations of concern for, or assisting to improve, the wellbeing and happiness of people. Definitions of humanitarianism include ideas around obligations to the welfare of all people or a belief in wanting to improve people's lives with dignity. These understandings place beneficence at the core of such acts, which are considered to be based on altruism and love. So, one would anticipate that a humanitarian system would embody such understandings, but it is never that simple. As with all systems, the humanitarian system has been constructed through favouring particular understandings and ignoring or marginalising others. It is as much about politics, economics and geopolitical power as it is about humanity (Barnett, 2011; Donini, 2012).

The humanitarian system as it is commonly understood today, with its architecture of International Non-Governmental Organisations (INGOs), the International Committee of the Red Cross (ICRC), United Nations organisations (UN), Red Cross/Red Crescent Societies, Non-Governmental Organisations (NGOs), and local civil society, is a relatively recent phenomenon. Modern humanitarian discourse and humanitarian action have been dominated by Western and particularly European perspectives. Scholars exploring the roots of the current humanitarian system point to the suffering of wounded soldiers in the 1859 battle of Solferino witnessed by Swiss businessman, Henri Dunant, who went on to be one of the founders of the ICRC in 1864 (Barnett, 2011). From this point of departure, the narrative has evolved across "three distinct ages" (Barnett, 2011) and distinct periods of influence (Davey et al., 2013), with each of these being dominated by Western history, culture and ideologies. The documented history of modern humanitarianism shows systematisation, professionalization and growth of a humanitarian enterprise that is dominated by Western donors, practitioners and institutions. This has culminated in a limited understanding of what constitutes 'humanitarian' work and who undertakes it. The marginalisation of alternative understandings of humanity and demonstrations of humanitarianism is increasingly being recognised, however resistance to change in the status quo is strong.

The narrow understanding of humanitarianism resists other modes of humanitarianism and diverse humanitarian narratives. Decolonial scholars, such as Smith (2012) and García (2020), warn us about the danger of a "universal", "chronological" and "totalising" history discourse with the notion of development and the myth of temporal and spatial colonial differences. Even in the attempts to contest the crooked history of modern humanitarianism, one can observe the lack of systematically recorded histories or stories of humanitarian work by non-Western actors being incorporated. The problematisation of the dominant narratives, singular history and European origin of humanitarianism sets the stage for our quest to understand diaspora humanitarianism from a different perspective.

The assumption of one systematic way of helping others in a crisis is no longer valid. What we have in the name of "humanitarianism" is a narrow definition of humanitarianism from the ICRC—"the independent, neutral, and impartial provision of relief to victims of armed conflicts and natural disasters" (Barnett & Weiss, 2011, p. 9)—which acts as the system's gold standard. This is not to dispute the values of compassion, humanity and alleviating suffering that underpin this understanding of humanitarianism, but to make a point: "there is no situation where humanitarian action is totally principled and allowed to operate as such" (Donini, 2012, p. 184). Barnett (2011, p. 10) argues, "We live in a world of humanitarianisms, not humanitarianism". Additionally, Bennett et al. (2016, p. 19) assert, "adaptation and change have always been part of humanitarian culture".

There has always been impetus to change and 'transform' the system to better meet the needs of affected people. This has come at a time of seemingly endless demand and stretched resources. Gatherings such as the World Humanitarian Summit (WHS) in 2016, which brought together a vast array of actors to Istanbul, put forward an "Agenda for Humanity" to prevent and reduce human suffering during crisis through major change initiatives, such as "New Ways of Working", "Grand Bargain" and "empower local humanitarian actors", and supporting locally led responses (OCHA, 2017). The WHS set out to address the malaise and frustration in the face of the growing scale and complexity of crises and to shift power to crisis-affected people and local actors. However, it has fallen short of expectations about system reform (Bennett et al., 2016; IARAN, 2018).

Shifting the focus to the local level and supporting locally led responses is understood as 'localisation'. The word was not officially used at the WHS but has been one of the most talked about 'transformations' stemming from the summit. There is seemingly much goodwill towards promoting the understanding of 'as local as possible and as global as necessary', which is one of the catch cries of the WHS. There is, however, no agreed definition of what 'localisation' is, which has left it open to interpretation.

In responding to humanitarian crises in their homeland, diasporas arguably straddle the local and global and demonstrate their 'humanity' in ways that demand greater recognition and respect. This alternative 'humanitarianism' is captured in the following:

> The WHS highlighted the importance of localisation, demand-driven humanitarian aid, centered on affected people, flexibility between humanitarian and development approaches, greater use of cash approaches, more person to person aid: this is what diaspora do already! Robert Smith, OCHA (IASC, 2017, p.2)

Diaspora Humanitarianism

The term 'diaspora' has proliferated from its meaning of Greek origin, dia speiro "to sow over" by which diaspora is understood as a "product of colonisation", and from its initial application to Jewish diaspora, concerned with "enslavement" and "exile" from Babylon (Cohen, 1997; Mohan & Zack-WIlliams, 2002). The proliferation of its meaning and application has taken place within and outside migration studies. As a concept, diaspora has been overstretched across various disciplines of social sciences and, often, gets trapped in clashes between diaspora related theories, policies and practices. "Dispersion", "homeland orientation" and "boundary maintenance" continue to influence the definitions of diaspora (Alexander, 2017).

In this chapter, we draw upon the broader literature on diaspora and present three relevant critiques Vivekananthan (forthcoming), as a prerequisite exercise to writing about 'diaspora humanitarianism': (1) the link between diasporic imaginaries and colonial or neo-colonial realities; (2) the exploitation of diaspora as a vehicle of neoliberal governance; and (3) the over-proportionate coverage given to remittances and their economic role.

Diasporic imaginaries and colonial or neo-colonial realities trap diaspora in racialised systems, body politics of invisibility and nation-centric identity discourse (Ndhlovu, 2015; Salih et al., 2020). Racial-capital systems in liberal democracies devise racial hierarchies, subordination, vulnerability and invisibility of black and brown bodies. Nation-centric identity discourse overlooks the realities of transnational and translocal interactions and other constructions and renegotiations of diaspora identity. While the understanding of the role of diaspora in international relations is not always inclusive of diasporic voices and worldviews, diaspora is arguably being used as a vehicle of neoliberal governance by powerful global institutions (Boyle & Kitchen, 2014). The profound importance given to economic remittances from diaspora is also problematic as it eclipses the other aspects of diaspora contribution to their communities and homelands (Horst et al., 2016). Remittance-centred rhetoric endorses diaspora as another promising agent in the development discourse but neglects the multi-directional flow of resources that sustain various diaspora networks. There is also a question of pre-existing class divisions and inequalities to consider in the backdrop of economic, social and cultural dynamics of diaspora groups. We need to be mindful of all these pitfalls before exploring the new conceptual domain of 'diaspora humanitarianism'.

Diaspora assistance to their people within and outside the imaginary borders of their homeland is not a new phenomenon. The development sector is far more advanced in recognising diaspora actors as potential development agents (Wall & Hedlund, 2016). The calls to engage systematically with diaspora in the formal humanitarian system are what appears to be a new direction in policy and practice (IOM, 2015).

Diaspora assistance in pre-crisis, crisis and post-crisis contexts ranges from individual to collective contributions that involve sending money and relief supplies, volunteering, skills and knowledge transfer, mobilising community support, and utilising social capital and advocacy (DEMAC, 2016; Esnard & Sapat, 2016; IOM, 2015; Le De et al., 2013). Diaspora engagement in a humanitarian crisis is driven by familial links, transnational civic responsibility, solidarity, duty, political motivations and commitment to the country of origin, or a combination of these factors (DEMAC, 2016; Horst et al., 2016). Diaspora communities are equipped with in-depth contextual knowledge, trust mechanisms, versatile social networks and compiling first-hand crisis information. They have access to non-traditional funding sources and affected communities that large humanitarian organisations have difficulty reaching. Furthermore, they demonstrate commitment well-beyond the short frame of crisis response (Andrew et al., 2016; DEMAC, 2016; IOM, 2015). Diaspora actions work across the 'nexus' and are inclusive of the development and humanitarian continuum (DEMAC, 2016, 2018). Diaspora actors bring their own set of ideas, skills, values, principles and approaches. Each diaspora is a heterogenic community, and their agenda in a humanitarian crisis is also heterogenic (Andrew et al., 2016).

We need to be cautious with calls to engage diaspora systematically in a Westernised, centralised and institutionalised humanitarian system. Any attempt to fully institutionalise diaspora engagement is a potential risk because it would be hindered by the current governance structure, bureaucracy and the flows of international humanitarian system (IOM, 2015; Vivekananthan & Connors, 2019). Horst, Lubkemann and Pailey argue that 'diaspora humanitarianism' differs fundamentally from the 'international' and 'local' humanitarian community. They highlight that "diaspora humanitarianism is assumed to be driven by motivations related to helping 'one's own'" (Horst et al., 2016, p. 225). The main difference in the modus operandi of diaspora is signified by more fluid and informal arrangements, as opposed to fixed, static, long-term structures inherent in the humanitarian system.

Diaspora engagement in humanitarian response is often criticised for a number of reasons, including being non-professional, ad-hoc, fragmented and prone to instability due to the voluntary affiliations and non-static nature of the members and the uncertain commitment of future generations (DEMAC, 2016). The traditional idea of upholding Dunantist humanitarian principles of impartiality, neutrality and independence as a distinguishing practice of life-saving assistance gatekeeps diaspora actors, who come with their own ideas and interpretations of legitimacy, accountability, transparency and fairness. The concerns expressed by the international humanitarian community regarding quality directly impute diaspora professionalism, knowledge of standards and the level of compliance with principles and codes of conduct which stem from the closed system thinking of humanitarianism. The level of commitment of diasporas to humanitarian principles differs with respect to their organisational characteristics and members' interests. Sezgin (2016) explains this behaviour with "associational theory". Complying with members' expectations is more essential for diaspora humanitarians to increase the legitimacy of their actions than complying with normative humanitarian principles. Despite the questioning of diaspora impartiality and neutrality, there is empirical evidence to suggest that diasporas deliver humanitarian relief to the affected population regardless of their kinship ties and associations (DEMAC, 2016). On the other hand, we need to acknowledge that one cannot dismiss the spirit of personal and professional affiliations of diaspora on the ground that characterise diaspora ways of helping their own.

There is a dearth of knowledge among academics, policymakers and traditional humanitarian actors about why and how diverse diaspora communities engage in humanitarian response and their coordination with other actors in this context (DEMAC, 2018; Horst et al., 2016; IOM, 2015; Wall & Hedlund, 2016). More research is required to understand the potential of diaspora humanitarianism. We have engaged long enough in judging the worth of diaspora humanitarianism based on the Dunantist tradition. What is required is a radical framework to understand diaspora humanitarianism outside the lens of old system thinking.

PACIFIC MIGRATION, REMITTANCES AND DISASTERS

Pre-colonial migration in the Pacific suggests free and frequent movements between islands (Lee, 2009). Colonial era migration involved both voluntary and forced movements beyond the Pacific. These movements created historical social networks within and beyond the Pacific, with New Zealand, USA and Australia being three key destinations of Pacific migration. These destinations are home to a Pacific diaspora population that is relatively large in comparison to the local population in the island homes.

Pacific Island Countries (PICs) are remittance-dependent and known to be heavily aid-assisted (Connell, 2015; Pyke et al., 2012). Remittances are crucial in PICs to sustain people's livelihoods. They serve as a reactive mechanism during crises (Le De et al., 2013). The increase in the level of remittances during crises helps affected communities with "short-term coping" and "long-term recovery" (Le De et al., 2015). Pre-existing vulnerabilities in communities are exacerbated during a disaster. Remittances increase the coping capacity of disaster-affected people as a "livelihood diversification strategy" with "multiplier effects" and particularly help those who lack access to resources due to failure of the formal society (Le De et al., 2013; Le De et al., 2015; Wall & Hedlund, 2016). Other scholars challenge the way the flow of remittances is considered as a one-way street, shining light on the specificity of Pacific transnational exchange networks where resources flow in multi-directions (Addo, 2009; Gershon, 2007).

PICs are highly exposed and vulnerable to natural disasters (Gero et al., 2013; Méheux et al., 2007; WB, 2019). The vulnerability is exacerbated by climate change, which acts as a threat-multiplier, adversely affecting peoples' livelihoods, economies and ecosystems. Climate-induced disasters cause deaths, displacements, loss of livelihood, environmental degradation and damage, or destroy infrastructure. Migration is a vehicle for providing transnational care and welfare in the Pacific (Connell, 2015; Pyke et al., 2012). Disaster acts as an emotional stimulus that reinforces social ties of diaspora and the diaspora identity (Le De et al., 2015). Pacific diaspora respond to disasters out of their sense of obligation to their family and kin, out of empathy drawn from their consciousness of the economic difficulties in island homes and from religious values. Nevertheless, there are few attempts by migrant-sending countries to engage with their diaspora communities at a macro-level (Connell, 2015). Limited data on diaspora and migration in PICs also poses a challenge for policymakers and researchers.

It is, thus, critical to better understand and acknowledge Pacific diaspora engagement during times of crisis in the Pacific. The lack of knowledge about why and how Pacific communities in Australia respond to disasters is a matter of concern, considering Australia is one of the main three destinations for Pacific migration and that PICs have strategic importance, historical relationships, and proximity to Australia. According to the 2016 census, Australia hosts 206,673 people of Pacific ancestry, excluding those claiming New Zealand, Maori and Fiji-Indian ancestries (Batley, 2017). The Pacific diaspora communities inside Australia and their transnational networks are a crucial link to Pacific island nations. Our research was an endeavour to understand the Pacific diaspora in a humanitarian context.

Methodology

Our research was initially designed to understand the role of the Pacific diaspora in humanitarian response to disasters. This was to be based on a comparative analysis of multi-stakeholder perspectives, that is, the perspectives of Pacific diaspora actors, traditional humanitarian actors and national disaster management officials of PICs. As we highlight in our research report,

> It became apparent during the early stages of data collection that a comparative analysis of perspectives cannot be methodologically justified due to the lack of knowledge about Pacific diaspora in humanitarian response and their invisibility in the traditional humanitarian system. (Vivekananthan & Connors, 2019, p.4)

Pacific diaspora communities were also not exposed to the internal structures, standards and operations of the humanitarian system. People-to-people connections, which lead the mobilisation of the Pacific diaspora in times of disaster, were not necessarily inclusive of traditional humanitarian actors in Australia or of national disaster management officials in Pacific island countries.

The preliminary research findings and our experiential learning led us to deviate from our initial research design. We separated the research inputs from Pacific diaspora participants and proposed understanding 'Pacific diaspora humanitarianism' from a diasporic perspective.

Methods

Relationship-building with Pacific diaspora leaders in Australia, data-gathering and meaning-making were carried out from 2018 to 2020, including post-research communications with Pacific diaspora leaders. Our list of research participants comprised 29 Pacific diaspora community leaders across Australia and 13 traditional humanitarian actors belonging to local, national and international humanitarian entities. Snowball sampling was used to reach out to Pacific diaspora communities in Australia and to invite community leaders as participants in this research. There were 25 interviews and 42 survey responses in total.

It took us a while to break the invisible wall between Pacific diaspora communities and our academia. The use of technical terms in our communication and documents as well as the impersonal nature of surveys posed a challenge in our initial data gathering. We learnt the significance of building relationships of trust, respect, cultural understanding and reciprocity. We learnt to simplify humanitarian jargon, including 'humanitarianism' and 'humanitarian' and academic concepts, including 'diaspora', for better understanding. Relationship-building was not just a matter of time but also a matter of language, communication and critical reflections from the researchers. We committed to creating a space, based on our initial learning and reflections, where Pacific diaspora leaders can be participants in the (re)creation of knowledge about the Pacific diaspora in humanitarian response to disasters in the Pacific.

The primary data for this research was gathered through an online survey and in-depth interviews. Official websites, media releases and dedicated public Facebook pages were used as secondary data sources to validate the primary data wherever available. We found that the online survey could not be optimised for many Pacific diaspora participants because of its impersonal nature and cultural inconvenience. These concerns were addressed during the face-to-face interviews, which we would like to call informal conversations. These informal conversations enabled mutual self-disclosure and trust-building. They created respectful and democratic spaces where Pacific diaspora participants were able to voice their agency and discuss their worldviews and lived experiences. Survey data and secondary data were, thus, applied as supplementary sources for the interview data. Inductive coding and thematic analysis were used for the purpose of analysis. Suspicious Interpretation (Willig, 2017) was used to analyse the inputs from traditional humanitarian actors, equipping our analysis with a technique to look beyond the surface meaning of text inputs and interpret the latent meaning.

In the research report (2019), 'Crossing the Divide: Pacific diaspora in humanitarian response to natural disasters', we proposed a model for understanding 'Pacific diaspora humanitarianism' built on a constructivist approach incorporating neo-institutionalist and diasporic perspectives (see Fig. 6.1). The model was modified in the latest work Vivekananthan (forthcoming) to reflect the decolonial lens the lead researcher used to centre the voices and worldview of Pacific diaspora communities as a means to understanding their responses to disasters in the Pacific.

'Pacific diaspora humanitarianism' is a previously unexplored territory. The available knowledge about the Pacific diaspora in disaster response was limited to remittances and their alleged role in sending unsolicited

Fig. 6.1 A Model for understanding diaspora humanitarianism

bilateral donations (UBD). The voices, worldviews and experiences of Pacific diaspora communities in Australia on this subject were largely absent in the academic literature and humanitarian discourse.

Our concern was, how do we bring out the voices, worldviews and experiences of Pacific diaspora people without tempering them by the cognitive, normative and regulative frameworks that govern the humanitarian system? Nakhid (2009, p. 216) argues that "the perspectives of people that have become Pacific transnationals" is one way of understanding Pacific transnationalism. Lee (2009, p. 30) emphasises, "Any issues facing Pacific peoples must be discussed in the context of both the islands and their diasporas, taking the processes of 'world enlargement' and transnationalism into account." Le De et al. (2015) provide an example for incorporating migrants' perspectives in a disaster context, challenging the conventional understanding of remitting behaviours in relation to the economic role of diaspora and the global neoliberal agenda.

How do we pave pathways for alternative realities and ideas while working within a Westernised academia and a humanitarian system? The starting point is being critical of system thinking and mainstream dialogues about the 'formal', 'authentic', 'professional' and 'systematic' ways of helping the distant others. We embrace decoloniality as a mechanism to lay the foundation for diaspora communities to express why and how they engage in humanitarian contexts with a sense of authentic humanity and agency. Decoloniality is "marked by a break and shift from European genealogy of thought and structure of feeling as the point-of-reference to the reconstruction of an-other episteme and ontology where decolonial options reside." (García, 2020, p. 307).

Smith (2012, p. 58) summarises researching "through imperial eyes" as "an approach which assumes that Western ideas about the most fundamental things are the only ideas possible to hold, certainly the only rational ideas, and the only ideas which can make sense of the world, of reality, of social life and of human beings." Decolonial scholars see decolonisation as an act of social justice, cultural survival, self-determination, restoration, reclaiming dignity, healing and resistance (Bahdia & Kassisb, 2016; Keikelame & Swartz, 2019; Salih et al., 2020; Smith, 2012). Bagele Chillisa, a Botswanan post-colonial scholar, asserts in an interview,

> For me, decolonising knowledge systems is a part of resistance against the domination of Western knowledge. I believe research needs to have a clear stance against the political, academic and methodological imperialism of whatever time and place we are in (Chilisa & Denborough, 2019, p. 13).

Decoloniality in this model works as an overarching principle holding non-Pacific researchers accountable to Pacific diaspora participants and their worldviews. However, we remain self-critical of the use of decoloniality in the research. Decoloniality challenges the Western representation of "ontologically inferior and epistemically irrational and deviant" others in the background of "Modernity/Coloniality", but analysing the "unequal nature of the other" or "plus and minus degrees of humanity" is not in its framework (García, 2020). One should be aware of the danger in producing "exceptional subjects" or universal solutions using the arguments of decoloniality.

Neo-institutionalist perspective is used by Horst et al. (2016) in their writing on 'diaspora humanitarianism'. Neo-institutionalist perspective presents an argument that diaspora actors can bring their own set of norms, values and expectations as the 'new' members of a broader humanitarian community and play a potential role in transforming the institutional structures of the international humanitarian system. Our model employs neo-institutionalist perspective to understand the underlying differences between diaspora humanitarian actors and traditional humanitarian actors. Our genuine concerns remain intact about membership of the humanitarian community. Do Pacific diaspora actors see themselves as part of a broader 'humanitarian' community? Is the label 'humanitarian' useful for them? Do they self-identify as 'humanitarians'? Will the existing normative, cognitive and regulative structures of the traditional humanitarian system persuasively assimilate diaspora actors and shadow the distinct qualities of diaspora humanitarianism? These are questions for the future.

The research paradigm of constructivism sets the stage for incorporating diaspora perspectives to understand disaster responses by the Pacific diaspora through their interpretation of their constructed realities. Constructivism, one of the postmodern paradigms, promotes relativism in the study of constructed realities. It uses a "hermeneutic/dialectic" methodology based on "trustworthiness and authenticity" (Lincoln et al., 2011). Constructivism proposes knowledge accumulation as an exercise of "more informed and sophisticated reconstructions" by individuals where the inquirer is the "facilitator of multivoice reconstruction". The philosophy underlying the constructivist approach enables the research to look at Pacific ways of responding to a disaster based on the worldviews of the Pacific diaspora. We use the constructivist approach as a way of preventing us from getting trapped into the constructed realities within the current humanitarian system.

We introduce 'diaspora perspective' in this proposed model as an encapsulation of diaspora voices and worldviews. Diaspora perspective makes space for diasporas' norms, values and expectations of each other in their transnational domains. It stands for their ideas, experiences and behaviours in responding to humanitarian crises. Fiddian-Qasmiyeh (2020) presents "South" as a metaphor for renouncing institutional and cultural practices associated with colonialism and imperialism in migration studies. She highlights the existence of multiple "Souths" within metropoles and peripheries. Recentring South can also mean recentring South voices and perspectives in the Global North. We draw upon her arguments on recentring South and call for recognising diasporic perspectives in humanitarian studies as the voices of South in Global North. Researchers have used positive stories of marginalised voices in disasters as a political act to overcome deficit thinking about how culture attributes to disaster response (Kenney et al., 2015). We centre diasporic perspective in the model as a deliberate political response to confront the incomplete narratives about diaspora humanitarianism in humanitarian studies.

LIMITATIONS

The Pacific diaspora in Australia is diverse in nationalities, ethnicities and tribal groups. We had only 29 Pacific diaspora participants, and the majority of them are of Fijian ancestry. The research findings do not represent the diversity of the Pacific diaspora. There were only a few responses from traditional humanitarian actors and national disaster management officials to our research invitation, which could be interpreted as a lack of interest in or exposure to humanitarian actions by diaspora in the Pacific context, if it was not due to the lack of capacity for their participation. The findings of this research are, thus, based on small sample size and not generalizable. They are focused on the positive aspects of the Pacific diaspora in humanitarian response. We encourage readers to use the findings as an entry point to understand Pacific diaspora humanitarianism from diasporic perspectives.

The Journey: Authors' Note

Jeevika Vivekananthan: When Phil suggested looking into how Pacific communities in Australia engage in humanitarian response, we did not have much to start with, as we have mentioned above, other than the literature on remittances in the Pacific and mainstream dialogues of the alleged role of the Pacific diaspora in sending unsolicited bilateral donations (UBD). Since that point, my journey as a lead researcher was like unfolding a mystery box. I was conscious of my colonised and westernised mind, lack of understanding about the Pacific context, and my knowledge influenced by the system thinking and academia to some extent. At the same time, I had the advantage of being a member of a diaspora community, with lived experience in humanitarian crises and experience in working with various diaspora communities in Australia. As I have written in a reflection article (Vivekananthan, 2020), a couple of incidents at the beginning of our research challenged me. They made me realise my agency as a researcher in the political act of knowledge production. Pacific diaspora community leaders have helped me grow as a considerate researcher. I hope our research has done some justice to Pacific knowledge, Pacific ways and the Pacific communities inside Australia in the humanitarian ecosystem.

Phil Connors: This research has both challenged and reinforced my belief in the power of storytelling in research. From a community development perspective, stories are an important part of meaning-making, and this research provided the opportunity to hear the story from those making the meaning. Working alongside Jeevika, a self-identified member of a diaspora, challenged me to reflect on my work as a researcher and practitioner in the humanitarian space. The whole process reinforced my belief in respecting local knowledge and in the diversity of humanitarianisms not being abstract but real, and then, in how this needed to be the future of humanitarian action. I also hope this research does justice to the deep knowledge of the Pacific diaspora in Australia and of how they work with affected people and communities in their homelands during crises.

Understanding Pacific Diaspora Humanitarianism

Pacific Diaspora: Who?

Defining diaspora is contextual. We define diaspora as follows,

> Diaspora is a transnational community whose members live outside of their self-identified homeland(s) on a temporary or permanent basis and remain connected to it (or them) through family, known and/or imagined community spheres while maintaining a group identity that may change through time and space. (Vivekananthan & Connors, 2019, p.12)

This definition is specific to the Pacific diaspora. We have drawn on the salient features of Grossman's (2019) "decontested definition" of diaspora and cross-checked them with the characteristics of the Pacific diaspora in our research. Homeland orientation is one of the salient features in defining the diaspora but not the central feature. The definition allows flexibility in terms of temporal and spatial differences. We acknowledge with 'maintaining a group identity that may change through time and space' that the way diaspora members construct and associate with identities constantly changes across time and space (Gershon, 2007).

Our Pacific diaspora participants come from diverse backgrounds, that is, nationalities and ethnicities. 'Pacific' in the term 'Pacific diaspora' blankets different identities, movements and associations of the members of this group. There are "culturally specific ways of constructing unities and of connecting people to places" (Gershon, 2007, p.485). The problem with the ways researchers and governments classify people is the homogenous identity that puts people with diverse backgrounds and experiences in the same category for convenience. 'Pacific diaspora' in our research stands for people who self-identify their origin with one or more Pacific Island nations. Some of them have multifaceted identities inherited from their ancestries, for example, "I am second-generation descendant from Vanuatu, with also heritage in Indigenous Torres Strait background. My father is also a West Indian from the Caribbean." Loyalty and belongingness are not always straightforward. Loyalty is divided between their self-identified homelands. One participant expressed the duality of belonging by mentioning, "I think I belong to both places. When I am in Fiji, I am a Fijian. When I am in Australia, I am an Australian." Pacific islanders take on migratory routes, mostly involving more than one destination, for example, "I am originally from Fiji islands and I left Fiji islands in 1974 to live in the USA and from there I came to Australia". Most of the migratory routes are neither linear nor uni-directional. Pacific islanders in Australia share specific values and ways that bring them together under a united 'Pacific' identity reflecting all these dynamics in identities, migration experiences and origins. When asked about any apparent divisions within the Pacific diaspora communities in Australia, one participant cheerfully told us, "unless it is on the football field. And then that is a different story. However, we understand one another's hardship. We understand one another's culture."

The social connections of Pacific diaspora participants transcend nation-centric borders. Their family, together with known and/or imagined community spheres, fosters transnational and translocal networks. We identified various links by which Pacific people in Australia connect and network: families; various communities including local communities in PICs, Pacific communities in Australia and non-Pacific communities in Australia; various organisations, both in PICs and Australia, including grassroots organisations, National Disaster Management Offices (NDMOs) and other government agencies, religious organisations, sports associations, local businesses and Australian Non-Government Organisations (ANGOs); industrial links; politicians. These various groups, communities and networks indicate that Pacific diasporas "operate in social fields that transgress geographical, political and cultural borders" (Nakhid, 2009, p. 217). Esnard and Sapat (2016) capture the transnational and translocal networks of diaspora as sources of "social capital", which is critical in a disaster response. The transnational and translocal networks of the Pacific diaspora represent the social capital, which comes in handy in responding to humanitarian crises in the Pacific.

Motivations: Why?

When a disaster strikes in the Pacific, Pacific islanders in Australia get involved in disaster responses. Pacific diaspora community leaders identified families, communal responsibility, sense of solidarity, empathy and loyalty as the motivations for their involvement. Family and communal responsibility are no surprise in the Pacific context. Pacific ethnographers see the Pacific as a "sea of families" (Gershon, 2007). Familial links are a central part of Pacific diasporic identity and transnational exchange networks. Families are understood as networks where each member is a node. A network analogy of scholars locates migrant families as part of a larger diaspora in which knowledge and resources are exchanged in multiple directions (Gershon, 2007). Our participants interpreted family in diverse ways. One participant said that family comes first for him during a disaster, and he continued, "Family becomes the whole country, the whole country is your family." One participant of Maori and Polynesian descent quoted, "it takes a village to raise a child" as a philosophy that guides Pacific communities through any crisis. There was "love" in helping families. There was an order of priorities, for example,

> The way I describe any disaster in Fiji is the immediate help we give, or my family here, we give it to our own family in Fiji. That's our number one priority. Once these families looked after then you extend it to your village. And then you extend it your district. Fiji is made up of different districts. Fiji as a nation comes last. It's fourth on the list.

This interpretation of family, extended family, village and country challenges our idea of family as a single unit. Diasporic perspectives provide insights into how communal responsibility is woven through culturally specific networks where families are the core. Communal responsibility ensures 'their people', whether members of immediate families or the broader community, are supported during challenging times. We argue that the humanitarian imperative of the Pacific diaspora is shaped by their cultural practice of looking after each other in times of suffering within their transnational networks.

Sense of solidarity for the Pacific diaspora means ethnic solidarity, Pacific solidarity and humanitarian solidarity. Ethnic solidarity and Pacific solidarity are influenced by how people identify themselves as a group when they come together for a common cause. When there was a cyclone in Samoa, a participant of non-Samoan background told us "we all got behind these communities." Pacific identity is the point of connection that brings various island communities together, reflecting, "we come as one, but we are many." Pacific diasporas show their solidarity to the affected communities by coming together and sharing resources that are required to go to these communities. Fijian diasporas with an Indian heritage responded to a disaster in Nepal in solidarity with Nepalese diasporas with an Indian heritage. It is an example of ethnic solidarity. These examples show how differently diaspora actors identify and associate themselves with the suffering of others, as they become part of a known or imagined community of unity and solidarity. Humanitarian solidarity motivates some members of the Pacific diaspora to respond to disaster anywhere in the world, based on values such as compassion, sense of humanity, lived experience and their improved standards of living in Australia. The discussion on the nuances of solidarity and the so-called invisibility of the Pacific diaspora in Australia strike a connection to what Salih et al. (2020) discuss as "an intersectional space of appearance". It is a space for "intersectionality of struggles". The intersectional space of appearance enables non-white bodies in liberal democracies to come into a space where they become visible to one another without getting overshadowed by the whiteness of mainstream solidarity.

Divided loyalty between self-identified homelands is another reason some people want to help across the borders of nation-states. It could be the country where their ancestors were, where they were born, where they spent a considerable time of their lives, or where they currently reside. Loyalty is influenced by their migratory routes and experiences. The research participants used duty, patriotism, gratitude and sentimental affection to explain their loyalty to one or more places. On the other hand, lived experiences of disasters make Pacific diasporas better able to empathise with the suffering and hardship of affected people in PICs. When asked, one of the participants asked back, "what happens in the night if you don't have a house or roof over your head? That's what we experienced. So that's what comes in your mind." The first-hand experience of disasters, relief and working with the national actors come in handy for diaspora actors during their disaster responses.

The motivational factors of diaspora humanitarianism from our study share similarities with Le De et al. (2015). The Pacific diaspora's assistance during a disaster extends from their families to the broader community. Helping local counterparts in a disaster is situated in their cultural values, social connections and religious obligations. Disaster acts as an emotional stimulus that evokes memories of lived experiences and diasporic sentiments and regenerates the social ties of the Pacific diaspora.

Humanitarian Actions: How? How different?

Pacific diaspora communities in Australia respond to disasters in the Pacific in different ways. Sending money and relief materials, organising cooked food on the ground, sharing timely information, fundraising for humanitarian initiatives, volunteering, programmes and projects, post-disaster reconstructions, medical assistance and providing emotional and physical support are part of their humanitarian assistance to disaster-affected communities in PICs.

Pacific diasporas find out what is needed on the ground through their connections to the local communities. These social connections include but are not limited to families, relatives, advisory councils, professional associations, religious organisations, military personnel, government ministers and community volunteers. A Fijian diaspora participant explained,

> when we hear the news, for example, if it says the hurricane hit the western part, we know exactly where it is hit. And then I have a very strong link with my teachers' union in Fiji. I was an executive of the teachers' union in Fiji. So, I just pick up the phone and I ring the secretary and I say to him 'mate that's what we have heard. You know I want you to identify some areas of the biggest concern'. And then through the link of the teachers all over the places, they will send out a letter to the teachers and the teachers will feedback 'oh my school is blown away and gone there's nothing standing here', 'The farms in my area are all gone'. So that's where we get the information and then we know exactly where to go.

People personally visit the villages and find out what is needed. They also make decisions based on their previous experiences, media information and inputs from government agencies in PICs, such as NDMOs.

The findings indicate that the Pacific diaspora use social connections, local knowledge and first-hand crisis information to identify and respond to the needs of the affected communities. Their actions are based on trust and relationships. One of the community leaders with years of experience explained, "Very important thing in life is to build trust. If you've got to trust with each other or any organisation… and if they trust you then you have no problems in getting any help from them." The Pacific diaspora use their transnational and translocal networks for mobilising communities and resources in assisting disaster-affected communities. Some of these networks get activated only in response to disasters. There is flexibility in the way the members network and organise the response, for example,

> What I have been able to do (is to) organise with different Fijian organisations in Melbourne to come together for disaster relief. What I have made it very clear to each and every organisation is that the group that we form is purely to assist for that particular disaster. As soon as the disaster help is done, we all go separate ways. We will only come together as a group when the next disaster happens. There is no committee, no organisational structure set up, it is purely based on voluntary and volunteers come on board.

Sending cash and goods across the transnational exchange networks is a customary practice for Pacific people. Some people send money, some send containers of relief supplies, and some consider both, for example,

> The first response that we would do is to send money, transfer money. Because it is much faster. That help is much faster. You can transfer money now and get it today. And then we can work along in pulling some, you know like food and other items together, to get across.

Pacific exchange networks are historically used to share knowledge and resources according to their customs. These exchange networks provide arenas for people to represent their extended families as unified networks in multiple communities, that is, local and transnational, and ritual events, such as civic events, church events and individual life events (Addo, 2009; Gershon, 2007). Diaspora perspectives in this research offer us an understanding that Pacific diaspora humanitarianism is a product of customary practice in the Pacific. Pacific diaspora humanitarian actions are transnational activities that provide arenas for the Pacific diaspora to express solidarity with people in PICs and exchange life-saving resources through their networks.

Linking Relief, Rehabilitation and Development (LRRD) is logically coherent and theoretically sound, but operationally the humanitarian sector and development sector are coexisting as two solitudes (Audet, 2015). The nexus of these solitudes is argued to be not viable for humanitarian organisations, who tend to develop institutional cultures, values and bureaucratic characteristics that are distinct from development agents. Our research findings show that Pacific diaspora actors do not fall into these solitudes. They rather fluidly move on the continuum of humanitarian assistance and development.

Pacific diasporic perspectives share ground with what Lee (2009, p. 15) explains as "The form of transnationalism with which Pacific peoples typically engage is shaped by this awkward relationship between state-imposed borders and cultural differences, and their own perceptions of social relatedness that transcend national boundaries and emphasise reciprocity, kinship and cultural identity". We, thus, define Pacific diaspora humanitarianism as "a transnational demonstration of solidarity by the Pacific diaspora operating in family and/or community spheres to support their homeland(s) and their people with humanitarian needs and recovery" (Vivekananthan & Connors, 2019, p. 12).

CONCLUSION: CROSSING THE DIVIDE?

The non-Pacific diaspora participants belonging to local, national and international humanitarian organisations identified diaspora actors as remitters, conduits, fundraisers, troublemakers, volunteers, service providers, solutions to brain-drain as well as a new option for walking the talk on localisation. However, the portrayal of diasporas as 'troublemakers' in sending UBD, the scrutiny of the level of diaspora's adherence to humanitarian principles and the system thinking dominated their perspectives. There was an emphasis on the international system, for example, "We need to prepare them, I think, in the sort of operation modality of the international system, so understanding everything from the cost to the principals to the targeting beneficiaries". The paucity of understanding among traditional humanitarian actors about Pacific diaspora engagement in disasters was also noted.

On the other hand, some of our diaspora participants expressed their concerns about traditional humanitarian organisations in terms of dominance, distrust and disconnect. At the same time, some had good opinions based on their previous working experiences. Nonetheless, Pacific diaspora community leaders prioritise local leadership and direct engagement with affected communities. Most of them believe that creating parallel structures with the formal humanitarian organisations is a risk for diaspora organisations. Therefore, diaspora organisations should be acknowledged for their unique way of responding to humanitarian crises. A holistic understanding of the diverse ways diasporas act on their urge to help their own may promote cooperation with other actors in the humanitarian ecosystem. It can help local and international actors to develop effective ways of meeting the needs of the affected population in times of crisis hand-in-hand with diaspora actors wherever viable.

Prompt response to a crisis, access to vulnerable people, acceptance from the local population, cost-effectiveness of humanitarian assistance, links with development agents and the possibility for increasing accountability underlie the rationale behind why we need to support local humanitarians (OECD, 2017). Diaspora actors share some of these strengths even though they cannot be categorised as local humanitarians. The similarity of attributes between diaspora and local actors open doors for meaningful and equal partnerships or collaborations. As cultural agents with proximity, Pacific diaspora can also play a role as enablers of localisation through their advocacy work with Australian-based humanitarian agencies and the Australian Government. Pacific diaspora community leaders are one step ahead in their advocacy work, noting, "Climate change is evident, and we need to get a lot more consciousness around and support our communities in the islands because they are sinking here, and you know Australia's got a lot to answer for the contribution that Pacific islanders made to this nation." We suggest at this point, if Australian-based humanitarian agencies and the Australian government want to cross the divide with the Pacific diaspora, they must start from understanding Pacific diaspora humanitarianism from a diasporic perspective.

Acknowledgements Pacific diaspora humanitarianism could not have been documented without the participation and contribution of Pacific diaspora community leaders. We extend our sincere gratitude to Pacific diaspora community leaders: Aneesh Singh, Annukar Mishra, Avreen Sharma, Asofitu Leatuavao, Awindra Prasad, Dev Anand, Dianne Austral-ombiga, Ema Vueti, Emelda Davis, Ganesh Sen, James Munroe, Jatish Puran, Jerry Ueseli Katarina Driu, Lesa Chang Wai, Martin Chanel, Mary Irene Bayldon, Maureen Mopio Jane, Raewyn Burton, Raj Bachu, Ravin Narayan, Sahiban Ali, Semi Meo, Simon Charan, Solomone T Koroi, Sullieni Layt, Surendra Prasad, Tere Brown and Uo Brown. We also thank our non-Pacific diaspora participants. We acknowledge the IKEA Foundation for funding this research undertaken by the Centre for Humanitarian Leadership (CHL).

References

Addo, P.-A. (2009). Forms of Transnationalism, Forms of Tradition: Cloth and Cash as Ritual Exchange Valuables in the Tongan Diaspora. In H. Lee & S. T. Francis (Eds.), *Migration and Transnationalism: Pacific Perspectives* (pp. 43–56). ANU Press.

Alexander, C. (2017). Beyond the "The 'diaspora' diaspora": A Response to Rogers Brubaker. *Ethnic and Racial Studies, 40*(9), 1544–1555. https://doi.org/10.1080/01419870.2017.1300302

Andrew, B., Brown, D., & Cechvala, S. (2016). *Humanitarian Effectiveness and the Role of the Diaspora: A CDA Literature Review*. CDA Collaborative Learning Projects.

Audet, F. (2015). From Disaster Relief to Development Assistance: Why Simple Solutions Don't Work. *International Journal, 70*(1), 110–118. https://doi.org/10.1177/0020702014562595

Bahdia, R., & Kassisb, M. (2016). Decolonisation, Dignity and Development Aid: A Judicial Education Experience in Palestine. *Third World Quarterly, 37*(11), 2010–2027. https://doi.org/10.1080/01436597.2016.1181521

Batley, J. (2017). *What Does the 2016 Census Reveal about Pacific Islands Communities in Australia?*. State, Society & Governance in Melanesia. http://bellschool.anu.edu.au/sites/default/files/publications/attachments/2017-09/ib_2017_23_batley_revised_final_0.pdf

Barnett, M. (2011). Introduction: The Crooked Timber of Humanitarianism. In *Empire of Humanity* (pp. 1–18). Cornell University Press.

Barnett, M., & Weiss, T. G. (2011). Humanitarianism: The Essentials. In *Humanitarianism Contested: Where Angels Fear to Tread* (pp. 37–63). Taylor & Francis Group.

Bennett, C., Kent, R., Donini, A., & Maxwell, D. (2016). *Planning from the Future: Is the Humanitarian System Fit for Purpose?* https://fic.tufts.edu/wp-content/uploads/pff_report_uk.pdf

Boyle, M., & Kitchin, R. (2014). Diaspora-centred Development: Current Practice, Critical Commentaries, and Research Priorities. In S. Sahoo & B. K. Pattanaik (Eds.), *Global Diasporas and Development* (pp. 17–38). Springer. https://doi.org/https://doi-org.ezproxy-f.deakin.edu.au/10.1007/978-81-322-1047-4

Chilisa, B., & Denborough, D. (2019). Decolonising Research: An Interview with Bagele Chilisa. *The International Journal of Narrative Therapy and Community Work, 1*, 12–18.

Cohen, R. (1997). *Global Diasporas: An Introduction*. Taylor & Francis Group.

Connell, J. (2015). The Pacific Diaspora. In W. H. Khonje (Ed.), *Migration and Development: Perspectives from Small States* (pp. 224–264). Commonwealth Secretariat.

Davey, E., Borton, J., & Foley, M. (2013). *A History of the Humanitarian System: Western Origins and Foundations.*

DEMAC. (2016). *Diaspora Humanitarianism: Transnational Ways of Working.* http://www.demac.org/content/5-news/5-demac-report/final_report_web.pdf

DEMAC. (2018). *Creating Opportunities to Work with Diasporas in Humanitarian Settings.* https://reliefweb.int/report/world/creating-opportunities-work-diasporas-humanitarian-settings

Donini, A. (2012). Humanitarianism, Perceptions, Power. In C. Abu-Sada (Ed.), *In the Eyes of Others: How People in Crises Perceive Humanitarian Aid* (pp. 183–192). MSF-USA.

Esnard, A.-M., & Sapat, A. (2016). Transnationality and Diaspora Advocacy: Lessons from Disaster. *Journal of Civil Society, 12*(1), 1–16. https://doi.org/10.1080/17448689.2015.1114737

Fiddian-Qasmiyeh, E. (2020). Introduction. *Migration and Society, 3*(1), 1–18. https://doi.org/10.3167/arms.2020.030102

García, R. (2020). Decoloniality and the Humanities: Possibilities and Predicaments. *Journal of Hispanic Higher Education, 19*(3), 303–317.

Gero, A., Fletcher, S. M., Rumsey, M., Thiessen, J., Kuruppu, N., Buchan, J., Daly, J., & Willetts, J. (2013). *Disaster Response and Climate Change in the Pacific.* National Climate Change Adaptation Research Facility.

Gershon, I. (2007). Viewing Diasporas from the Pacific: What Pacific Ethnographies Offer Pacific Diaspora Studies. *The Contemporary Pacific, 19*(12), 474–502.

Grossman, J. (2019). Toward a Definition of Diaspora. *Ethnic and Racial Studies, 42*, 1263–1282. https://doi.org/10.1080/01419870.2018.1550261

Horst, C., Lubkemann, S., & Pailey, R. N. (2016). The Invisibility of a Third Humanitarian Domain. In Z. Sezgin & D. Dijkzeul (Eds.), *The New Humanitarians in International Practice: Emerging Actors and Contested Principles* (pp. 213–233). Taylor & Francis Group.

IARAN. (2018). *From Voices to Choices.* https://static1.squarespace.com/static/593eb9e7b8a79bc4102fd8aa/t/5be216ff562fa77a94 1b14eb/1541543685634/Voices2Choices_FINAL-compressed.pdf

IASC. (2017). *Key Highlights from the Panel Discussion: Strengthening Collaboration with Diasporas in Humanitarian Response.* https://interagencystandingcommittee.org/system/files/key_notes_from_iasc_event_on_diaspora_final.pdf

IOM. (2015). *The Role of Diaspora in Humanitarian Response [Summary].* IOM Migration Series, UNHQ, New York. https://unofficeny.iom.int/sites/unofficeny/files/%5BInternational%20Organization%20for%20Migration%5D%20Role%20of%20Diaspora%20in%20Humanitarian%20Response.pdf

Keikelame, M. J., & Swartz, L. (2019). Decolonising Research Methodologies: Lessons from a Qualitative Research Project, Cape Town, South Africa. *Global Health Action, 12*(1), 1. https://doi.org/10.1080/16549716.2018.1561175

Kenney, C. M., Phibbs, S. R., Paton, D., Reid, J., & Johnston, D. M. (2015). Community-led Disaster Risk Management: A Maori Response to Otautahi (Christchurch) Earthquake. *Australasian Journal of Disaster and Trauma Studies, 19*(1), 1.

Le De, L., Gaillard, J. C., Friesen, W., Pupualii, M., Brown, C., & Aupito, A. (2015). Our Family Comes First: Migrants' Perspectives on Remittances in Disaster. *Migration and Development, 5*(1), 130–148. https://doi.org/10.108 0/21632324.2015.1017971

Le De, L., Gaillard, J. C., & Friesen, W. (2013). Remittances and Disasters: A Review. *International Journal of Disaster Risk Reduction, 4*, 34–43. https://doi.org/10.1016/j.ijdrr.2013.03.007

Lee, H. (2009). Pacific Migration and Transnationalism: Historical Perspectives. In H. L. A. S. T. Francis (Ed.), *Migration and Transnationalism: Pacific Perspectives* (pp. 7–41). ANU Press.

Lincoln, Y., Lynham, S., & Guba, E. (2011). Paradigmatic Controversies, Contradictions and Emerging Confluences. In N. L. Denzin (Ed.), *Handbook of Qualitative Research* (pp. 97–128). SAGE.

Méheux, K., Dominey-Howes, D., & Lloyd, K. (2007). Natural Hazard Impacts in Small Island Developing States: A Review of Current Knowledge and Future Research Needs. *Natural Hazards, 40*(2), 429–446. https://doi.org/10.1007/s11069-006-9001-5

Mohan, G., & Zack-WIlliams, A. (2002). Globalisation from Below: Conceptualising the Role of the African Diasporas in Africa's Development. *Review of African Political Economy, 29*, 1. https://doi.org/10.1080/03056240208704610

Nakhid, C. (2009). Conclusion: The Concept and Circumstances of Pacific Migration and Transnationalism. In H. Lee & S. T. Francis (Eds.), *Migration and Transnationalism: Pacific Perspectives* (pp. 215–230). ANU Press.

Ndhlovu, F. (2015). A decolonial critique of diaspora identity theories and the notion of superdiversity. *Diaspora Studies, 9*(1), 28–40. https://doi.org/1 0.1080/09739572.2015.1088612

OCHA. (2017). *OCHA on Message: Agenda for Community* (Agenda For Humanity Resources). https://agendaforhumanity.org/sites/default/files/OOM%20Agenda%20for%20Humanity.pdf

OECD. (2017). Localising Response (The Commitments into Action Series). https://www.oecd.org/development/humanitarian-donors/docs/Localisingtheresponse.pdf

Pyke, J., Francis, S., & Ben-Moshe, D. (2012). *The Tongan Diaspora in Australia: Current and Potential Links with the Homeland*.

Salih, R., Zambelli, E., & Welchman, L. (2020). "From Standing Rock to Palestine we are United": Diaspora Politics, Decolonization and the Intersectionality of Struggles. *Ethnic and Racial Studies, 44*(7), 1135–1153. https://doi.org/1 0.1080/01419870.2020.1779948

Sezgin, Z. (2016). Diaspora Action in Syria and Neighbouring Countries. In Z. Sezgin & D. Dijkzeul (Eds.), *The New Humanitarians in International Practice: Emerging Actors and Contested Principles* (pp. 232–255). Taylor & Francis Group.

Smith, L. T. (2012). *Decolonising Methodologies* (2nd ed.). Zed Books.

Vivekananthan, J. (2020). The 'Naked' Researcher. Convivial Thinking. https://www.convivialthinking.org/index.php/2020/04/08/the-naked-researcher/

Vivekananthan, J. (forthcoming). Pacific Diaspora Humanitarianism from a Diasporic Perspective.

Vivekananthan, J., & Connors, P. (2019). *Crossing the Divide: Pacific Diaspora in Humanitarian Response to Natural Disasters.* Centre for Humanitarian Leadership. https://centreforhumanitarianleadership.org/wp-content/uploads/2019/10/Crossing-the-Divide_Pacific-diaspora-in-response-to-natural-disasters_Full-Report.pdf

Wall, I., & Hedlund, K. (2016). *Localisation and Locally-led Crisis Response: A Literature Review.* https://usercontent.one/wp/www.local2global.info/wp-content/uploads/L2GP_SDC_Lit_Review_LocallyLed_June_2016_revised-Jan_2017_online.pdf

WB. (2019). The World Bank in Pacific Islands. WB. Retrieved 1 July, 2019, from www.worldbank.org/en/country/pacificislands/overview

Willig, C. (2017). Interpretation in Qualitative Research. In C. Willig & W. S. Rogers (Eds.), *The SAGE Handbook of Qualitative Research in Psychology* (pp. 274–288). SAGE Publications Ltd.. https://doi.org/10.4135/9781526405555.n16

CHAPTER 7

Diaspora Peacebuilding Through Inter-Ethnic Harmony: The South Sudanese and Sri Lankan Diasporas in Australia

Atem Atem, Jennifer Balint, Denise Cauchi, and Shyama Fuad

INTRODUCTION: INTER-ETHNIC HARMONY IN THE CONTEXT OF DIASPORA COMMUNITIES

This chapter focuses on migrants' and refugees' activities to address intra-communal discord in Australia that arises from the escalation of political conflict or violence in the country of origin, and how this can be

---

A. Atem
Australian National University, Canberra, ACT, Australia

J. Balint
The University of Melbourne, Melbourne, VIC, Australia
e-mail: jbalint@unimelb.edu.au

D. Cauchi (✉)
Consultant, Brunswick East, VIC, Australia

S. Fuad
Psychologist, Oakleigh South, VIC, Australia

© The Author(s), under exclusive license to Springer Nature Switzerland AG 2022
M. Phillips, L. Olliff (eds.), *Understanding Diaspora Development*,
https://doi.org/10.1007/978-3-030-97866-2_7

137

understood as a form of peace-making in the countries of origin. Through a focus on the peacebuilding activities undertaken by South Sudanese and Sri Lankan refugees and migrants in Australia and from an Australian base, it considers how inter-ethnic harmony is understood and utilised as a tool of peace by these diasporas.

Diaspora, for this chapter, will be defined narrowly as a category of practice (Brubaker, 2005, p. 1). Category of practice refers to the "everyday social experience, developed and deployed by ordinary social actors" (Brubaker & Cooper, 2000, p. 4). Therefore, diaspora as an identity "is used by lay actors in some everyday setting to make sense of themselves, of their activities, of what they share with and how they differ from, others" (Brubaker & Cooper, 2000). For South Sudanese and Sri Lankans, the focus of this chapter, the everyday setting is the interface between settling in Australia permanently and simultaneously maintaining connections with home countries (Erdal, 2020).[1] This interface can be challenging, as it influences, in significant ways, social experience in Australia for both South Sudanese and Sri Lankans. For both communities, this experience is marked by the struggle to achieve social and structural integration, fulfilling family obligations in Australia and the home country, disappointment with political events in the home country and the fall out within these communities in Australia over political events in the home country.

Although this chapter does not concern itself directly with settlement and integration of South Sudanese and Sri Lankan migrants and refugees, it is appropriate to point out that the research in Australia on settlement and integration tends to present each migrant community as homogeneous, cohesive and harmonious. Consequently, intracommunity discord and conflict in the course of settlement and integration are ignored. In addition, migrants' strong links with the home country due to family connections and other transnational interests that lead to transnational engagement and activities do not receive enough attention. However, when transnational engagement and transnational activities are perceived as threats to national security and community safety, settlement and integration come under the spotlight. For example, the participation of a small number of second-generation Lebanese-Australians in the war in Iraq in support of Islamic State and alleged youth crimes by South Sudanese young people prompted the former minister for the newly formed

---

[1] Marta Bivand Erdal discusses a multiscalar approach to explore the interaction between migrant transnationalism and integration/settlement (see: Erdal, 2020)

Department of Home Affairs to declare that it was a mistake to allow Lebanese, South Sudanese and other refugee communities to settle in Australia (Hurst, 2016; Murphy, 2016). In both Europe and America, transnational engagement and activities are perceived as a barrier to integration (Snel et al., 2006). However, there is no clear empirical evidence to support such a perception (Snel et al., 2006).

As this chapter demonstrates, conflict-induced migrants and refugees experience a significant amount of intracommunity conflict in their host country due to conflict in the home country. These intracommunity conflicts in countries of settlement are exacerbated by divergent norms, networks and preferences that different groups within a particular migrant community adopt, driven by their premigration and postmigration experiences (Williamson, 2015). Both the Sri Lankan and South Sudanese communities in Australia have experienced deep divisions that mirror the tensions in their countries of origin. Typically, when conflicts overseas escalate, relationships and networks in the diaspora deteriorate, resulting in hate speech, breakdown of friendships and associations between people of different political views. In some isolated instances, it has included physical aggression. This dynamic of deterioration of relations, reported by both communities, is frequently experienced by conflict-generated diasporas. These tensions affect social and psychological wellbeing, with community members frequently reporting distress, anxiety and feelings of increased social isolation. Community leaders' attention is also diverted away from other activities that enhance community wellbeing.

In responding to conflicts in country of origin, migrants often use their diaspora identities to take a conflicting stance towards the unfolding conflict in the home country and make claims about the conflict that legitimise their stance. In this way, we can understand diaspora as an identity and category of practice. Positions are taken that are not necessarily based on ethnic identity, but that occupy a difficult 'third' space that is neither about origin nor settlement country (Bhabhna, cited in Rutherford, 1990) but about legitimising a stance in relation to the conflict in the home country as a means of resolving it and about residing in country of settlement. The claims made to justify taking a stance are often based on the historical understanding of the conflict embedded in social relations that place certain groups in opposition, for example, the Dinka and the Nuer in the South Sudanese context and the Tamil and the Sinhalese in the Sri Lankan case.

140   A. ATEM ET AL.

In its attention to the particular initiatives of diasporas that focus on inter-ethnic harmony, and their motivations, this chapter draws out the dual focus of this work—on conflict and inter-ethnic harmony in countries of settlement as well as in home countries. In so doing, it aims to unsettle the linear settlement narrative, that 'leaves behind' the home country and has an 'integration' focus.

Intracommunity discord and the need to urgently resolve conflict motivates some members of the affected migrant community to act. The conflict in country of origin drives intra-community discord in host countries, resulting in diaspora involvement in home country conflict resolution which is motivated, at least in part, by the need to resolve intracommunity discord in host country. The result is the activation of transnational capacities, that is, the "willingness and ability to engage in activities that transcend national borders" (Al-Ali et al., 2001, p. 581).

The empirical evidence provided in the following two sections of this chapter details the transnational activities South Sudanese and Sri Lankan community members engage in, particularly in Australia but also in Sri Lanka and South Sudan, to address intracommunity conflict in order to achieve intracommunity harmony. The work draws from the project and subsequent research *Long distance peacebuilding: the experiences of the South Sudanese and Sri Lankan diasporas in Australia* by the author (Cauchi, 2018). The qualitative research involved interviews and focus groups with members of twelve multi-ethnic diaspora-led organisations from the Sri Lankan and South Sudanese communities. The two communities were identified as suitable for the research because both were known to be implementing peacebuilding and inter-ethnic harmony initiatives in Australia. The significant differences in their migration patterns and motivations, and length of time in Australia, lent richness to a comparative study: the majority of South Sudanese Australians had started to arrive via the humanitarian programme during the civil war in the early 2000s, while the Sri Lankan diaspora's 150-year history in Australia has occurred through distinct waves of migration, not all of which were conflict-induced. This work arose from the author Cauchi's long-standing collaboration with many of these organisations, in her capacity as then Executive Director of Diaspora Action Australia. Unless otherwise noted, interviews cited in this chapter are from the report.

This chapter is written by four authors coming from diverse and lived perspectives. One author is a PhD candidate who is also from South Sudan and has long experience working with the South Sudanese diaspora communities. One author is from Sri Lanka with long peacebuilding experience—working both in Sri Lanka and with diaspora communities in Australia—as a medium and bridge builder between the two spaces. One author has long experience working with diaspora communities on issues related to peace and armed conflict, and is the author of the report that forms the basis of this chapter, and one is an academic working in the area of conflict and justice. These differences bring a strength to the chapter and our work, and are also reflected in the diversity of terminology in the chapter and the ways we approach these issues.

Conflict resolution activities in the host country, as the South Sudanese and Sri Lankan diasporas are convinced, contribute positively to addressing conflicts in their home countries. As discussed in the chapter, South Sudanese and Sri Lankans also engage in transnational peacebuilding activities addressing the social, political and economic needs of people they left behind in their home countries. Together, this is a part of the settlement narrative that is missed. This has prompted community leaders to develop a range of initiatives to bridge these divides, fostering tolerance and co-existence, creating shared histories and establishing unified, multi-ethnic community structures. The following section outlines some initiatives developed by the South Sudanese and Sri Lankan diasporas in Australia, the strategies employed and motivations, including the need for shared narratives.

Achieving Inter-Ethnic Harmony from and in Diasporas: Projects, Strategies, Approaches and Motivations

South Sudanese Communities in Australia

The South Sudanese diaspora began to understand the role they could play as peace-makers through exposure to Australian and Western institutions and their practices of accountability, diversity and democracy. They also observed the approaches of development NGOs and studied in fields such as international development and international relations, all of which provided exposure to new ideas about peace-making. Therefore, by South Sudan's independence in 2011, South Sudanese in Australia were looking for opportunities to apply their newly found understandings of peacebuilding.

One of the earliest examples within the South Sudanese communities was the establishment of the South Sudan Diaspora Network (SSDN) in

New South Wales (NSW) in 2012. SSDN was established to support South Sudanese and their organisations who were either delivering or planning development projects and programmes in South Sudan. SSDN's focus was on capacity building and linking up individuals and organisations with Australian government aid programmes and international development organisations including those based in Australia. In addition, SSDN engaged in raising awareness among the wider Australian community about the political and economic situation in South Sudan to mobilise host community support, including resources. The SSDN convened a series of community workshops and meetings, and produced publications, aimed at drawing out and engaging with the differing views within the community as a starting point for community harmony and potential collaboration on peacebuilding in South Sudan.

Several years later in Victoria, the deterioration of the conflict in South Sudan in 2013 and consequent rising tensions among the diasporas prompted a group of community and church leaders from different denominations and tribal backgrounds to initiate a state-wide process of unification. The South Sudan Unification Committee (SSUC) undertook an 18-month process of travelling around Victoria speaking with community leaders, to encourage them to work together towards peace within their own sub-community groups. As part of this work, two rival community associations that were divided across tribal lines were disbanded in order to form one inter-ethnic umbrella organisation. This was intended to represent the voices of all South Sudanese communities in Victoria along with the promotion of human rights and development in South Sudan. With the renewed conflict in South Sudan, the formation of this new organisation ceased, however it began again a few months later, and culminated in a peacebuilding retreat attended by 62 leaders from across Victoria, in which a constitution was agreed upon and a new organisation established a few months later.

The SSUC were motivated by the need to establish a representative body that could liaise with government on settlement issues, as well as foster unity within the community so that they were better able to contribute to peace in South Sudan. They were also interested in establishing a structure that could be a model for other communities in Australia and in other parts of the world. The unification process did in fact attract the attention of online media and radio in South Sudan and internationally, aided by the connections of the SSUC and others in the community with counterparts in the UK, US, Canada and several African countries.

7 DIASPORA PEACEBUILDING THROUGH INTER-ETHNIC HARMONY... 143

Sri Lankan Communities in Australia

During the civil war in Sri Lanka (1983–2009), some members of the Sri Lankan diasporas saw the need to ease tensions between different ethnic groups, particularly the Tamil and the Sinhalese. Prompted in fact by the rise of the divisive and racist One Nation political party, People for Human Rights and Equality (PHRE) was established in 1996 by former political and social activists from Sri Lanka. By promoting the values of multiculturalism in Australia within their own communities, they saw the potential of the diasporas to diffuse tensions within Sri Lanka as well. Over many years, they held public events, lectures, community meetings and dialogues, set up a radio station and published a range of publications to promote, as they outlined on their website, "the values of multiculturalism and pluralism within the Sri Lankan community in Australia and a just and peaceful settlement to the ethnic conflict in Sri Lanka" (People for Human Rights and Equality, 2009). PHRE's activities were designed to include members of different ethnic groups to create a space for dialogue and foster willingness to collaborate. This in itself created challenges however, ranging from low involvement of one main ethnic group, to active attempts at sabotage by pro-government groups.

Communities have also created their own spaces for this work within government-held multicultural initiatives, for example, the Victorian state government's annual Harmony Day. The Sri Lankan diaspora, through the Uniting Church, convened social and cultural events on Harmony Day from 2014–2017, that focused on bringing people together from different Sri Lankan ethnicities. These events were organised as non-confrontational events to build a sense of familiarity and connection between antagonistic ethnic groups. These included non-direct approaches such as sharing food and music, and playing sport together:

> We said, come play cricket, come and listen to some lovely music, come and eat hoppers and we will make them for you and then we'll talk a little about how we can help, and how by us being together in this peaceful and lovely country where we live together without anger and hate, then maybe we will have something to offer back home. (Interviewee 8)

It also included more direct approaches, such as conflict resolution theatre, and the ConChord choir, comprised of over 60 Tamils, Sinhalese, Hindus, Christians and Muslims, who sang the national anthem together—a significant act. The idea behind these initiatives was to build a sense of

144 A. ATEM ET AL.

unity as to a common identity and shared nationality: based on the understanding that they could not do anything to further peace in Sri Lanka if they could not come together in Australia.

Moreover, these government initiatives such as Harmony Days, intended to promote social harmony between different ethnic groups, are being put to an additional purpose by diasporas, beyond what is envisaged by government. Settlement programmes and host governments do not usually think about settlement in a translocal way in relation to diasporas and countries of origin—the sole focus is on the country of settlement (Halilovich, 2012). The way settlement is thought about is often very restrictive because as it fails to recognise people's full sense of belongings to specific localities, ethnicities and social groups (Marlowe, 2018). These diaspora initiatives and the purposes to which they are put outline this clearly.

Building Shared Narratives

The importance of developing shared narratives, truth-telling and 'myth busting' has been seized as critical by some in the diaspora communities we investigated and this can be understood as a key component of this work.

Understandings of the facts and events of both conflicts among the diasporas have been highly polarised, influenced by a range of factors including migration waves and patterns, length of time in Australia, connections with country of origin, and information sources. These divides are not only between different ethnic groups but also within them, along generational and age lines, and migration times—when people had migrated, and their experiences in countries of origin and transit. These experiences create very different versions of history and identity within the diaspora which can also lead to tensions. Within the South Sudanese diaspora, for example, the differences between an ex-combatant who lived through the war and a younger member of the community who grew up in Australia can be so great as to give rise to divergent perspectives and narratives about the war. According to one community leader, it has also led to competing claims over who has the right to call themselves 'authentically' South Sudanese, and who can legitimately hold views about the conflict (Interviewee 5). Legitimacy is contested between tribes, within tribes and across generations.

Divergent narratives are also due to the fact that diasporas receive information about the conflicts from a range of sources: traditional media in country of origin, ethno-specific media in Australia, social media, as well as from family and friends. The rise of social media has had a significant effect on the conflict in South Sudan. A 2018 report commissioned by the Australian government highlighted the ways in which the diasporas have manipulated news via social media to spread misinformation and exacerbate the conflict (Barnes et al., 2018).

An example of building shared narratives is the work of the South Sudanese Diaspora Network (SSDN) in attempting to build a shared understanding: "we haven't got a common starting point—socially, culturally, historically, politically" (Interviewee 5). A further example of building shared narratives and how these narratives alter beliefs and perspectives is the example of Bridging Lanka, who have invited the diaspora to Sri Lanka to play a part in various conversations and projects with an underlying reconciliation theme. Inter-ethnic networks are established and diasporas whose views were shaped by memories of wartime atrocities and ethnic riots have the space to navigate their own conflict within partially guided frameworks that raise issues of concern and conflict. Other Sri Lankan organisations like PHRE have chosen to bring speakers to Australia for this purpose in the hope of encouraging the diaspora to discuss and clarify misinformation that divides and ignites division between inter-ethnic communities.

This task of building a shared history is difficult work. The tensions within communities can result in backlash as it challenges authority within communities. Established leaders can see attempts to build new narratives as a challenge to community structures. People doing this work have been seen as traitors to their own ethnic groups. One Sri Lankan respondent talked about being shunned by their community:

> We were all labelled as traitors by the majority of the community because we were promoting a political solution to the problem—because they wanted to defeat it militarily. (Participant, Focus Group 2)

In general, community members doing inter-ethnic harmony work are viewed with suspicion. Building bridges can be seen as aligning with the 'other side'. For the SSDN, their attempts to draw community members together were viewed with such suspicion by some leaders that the organisation indefinitely halted its activities. A South Sudanese participant said his organisation faced "accusations that we were selling [out] the nation. I, as Dinka, was selling the Dinka because we were engaging with the

Equatorians, and so Facebook went into action and terrible things were said" (Interviewee 5).

For the younger generation of South Sudanese who were born in Australia or who arrived as young children and grew up in Australia, there were further challenges to legitimacy. In not having the direct experience of conflict as their parents' generation, they have not been seen as having the authority to carry out this inter-ethnic work and have also suffered consequences when they do. In one case, Nuer youth defied their parents' bans on attending a multi-ethnic event in a location considered predominantly Dinka. One of the young men who attended made a speech about the youth becoming "prisoners of the elders' perceived perceptions and bitterness". While this was heard by elders in the community, "Grandmothers were crying because they can see that, they are aware of it" (Interviewee 3), there were consequences, in particular for the women who attended, as one young woman articulated:

> The young men that were there who were making the speech were saying 'we have come today against our elders' wishes and against our parents' wishes, and when we go back to our homes tomorrow or later tonight we won't get in trouble but our sisters will get in trouble'. (Interviewee 3)

This inter-ethnic work models tolerance and collaboration, as the people involved in this work must confront their own biases and those of the people close to them. For both communities, clarifying the truth, understanding and accepting different perspectives, and challenging polarised narratives have been central to their work in building community harmony in Australia. Acceptance of the 'other' is a healing element in the reconciliation process.

SOCIAL CHANGE AND LONG-TERM PEACE: PERCEPTIONS OF SOUTH SUDANESE AND SRI LANKAN DIASPORA PEACE-BUILDERS

Diasporas as Connected Communities

The first observation that arises from this work of inter-ethnic harmony and peacebuilding is that diasporas are connected communities. Community harmony activities among the diaspora are designed to heal divisions in Australia that would enhance co-existence and life in Australia, however they are also intended to contribute to healing ethnic and political divisions in countries of origin. These assumptions—that social change in one country leads to change in another—reflects the diaspora dynamic that links country of origin and country of settlement together (on this, see Olliff, 2018), and challenges the accepted settlement dynamic that insists on a separation between the two. Diasporas are not just peoples who have crossed international borders. Rather, they represent reconfigured communities residing in multiple geographic locations: they are still members of their communities from country of origin, and of communities in country of settlement, as well as part of a wider diaspora around the world. These dynamics play out through the peace-building initiatives and their deliberate design to influence community at country of origin.

In this way, we can also understand this work of diasporas as a form of what Cindy Horst (2013) has termed "civic participation". In understanding diaspora engagement as a form of civic participation—in both countries of origin and settlement—it offers a way out of the quagmire of risk aversion that has impeded more substantial engagement between diasporas, government and NGOs in Australia.

This interconnectedness has implications for the modes of action available to the diaspora, and lies at the heart of the theories of change articulated by the peacebuilders of both communities. The approach of bringing together people across ethnic, tribal and religious divides in Australia, in order to contribute to peace in countries of origin, was encapsulated in the words of a South Sudanese community leader: "If we are united here, this will impact the lives of people back home and our politicians there" (Interviewee 6). What this shows is that the work done at sites of settlement is consciously directed to ongoing peace-building in countries of origin.

The potential to bring about change in countries of origin is also exercised through the influence exerted via familial connection, community/professional networks and links to political decision makers. The community diaspora peacebuilders consciously use their informal influence to bring about behaviour change through these networks. As an example, the Melbourne-based Union of Greater Upper Nile States (UGUNS) mobilised its Australian-based members to actively communicate messages of peaceful coexistence and national unity through family networks in South Sudan. Another South Sudanese community leader identified the influence that comes from financial support: "We send so much money that one day if we stop sending that money and we tell everybody 'this is what we want, if they don't do it, we are not sending the money', I'm sure they'd behave!" (Interviewee 5).

Given the level of influence of the diaspora, and their interconnectedness to communities in home countries as well as in other parts of the world, the views and values of the diaspora are of critical importance. Leaders from both the Sri Lankan and South Sudanese communities shared strong beliefs in the need to change attitudes and mindsets among the diaspora in Australia—to model constructive behaviour, foster collaboration, minimise negative practices (such as sending money to armed actors in the conflicts), and inform their interactions with family, friends and colleagues around the world.

Social Change Is Reliant on Shifting Mindsets

These diaspora initiatives further reflect a view that deep-seated conflicts are resolved not only through formal agreements and mechanisms but also through change of mindsets and attitudes. Underlying the various approaches to building harmony and reconciliation is a belief that change occurs through shifting mindsets and values away from polarised positions vis a vis the conflict and entrenched beliefs about 'the other', and towards increased tolerance of different perspectives, pluralism and values such as multiculturalism, diversity and co-existence. This reflects a conceptualisation of sustainable peace as a long-term process that rests with individuals rather than, or in addition to, formal political or military solutions. Many are disillusioned with political leaders' handling of peace negotiations or post-conflict reconciliation, or frustrated by top-down approaches that did not involve affected communities. Their work seeks to fill these gaps or to bring the grassroots into a national level dialogue.

Most of the initiatives from both communities have been based on the premise that increased familiarity and understanding of 'the other' underpin sustainable conflict resolution. This involves not only dismantling stereotypes but also ultimately challenging the fixed dichotomies of right and wrong, and victim and perpetrator. Recognising the suffering of the other side entails, by definition, an openness to accept that suffering was caused by one's own ethnic, tribal, religious or political grouping.

This is exemplified by a reconciliation tour of Sri Lanka undertaken by members of the diaspora in 2016. Organised through the Uniting Church, it involved a group of Buddhists, Muslims, Hindus and Christians visiting sites of religious and personal significance. Some were returning to family homes and other remembered places for the first time since they had left Sri Lanka, and were confronted with an altered version of history. One of the organisers described a visit to a mosque that had been the site of a wartime massacre:

> There were people who actually could not believe what they were seeing and had to cry and had to apologise to the next Muslim man they saw, saying: 'I didn't know this, I didn't know this was the level of hatred and violence that my people committed'. So that was a really defining moment and it opened up the discussion about what sort of peacebuilding do we need to do in the hearts of people to actually try and reconstruct Sri Lanka. (Interviewee 8)

The tour had a profound effect on the diaspora, challenging their perspectives, and in some cases redefining their understanding of their roles as members of the diaspora. It also increased their commitment to inter-ethnic harmony, with several participants subsequently returning to Sri Lanka to continue their peacebuilding work.

Harmony Increases Potential for Necessary Collaboration and Political Change

Community harmony also serves a more instrumental function: the ability to coordinate on a large scale and also to advocate to the Australian Government on foreign policy related to countries of origin. The potential to achieve political change through inter-ethnic collaboration was exemplified during the referendum on the independence of South Sudan in 2011. United by a common goal, the South Sudanese diasporas in Australia coordinated a mass mobilisation that enabled the community to vote. The result saw Australia with the highest numbers of out-of-country voters outside Africa (ABC News, 2011).

Most diasporas were also advocating to the Australian government to exert influence on Sri Lanka and South Sudan. They observed that inter-ethnic interventions that showed a united front were more readily received by government departments.[2] The government's calls for a unified voice place a subtle pressure on the community, even though they may also aspire to it in principle. As one leader pointed out, the government's insistence on a unified voice, while desirable, "places an unrealistic expectation

---

[2] Personal correspondence.

on the South Sudanese community here. I don't know any community on earth that agrees on everything, including the Australian community". (Interviewee 5) (see further Horst, 2013).[3]

Personal Transformation and Motivation

Community organisations who do this work are often consciously multi-ethnic or multi-tribal, as a means to model harmony and through this to shift community mindsets. For a Tamil member of Australian Advocacy for Good Governance in Sri Lanka (AAGGSL), working with Sinhalese colleagues has been a process of building trust so that robust discussion can occur:

> I am learning from them, I am able to understand their views, their struggles, their limitations, and their fears. And at the same time, I am able to tell them ... from a Tamil perspective ... that you guys can do better. (Interviewee 10)

Core to this is personal transformation, a conscious examination and challenging of long-held views and addressing their own personal biases and antagonisms. For many, this has meant working through experiences of grief and trauma, towards forgiveness and reconciliation. This was particularly the case for the South Sudanese community, where a significant number of community leaders involved in inter-ethnic harmony work had been ex-combatants, including the Lost Boys of Sudan.

Community leaders involved in this work recognise the need to confront their own prejudices. It necessitates a process of personal transformation in order to both be able to do the work, and to model this change. Across both communities, community leaders described a strong sense of responsibility to help families and communities, combined with a broader moral obligation to contribute to peace. As summed up one participant:

---

[3] Peace researcher Cindy Horst has critiqued the expectations of host governments and NGOs that diasporas be "impartial, neutral and unified" as being not only unrealistic but also ultimately disempowering for communities. She argues that differences of political opinion stem from the actual context of contested power relations in countries experiencing conflict, and therefore "the fact that authorities and NGOs in Europe and the Horn of Africa, as well as diasporas themselves, contribute to a discourse that seeks to deny the political nature of refugee diasporas is problematic" (Horst, 2013). This expectation is also potentially problematic if it is intended or perceived as a prerequisite for effective advocacy to government.

"It's something I need to do. I have no choice. ... If I don't, who will do it?" (Interviewee 5).

A sense of duty frequently extends beyond the immediate families and contacts of diaspora leaders (see Olliff, 2022). Shared experience can further provide personal motivation, as described by a former child soldier, now community leader:

> I often look back to when I was a child in the war and some of the things that we did as children in the war or we were made to do. When I look back at that I always say there is no way we can allow any of that, there's no way I can allow any other child to go through the same thing again and that is my motivation. When I look at it then I ask myself, 'How can I solve that?' and one way of solving it is to work hard to bring peace in South Sudan. (Interviewee 1)

Many leaders also expressed a sense of moral obligation to use their position of relative economic and educational privilege in Australia and freedom to speak out. Skills gained such as critical thinking through formal education can be seen as an important contribution:

> I've seen the suffering, I grew up through the suffering ... and I thought, being someone who have read and been to university, I can use my intellectual capacity and understanding to mobilise people around myself. And to tell the fact, yes, to tell the fact as it is: I know the war will not bring peace in South Sudan. (Interviewee 4)

This sense of responsibility extends to countering the contribution of the diaspora to division and conflict:

> The war [in Sri Lanka] could not have continued without the help of the diaspora. The diaspora was an enormous problem ... So the building of peace, the language of peace, the lobbying for peace, we think should come from these people, from us. (Interviewee 8)

Finally, for some leaders, the experience of living in Australia's multicultural society offers an example of how peaceful co-existence can be applied in contexts struggling with ethnic, religious or tribal tensions:

> If we're going to talk peace and reconciliation we can't leave it to shady politicians after the war. It has to come from those of us who have experienced

152   A. ATEM ET AL.

peace and live with it, and live with multiculturalism, and live with multi faith, and we talk it and we experience it ... back home it should be just like it is in Australia at its best. (Interviewee 8)

As these examples illustrate, the inter-ethnic harmony work of diaspora community peacebuilders is informed by a range of experiences and motivations gained in both countries of origin and settlement, and relies on their own personal transformations. As diasporas are connected communities, their work to bring about social change in countries of settlement and of origin is dependent on their ability to model the change they seek and utilise this to influence the behaviour of others.

The discussion above has focussed on diaspora activities in Australia; however, community leaders also use their mobility to take peacebuilding work into countries of origin. The following section considers two examples of how diaspora approaches to peace through interethnic harmony have been applied in Sri Lanka.

Significance of Inter-Ethnic Harmony for Long-Term Peacebuilding in Countries of Origin

Empathic reflection followed by common sense is a precursor and a necessity for any inter-ethnic harmony—the glue for long-term peacebuilding—but it appears this process is transient among warring factions in a conflict or post-conflict context. This final part of the chapter reports attempts made by a small segment of the Sri Lankan diaspora practising inter-ethnic inclusion to find 'wriggle room' amidst resisting inter-ethnic groups. The quest for a robust form of interaction that soothes factional dissent reveals the ongoing fragile nature of these challenges that make this a lifetime pursuit.

It is challenging to set markers for how inter-ethnic harmony for long-term peacebuilding is achieved, as this process is dynamic and volatile. In the Sri Lankan context, past wounds of inter-communal discord between the majority Sinhalese community and minority Tamil and Muslim communities are still deep. It only takes one incident to set off emotionally charged violent destruction of property and lives that dismantle any fledgling security and trust previously gained.

To satisfy the conditions necessary for such a paradigm shift in broken relations, dialogue must occur but given the precarious state of relations and deep levels of mistrust among the majority and minority factions,

Bridging Lanka a diaspora-led NGO operating in both Australia and Sri Lanka, realised that a 'dialogue of action' must necessarily occur prior to a 'dialogue of words'—the latter requiring a substantial level of trust not yet present. Most diaspora factions would prefer to hold onto past beliefs based on hurtful personal experiences rather than querying the longer-term impact of viewing inter-ethnic relations through any other lens.

The journey towards long-lasting peace is lengthy, incremental and uncertain. Valuing moments of reconciliation are crucial, as diaspora communities will face multiple snags and roadblocks along the way. It could be observed that when a critical mass of 'moments of reconciliation' is reached, a tipping point may well occur towards more enduring and positive inter-communal relations, and a miracle realised. Working towards shared goals common to all divided communities, such as post-conflict rebuilding of physical infrastructure, prosperity through business and job creation and tending to the survival needs of victims, can provide the foundation for longer-term peacebuilding.

The Australian and UK embassies based in Sri Lanka have funded programmes with a view to understand post war inter-ethnic conflict. An underlying hope of uncovering pathways of reconciliation and harmony is assumed. The geographical placement of where such conversations and interventions occur provide a trans locality lens that then filters the dynamic and fluid nature of these inter-ethnic relationships. The heart and mindsets from these experiences shift, and the lens used by diaspora pre and post such experiences influence the same actors to think and behave differently. Real-time interventions for long-term peace building by diaspora groups thus take on a tailored dichotomous trajectory from country of origin to country of settlement and in reverse.

Two such interventions have been selected to unpack this dynamic. In the first, International Alert (IA) a UK based peacebuilding organisation discovered that changing the perspectives of generational actors can substantially influence and manipulate inter-ethnic landscapes in Sri Lanka along multiple social, political, economic and ideological fault lines both in their country of residence as well as in their country of origin. In their 2015 report, they outline how through this 'generational lens' positional disparity is found among first, second and third generations within the same family (Perera & Yacoub, 2015). Listening to all perspectives revealed multi-layered motivations behind either engaging or not in peacebuilding. International Alert's paper emphasises the need to deeply understand the assumptions made by particular UK diaspora collectives based on misinformation and bent on sabotaging and driving division between inter-ethnic groups. IA worked with Sri Lanka's diaspora communities for over four years examining the dynamic and capacity building of diaspora as a cross-community partner with the objective of long-term peace in Sri Lanka. Focus group discussions followed by crucial conversations with many political, social and local communities were facilitated to mediate peace building initiatives in country of settlement and heritage.

In response to the question posed, "Can pro-peace, conflict-sensitive approaches ever be a worthy adversary to traditional and divisive community rhetoric?", International Alert asserts that safe platforms that build trust are undoubtedly essential for open discussion enabling a cross fertilisation of values and principles among inter-ethnic diaspora communities to build and encourage acceptance, tolerance and forgiveness of 'the other'.

A second example shows the limitations of a 'dialogue of words' approach. Through observing numerous well intentioned and meticulously conducted dialogue initiatives in Australia, Bridging Lanka came to understand the limitations of a 'dialogue of words' approach where little pre-existing trust-building groundwork had been attempted. Although Bridging Lanka's 'dialogue of action' method remained unpredictable and often vexed, it witnessed more 'moments' of reconciliation through such an approach. Through community engagement with a diverse range of individuals, groups and government and non-government agencies, community-driven endeavours are arrived at. They are involved in environmental, educational and the 'towards religious harmony' project, which is covered further down in this section. 'Common good' projects are 'trojan horses' for the underlying aim of peacebuilding in a country context highly suspicious of 'reconciliation' and 'peacebuilding'. Through this covert approach inter-ethnic relationships are being crafted and re-crafted with an underlying attempt to transform the heart and mindsets of the aggrieved both in-country and overseas.

A quote from one youth witnessing the rebuilding of his town outlines this clearly:

> I was badly affected by the war. I saw my young brother being killed. ... We are surrounded by destruction—buildings scarred by bomb blasts, roads turned into rubble, churches and community centres destroyed. When they start to repair buildings and roads out there, I start to repair inside. (Liyanage, 2013, p. 24)

Such statements attest to the deeper transformative work of the "dialogue of action" approach (Liyanage, 2016). Inter-ethnic communities joining forces in one's place of origin to rebuild what was destroyed could then create an inner space of healing. Many such experiences could wire together to strengthen the pursuit of inter-ethnic harmony, repairing past hurt and coaxing reconciliation ideals to influence both heart and mindsets.

Bridging Lanka has sought to provide the means to coaxing heart and mindset change in the Sri Lankan diaspora by offering an immersion experience. Through Bridging Lanka, diaspora members from Muslim, Tamil, Sinhalese, Burgher as well as non-Sri Lankan backgrounds are volunteering in Mannar in north-west Sri Lanka to work on an array of projects—educational, environmental, urban planning, social cohesion, youth, livelihood, tourism and animal welfare related. Practical action for the common good has brought hundreds to Mannar. They work alongside each other, rub shoulders, and slowly suspicion subsides and a normalising of relations grows. The heart space is unlocked to feel the value of a shared experience that transforms and connects across divides.

Just as the country was coming out of a 27-year-old war, the past ten years has seen a surge in attacks on Muslim homes, mosques and businesses across the country by Sinhalese factions. The Towards Religious Harmony project funded by the Australian High Commission in Colombo sought to unpack and understand the underpinnings of how Sri Lanka had relapsed into another ethnic calamity, this time with the Muslim minority as victims. Bridging Lanka gathered an inter-ethnic diaspora and 'in country' research team to visit the Digana-Teldeniya areas on fortnightly exploratory visits when the conflict was at its peak. Contact was made with Muslim victims, clerics and residents, Buddhist perpetrators and sympathisers, their families and the religious fraternity. Interviews were also conducted with academics, NGOs and groups of locals to understand the historical context underpinning this riot. The interviews and interactions extended to hundreds of hours of listening—without judgement. It was also a way of sourcing bridge builders who would be the change agents undertaking small experimental actions to encourage a return to more amicable relations. One commentator raised a poignant point worthy of mention:

> the former administration wanted to teach the Tamils and Muslims a lesson: that they are tolerated as long as they know their place as minority communities. (Liyanage, 2018, p. 5)

While interviewees suggested interfaith committees, visits to mosques and temples, intercultural exchanges and religious festivals as means of 'civic repair', a more rigorous approach was required for this diabolic state of conflict. Other suggested interventions were awareness workshops for Buddhist monks and the bringing together of Sinhala and Muslim core groups to work on conflict reduction strategies that include reconciliation protocols involving authorities. These interventions along with 'early warning' mechanisms to predict future 'hot spots' will be trialled when the timing favours these engagements. A selected group of bridge builders from Sinhalese and Muslim communities has been chosen and coached to understand the role of 'cognitive dissonance' and the confusion of stubborn and resistant minds through doing good to those labelled, 'enemy'.

Diaspora members in Australia have done their part by sending petitions to members of parliament, organising protest rallies and holding vigils vehemently wanting an end to discriminatory practices towards ethnic minorities. What happens in country of origin affects those in country of settlement. Diaspora are seen to take on roles as bridge builders to bring calm to aggrieved parties based on their encounters and experiences from their country of origin. This process is fluid and ever changing and there is never a 'one size fits all' approach. While all these bring international publicity, 'robust interaction' among aggrieved factions on an ongoing basis is required for longer lasting change to occur.

We can further understand this as a means of translocality. As discussed earlier in this chapter, diasporas are part of a living community that spans two or more countries (and regions within those countries) and what happens in one country affects what happens in another and vice versa. This complex interplay affects the way diasporas think and behave.

For those sceptical about or opposed to reconciliatory overtures, there is work to be done in creating the 'wriggle room' for these inter-ethnic diaspora–country of origin encounters. From our experience, the pursuit of common and shared action until relations normalise to some extent is the basis for the next stage when genuine empathetic listening, without judgement or correction, comes into play. The germination of such a neutral space will continue to cultivate the precious ingredient of trust and thus allow deeper levels of grief and pain to surface until at some point they no longer have their sting. Then there will be mutual agreement that the 'struggle against' will be merged into one common 'struggle with' for the common good and an enduring peace prevails.

CONCLUSION: REBUILDING PEACEBUILDING

Diaspora involvement in resolution of conflicts and peacebuilding in countries of origin is not new. For as long as people have fled conflicts and resettled in other parts of the world, they have also worked to resolve that conflict, through direct involvement in regime change, human rights advocacy, and in some cases, participation in peace processes and transitional justice mechanisms. The recognition of diasporas as extended or translocal members of 'homeland' communities provides an important perspective on the way in which diasporas are connected to the social and political life of countries of origin.

This chapter has shown how the work of inter-ethnic harmony in countries of settlement is incremental work designed to contribute to peacebuilding and conflict resolution in home countries. This work of community harmony in Australia, for the Sri Lankan and South Sudanese diasporas, plays a significant role in conflict resolution and peace-making in the countries of origin and, as we have shown through this chapter, it is consciously designed to do so. It is a core part of the work and practice of settlement that has largely remained unrecognised or underutilised.

The experience of settlement also fertilises the ideas of the diaspora and provides a secure base from which they can carry out their work. The examples of diaspora organisations operating in Sri Lanka show how they utilise their advantages provided by countries of settlement, together with their mobility and connectivity, to become bridge builders between divided communities. The peace-building work carried out by South Sudanese and Sri Lankan diaspora organisations in Australia demonstrates that while these activities predominantly take place in Australia—and seek to heal rifts in relationships among diasporas—they are designed with a broader and ongoing purpose: to influence prospects for long-lasting peace in Sri Lanka and South Sudan. And it is work that continues in spite of all challenges and setbacks.

Acknowledgments The authors of this chapter are indebted to many people: Our most heartfelt thanks go to the South Sudanese and Sri Lankan community leaders who generously shared their wisdom and experience in interviews and revision of the original research; to the University of Melbourne Social Equity Institute, who provided the Honorary Fellowship for the original research this chapter is based on; to Diaspora Action Australia, from where Denise Cauchi undertook the fellowship and where these ideas took shape; to the book's editors, Louise Olliff and Melissa Phillips, for their invitation to participate and their encouragement throughout.

REFERENCES

ABC News. (2011, January 20). Australia's South Sudanese Vote for Secession. *Australian Broadcasting Corporation News*. Retrieved June 3, 2021, from https://www.abc.net.au/news/2011-01-20/australias-south-sudanese-vote-for-secession/1912256

Al-Ali, N., Black, R., & Koser, K. (2001). The Limits to 'Transnationalism': Bosnian and Eritrean Refugees in Europe as Emerging Transnational Communities. *Ethnic and Racial Studies, 24*(4), 578–600.

Barnes, C., Carver, F., Deng, S., Kiir, G., Kindersley, N., Lorins, R., & Maher, S. (2018). *The Role of Transnational Networks and Mobile Citizens in South Sudan's Global Community: A Pilot Study Focused on Melbourne and Juba*. Rift Valley Institute, Australian Government Department of Foreign Affairs and Trade. Retrieved June 4, 2021, from http://diasporaaction.org.au/wp-content/uploads/2018/09/The-role-of-transnational-networks-and-mobile-citizens-in-South-Sudan's-global-community-RVI-2018.pdf

Brubaker, R. (2005). The 'Diaspora' Diaspora. *Ethnic and Racial Studies, 28*(1), 1–19.

Brubaker, R., & Cooper, F. (2000). Beyond 'Identity'. *Theory and Society, 29*(1), 1–47.

Cauchi, D. (2018). Long Distance Peacebuilding: The Experiences of the South Sudanese and Sri Lankan Diasporas in Australia. https://socialequity.unimelb.edu.au/__data/assets/pdf_file/0003/2930880/Long-distance-peacebuilding-the-experiences-of-the-South-Sudanese-and-Sri-Lankan-diasporas-in-Australia-Denise-Cauchi.pdf

Erdal, M. B. (2020). Theorizing Interactions of Migrant Transnationalism and Integration Through a Multiscalar Approach. *Comparative Migration Studies, 8*(1), 1–16.

Halilovich, H. (2012). Trans–Local Communities in the Age of Transnationalism: Bosnians in Diaspora. *International Migration, 50*(1), 162–178.

Horst, C. (2013). The Depoliticisation of Diasporas from the Horn of Africa: From Refugees to Transnational Aid Workers. *African Studies*. https://doi.org/10.1080/00020184.2013.812881

Hurst, D. (2016, February 5). Refugees May Face Monitoring and Further Restrictions, Leaked Document Suggests. *The Guardian*. Retrieved June 3, 2021. from https://www.theguardian.com/australia-news/2016/feb/05/refugees-may-face-monitoring-further-restrictions-leaked-document

Liyanage, J. (2013). Can the Built Environment Impact Reconciliation in Post-conflict Sri Lanka? *Planning News, 39*(5), 24–26.

Liyanage, J. (2016). Transcending Dissention: The Sri Lankan Diaspora in a Dialogue of Action for Reconciliation. In *Diaspora Action Australia Diaspora Conference*. Diaspora Action Australia.

Liyanage, J. (2018). Getting into Our Hearts and Over Our Heads: A Diaspora's Hope for Reconciliation in Sri Lanka's Religious 'Hotspots'. In *Identity: Community, Culture, Differencedeas, Capital & People on the Move: Conference on Diaspora Engagement in Sri Lanka's Post-War Development and Sustainable Development*. Centre for Poverty Analysis (CEPA).

Marlowe, J. (2018). *Belonging and Transnational Refugee Settlement: Unsettling the Everyday and the Extraordinary*. Routledge.

Murphy, K. (2016, November 21). Peter Dutton Points Finger at Muslims of Lebanese Background in Immigration Row. *The Guardian*. Retrieved June 3, 2021, from https://www.theguardian.com/australia-news/2016/nov/21/peter-dutton-most-terrorism-charges-lebanese-muslims

Olliff, L. (2018). From Resettled Refugees to Humanitarian Actors: Refugee Diaspora Organizations and Everyday Humanitarianism. *New Political Science, 40*(4), 658–674.

Olliff, L. (2022). From Resettled Refugees to Humanitarian Actors: The Transformation of Transnational Social Networks of Care. In M. Phillips & L. Olliff (Eds.), *Understanding Diaspora Development: Lessons from Australia and the Pacific*. Palgrave Macmillan.

People for Human Rights and Equality. (2009). Retrieved June 3, 2021, from https://www.phre.org.au/about_us.htm

Perera, D., & Yacoub, M. (2015). What's Diaspora Got to do With It? Reflections on Engaging Sri Lanka's Diaspora Communities in Peacebuilding, (February), 1–16.

Rutherford, J. (1990). The Third Space: Interview with Homi Bhabha. *Identity: Community, Culture, Difference, 1990*, 207–221.

Snel, E., Engbersen, G., & Leerkes, A. (2006). Transnational Involvement and Social Integration. *Global Networks, 6*(3), 285–308.

Williamson, A. F. (2015). Mechanisms of Declining Intra-ethnic Trust in Newly Diverse Immigrant Destinations. *Journal of Ethnic and Migration Studies, 41*(11), 1725–1745.

CHAPTER 8

South Sudanese Australians: Transnational Kinship During Conflict and Economic Crisis

Sara Maher, Nicki Kindersley, Freddie Carver,
and Santino Atem Deng

INTRODUCTION

The chapter will discuss how the two phases of the project detailed the ways in which the complex pressures limited transnational practical, social and emotional support, deepened division and distance between kinship networks, and challenged possibilities for mutual support, communication

S. Maher (✉)
The Centre for Multicultural Policy & Program Evaluation, Melbourne, VIC, Australia
e-mail: sara.maher@multiculturalprogramevaluation.com.au

N. Kindersley
Cardiff University, Cardiff, Wales, UK

F. Carver
Rift Valley Institute, Nairobi, Kenya

S. A. Deng
African-Australian Family and Parenting Support Services, Melbourne, VIC, Australia

© The Author(s), under exclusive license to Springer Nature Switzerland AG 2022
M. Phillips, L. Olliff (eds.), *Understanding Diaspora Development,*
https://doi.org/10.1007/978-3-030-97866-2_8

161

and collective action. It will also discuss the interconnectivity of South Sudanese urban and borderland communities with their Australian diaspora especially since the civil war began in 2013, and also, how the war has changed and challenged the nature of these connections.

South Sudan's long history of civil war has caused mass migration and displacement in the region since the 1960s. By the end of the last century, approximately four million of its roughly twelve million estimated residents had fled across the country's multiple borders. Of those regionally displaced, tens of thousands of refugees were resettled in the Global North, with the largest numbers in Australia and the USA, followed by Canada and the UK (Barnes et al., 2018). Refugee resettlement programmes of the 1990s and 2000s played a key role in bringing significant numbers of people to the Global North, with greater access to resources even for those outside the political elites. Access to these resettlement schemes has been uneven, depending on communities' proximities to borders, trade systems and refugee camps across South Sudan's six borders. Because of these generations of displacement and resettlement from different conflict arenas in South Sudan, South Sudan's internal diasporic networks are diverse and variegated—some communities have extensive connections to the near and far diaspora, and others have very little connection.

The conflicts that caused this displacement started in the 1950s, while Sudan was still under Anglo-Egyptian colonial rule. This first civil war, over the exploitation, underdevelopment and racist governing of the Southern region, ended in 1972. A second civil war broke out in 1983 and ended in 2005 with the Comprehensive Peace Agreement (CPA) (Deng, 2017a). The CPA gave the South Sudanese the right to secede as a separate state, which led to South Sudan's independence in July 2011. Unfortunately, South Sudan only enjoyed about two years of relative peace before another war broke out in December 2013; it was caused by the political differences within the ruling party, the Sudan People's Liberation Movement (SPLM) and the many SPLM factions (Deng, 2017a). The December 2013 violence, which reignited again in Juba in July 2016, forced at least 1.5 million residents to flee once more (Barnes et al., 2018), and there has been little sign of the violence abating. Several peace agreements have been reached and signed between the government and the main rebel groups, which led to the implementation of a revitalised government despite many obstacles and a very fragile peace. Nonetheless, in 2021, the country was described as experiencing an escalation of violence exceeding the events of December 2013 (UNHCR, 2021).

The migration flows caused by these conflicts have never been one way; refugees returned after signing the CPA in 2005 and 2011 after independence was declared, and cross-border movement has ebbed and flowed since 2013. These dynamic migration flows have created and sustained a political culture linking South Sudanese communities to regional and global networks. During the second civil war (1983-2005), these networks fragmented into regional factional conflicts and militias through the 1990s (Johnson, 2016). People displaced by the war survived in regional refugee camps and displaced urban settlements. Those refugees who managed to gain resettlement in the Global North built economic foundations and diaspora organisations. By the 2000s, diaspora emergency aid and funding were having an impact on the country. However, their input has also built a continuing set of negative assumptions about diaspora connectivity, including continued international funding of armed groups, diaspora members returning to join those groups, and how propaganda from the diaspora—both online and through radio and print media–has been used for decades to incite ethnicised hatred and propagate political division (Falge, 2015; Foltyn, 2017; Getahun & Dejene, 2021; Quinn, 2017; Walters, 2016).

The 2013 conflict and ensuing civil war polarised the country's political culture locally and internationally. Funding and organisation of many parties in the war drew on the extensive diaspora regional and global networks and associational life, allowing the movement of money and goods through international and internal connections (Barnes et al., 2018). However, this conflict created a significant economic crisis that changed and challenged the nature of those connections. Regional demand for diaspora practical help (housing, food, child and elderly care) and financial support increased significantly. Kinship systems and personal actions were re-politicised—placing social and familial networks under considerable strain and exacerbating tensions within the diaspora. South Sudan is inhabited by at least 64 ethnic groups who speak different languages, and the war was precipitated and fuelled by internal and ethnicised competition over central state power. It involved collective brutalities against ethnic groups on all sides, and it created hyper-politicised ethnic identities, as well as an environment *'where any action could be interpreted in multiple ways'* (Barnes et al., 2018, p. 3). Working with, or for, a specific ethnic group could be seen to emphasise that identity in a way that resulted in a national identity being discredited. Wealthy political, commercial and military elites based in South Sudan, but with diaspora citizenship rights and family networks, risked harming the reputation of the wider transnational communities, who were already facing often extreme difficulties in their places of resettlement. This is especially so in Australia, where the South Sudanese community has experienced ongoing racism and discrimination to the degree that a sense of exclusion from public life is prevalent (Maher et al., 2018). Marginalisation and stress have been further exacerbated by the ongoing conflict in their homeland and the overwhelming emotional and financial burden this placed upon them.

LITERATURE REVIEW

Before resettling in Australia and other Western nations, typically South Sudanese refugees spent many years displaced in refugee camps in Ethiopia and Kenya and urban settings like Cairo in Egypt (Barnes et al., 2018; Deng, 2017a; Marlowe, 2011; Marlowe et al., 2014). The relocation and disruption caused changes in traditional family beliefs, structure and parenting practices. Resettlement challenges for new refugees have impacted on community reconstruction in their new environment (Deng, 2017a, 2017b; Deng & Marlowe, 2013; Deng & Pienaar, 2011).

There is extensive research within South Sudanese diaspora communities, particularly in the USA, often focused on cultural change and relationships with 'home' (Barnes et al., 2018; Deng, 2017a; Ensor, 2013b, Ensor, 2016; Falge, 2015; Marlowe, 2010, 2011; van der Linden et al., 2013; Faria, 2010, 2013, 2014, 2017; Wilcock, 2018; Holtzman, 2007; Shandy, 2002, 2005). In Australia, South Sudanese families and individuals often talk of their concerns about their relatives overseas but are also just as worried about the challenges they are facing in their new home, particularly regarding allegations of youth criminality. This issue has led to racist characterisation or vilification of the community by some media, individuals and politicians, and has incited racism and discrimination against community members (Benier et al., 2018; Deng, 2017a, 2017b). This, of course, increases stress as community members feel othered in their new environment, while the news about the country of origin remains traumatic and stressful due to ongoing conflict (Benier et al., 2018).

Significant ethnographic research focuses on these socio-cultural and personal impacts of transnational resettlement and adjustment within diaspora communities. Research indicates that this occurred due to acculturation in which groups of people from different cultures meet first-hand experiences with associate alterations in the original culture of another group, which contributed to their resettlement challenges (Berry, 1997; Deng, 2017a). These cultural encounters lead to behavioural and psychological changes impacting individuals' behavioural outcomes, ethnic identity, attitudes and values (Berry, 1997; Deng, 2017b; Miller & Kerlow-Myers, 2009). These adaptations to new norms and environments lead to changes in gender roles, social support, and to a new legal framework, often leading to feelings of status loss, particularly for men (Deng, 2017a; Deng & Marlowe, 2013). Like other former refugees, many South Sudanese refugees were deprived of education due to the civil wars and gender bias, and their differences in education and language skills create significant intergenerational gaps as children acquire the new skills more quickly than their parents (Deng & Pienaar, 2011; Duff, 2012; Khawaja & Milner, 2012; Shakespeare Finch & Wickham, 2010). As children adapt quickly to their adopted, locally dominant culture and start embracing its values, parents see these transformations as diversions from their traditional beliefs and moral standards, leading to tension, conflict and stress within the family. Consequently, children may find themselves trapped in the middle as they attempt to accommodate both their parents and the new culture (Deng & Pienaar, 2011; Khawaja & Milner, 2012).

Across diaspora studies, new research focused on 'the microfoundations of diaspora politics' has explored the economic and political impacts and organisation of diaspora communities at both local and global levels (Délano Alonso & Mylonas, 2019, p. 473). This work increasingly links the social and ethnographic work focused on diaspora communities in their places of resettlement with studies of diaspora organisations, transnational churches and businesses, trade networks and political influence (e.g. Carment & Calleja, 2018; Faria, 2017; Horst, 2018; Karabegović, 2018; Steel, 2021). This chapter is situated at this connection between South Sudanese diaspora members' personal, social, economic and political lives.

METHODOLOGY

The research for this chapter was driven by the lack of substantive knowledge about the dynamics of South Sudanese diasporas and their impact within South Sudan. While some studies have explored the internal dynamics of the South Sudanese diaspora within Australia (Marlowe et al., 2014), the study looked instead at diaspora influence and activities from the perspective of their effects within South Sudan. Pilot research was conducted in 2018 in Juba, the capital of South Sudan, and in Australia's second largest city of Melbourne, the site of the largest South Sudanese diaspora in the country. A second case study was conducted in 2019 across four sites, with residents in Gambella, a region on the Ethiopia-South Sudan border with an extensive Nuer-speaking global diaspora, and with members of this Gambella diaspora in Juba, Melbourne and the UK. There was a degree of dialogue between research findings in each of the research sites in both instances.

All sites required careful considerations given the tense political climate and breakdown of trust within communities during the civil war. For the first study, data collection in Juba occurred on the campus of Juba University due to broad insecurity in the capital. Focus groups in Melbourne required lengthy negotiations with participants, given their concerns regarding the focus and purpose of the research. It was quickly made clear that the process of building informed consensual and ethical research reflected how South Sudanese diaspora residents' energies, emotions and trust were being stretched thin by the divisive dynamics of the civil war. This process also highlighted the fundamental challenges for community reconstruction and reconciliation in the aftermath of this deeply destructive conflict. It was notable that tensions were less severe in the second study largely due to the focus on a single ethnic group, reducing the need to bring different groups together.

This chapter is based on extensive interview and qualitative survey material collated over the course of the two research projects. In 2018, a team from the Department of Mass Communication at the University of Juba conducted focus groups, a 200-person survey and a series of interviews with South Sudanese Australian residents, government workers, money transfer agents, journalists and church members. In Melbourne, another team conducted focus groups at Monash University that were cross-representative of the highly diverse South Sudanese–Australian community. This process was intentionally connected and reflective: Melbourne focus groups considered the findings of the Juba research, and this was fed back to the Juba team for further reflection in focus groups. During the second project in 2019, this reflective process was continued, with initial interviews by the multi-national research team with Gambella residents and diaspora members in the UK, Australia, South Sudan and Ethiopia, which set the priorities for in-depth qualitative fieldwork in Gambella about diasporic connections and impacts. The Gambella fieldwork was then reflected on focus group discussions and follow-up interviews in the UK, Australia and South Sudan.

The research process reflected many of the challenges and tensions faced by South Sudanese transnational diaspora groups. This included the immediate practicalities of communicating, connecting and sharing analysis amongst an international team made up of South Sudanese and non-South Sudanese members located in four countries across an 11-hour time difference. It also involved navigating the changing but tense political climate and lack of trust throughout South Sudanese communities in Juba and Melbourne. This chapter is a product of sustained mutual support, reflection and collaboration between this transnational research community and with our South Sudanese research participants.

PART 1: DIASPORA, PLACE AND CHANGE OVER TIME

The South Sudanese community globally had perhaps its most positive collective experience around the independence referendum of 2011. With voting centres established around the world, focusing on the countries where significant numbers of people of South Sudanese origin were living, the process became an opportunity for different communities to come together around a shared identity and excitement at the opportunities presented by the potential formation of an independent South Sudan. Australia was the country with the third highest number of votes cast outside Sudan, almost 10,000 in total. This became a publicly visible manifestation of the existence of a major locus of South Sudanese society across Australia, North America, the UK and Europe.

The growth of South Sudanese diaspora communities reflects multiple generations of displacement, creating a diaspora with significantly different internal class, ethnic and educational backgrounds. While the international dispersal of South Sudanese communities took place over the course of the twentieth century, it accelerated significantly towards the end of the century as a result of refugee resettlement programmes, particularly to the US, Australia and Canada. Whereas previously the ability to emigrate had primarily relied on access to finance or education, making it almost exclusively the domain of the wealthier sections of South Sudanese society, these programmes created more widespread opportunity (Collier & Hoeffler, 2004).

These new refugee resettlement opportunities were framed—at least for some—as part of a communal effort to benefit one's wider community:

for example, Nuer interviewees described how, in the 1990s, Nuer communities worked together to select individuals who could be "trusted" to retain connections with their places of origin, and then collectively funded them to reach key locations like Kakuma refugee camp in Kenya where resettlement opportunities were most available. This focus on community solidarity had a political element as well, with, for example, Riek Machar[1] explicitly calling for Nuer people to seek such opportunities at a time when he had recently split from the SPLA leadership and was seeking to corral support and solidarity along ethnic lines.

Whether framed politically or not, this support and solidarity have been at the core of diaspora connections, with the nature and direction of this support depending on both place and time. There is a strong emotional and moral connection between friends and family that is facilitated by digital communication on an everyday basis. Evidence gathered on Nuer networks in Gambella suggests that financial support is also an important aspect of these connections, with money being provided to family and kin at particular times of need or for particular purposes—such as during the "hunger gap" in South Sudan during dry seasons when food supplies run low, which diaspora and South Sudan residents called a 'season of support' due to increased reliance on money from family and friends elsewhere. This financial support takes many different forms. The evidence suggests that the majority is provided for specific purposes and on a time-limited basis, whether because of a personal or community crisis—a medical emergency, responding to conflict, helping people in times of hunger—or to support a critical moment in people's lives. Providing sponsorship for education is a powerful theme, whether paying for people's fees or for the purchase of books, mobile phones or laptops as necessary. Beyond the family level, there are also many examples across Australia of community support projects, often run through churches or community associations, where in-kind contributions or cash are gathered and sent to South Sudan.[2] Small individual payments made through money transfer agencies amounted to considerable sums:

---

[1] Riek Machar is currently the 1st Vice-President of South Sudan and has been in similar posts since the formation of the Government of Southern Sudan in 2005. He has been a figurehead for the Nuer-speaking peoples of South Sudan since the 1990s, whether leading various iterations of armed groups or in government positions.

[2] A recent example is fund raising by a group of Tonj women in Melbourne to build a clinic in their homeland (SBS, 2019).

A Dahabshiil branch manager in Juba estimated there are about 250 to 350 transfers from Australia to South Sudan per day, increasing in times of crisis and at Christmas to over 500 transfers per day, and these numbers are continuing to increase each year. These are often small sums, USD 50 to USD 300 per transfer, from both regular and irregular customers abroad. Smaller regional money transfer companies operating for specific regions and towns within South Sudan also process considerable amounts of remittances. One small agency, founded by a South Sudanese-Australian returned refugee, receives around 50 transfers per day from Australia, mostly of amounts averaging USD 150 but ranging between USD 50 and 5000 (Barnes et al., 2018, p. 12).

Examples of the provision of one-off funds to enable migration or help start small business were also identified in Juba and Gambella (DIP1 and DIP2). One respondent described how important they saw this support to be:

I wanted to say that it is really good that the community, the South Sudanese community, is keeping family financially. Why—because it happened in 2016, when the war broke out, it was really very hard for people who don't have relatives outside to get what to eat. It happened that a lot of people are suffering because there's no food, and the villages where people are cultivating, nothing is in the village: so it happened that these South Sudanese who were in Australia formed a group [to contribute], and they opened an account, naming it the South Sudanese Suffering in South Sudan, and they were contributing—each and every one was coming with anything that they feel of giving—and then when this money was at least something that could help, they all came, and they contributed the money (Barnes et al., 2018, p. 10).

But others did not receive reliable financial assistance or see the diaspora as a key form of support. One respondent in Juba noted that the diaspora is not necessarily well-off and others were keen to emphasise their own coping mechanisms as more important than support received from outside. Conversely, many within the South Sudanese diaspora have benefited from investment and employment within the post-2005 state. From the signing of the Comprehensive Peace Agreement in 2005 through independence until the start of the civil war in 2013, it was an economic boom period that drew in diaspora residents and networks. During this time, the capital Juba became a boom town, as significant oil resources flowed into the government's coffers for the first time. The 'big tent' approach to politics that President Salva Kiir espoused at this time incorporated many old warring factions into the rapidly growing government and civil service, and this meant that the majority of South Sudan's communities were able to access state resources to some degree, both through the massive expansion of military and civilian public payrolls as well as through more illegitimate opportunities for resource extraction (de Waal, 2014).

While some of these resources and investments went directly to communities in rural areas, there were also strong incentives to remove funds from the still unstable country. During this period, many diaspora communities were net beneficiaries from these connections. Some diaspora residents sought high-paid government, NGO and UN employment in South Sudan; other diaspora families supplemented whatever income they could generate in their new homes with financial support from well-employed relatives in Juba (Ensor, 2013a; Erickson & Faria, 2011; Grabska, 2011; Newhouse, 2012). Additionally, those in Juba with strong diaspora connections were better able to invest their resources outside the country, build their capital base, buy homes and support their children to be educated elsewhere. At this time, new South Sudanese middle and upper classes were created to move flexibly between different diaspora locations and take maximum advantage of the new resource flows for themselves, their families and their communities. New inequalities emerged during this period: while nearly all the wealthiest South Sudanese elites developed well-established bases and investments outside the country, not all diaspora communities are part of these elite circles, with a highly diverse range of experiences amongst different groups.

The Impact of the 2013 Conflict

The start of the December 2013 conflict had a transformative effect on South Sudanese communities worldwide. The new civil war involved elite factions' military forces as well as militias and local armed groups mobilised by community leaderships and individual military and political actors. Violence was often directed more at the ethnic communities believed to be aligned to opponent forces than at opponent forces themselves, creating the conditions for horrific violence against civilians, mass displacement, atrocities and looting (African Union, 2015). This section outlines the immediate interpersonal and financial impacts of the war and these forms of violence within diaspora networks. The following section then explores the societal changes within the diaspora that these impacts created.

Information Sharing as Polarising Re-traumatisation

There has been a collective trauma enacted within diaspora groups through the process of information sharing and verification among family, friends and kin. With publicly available information very limited and often unreliable, the information coming directly from trusted sources—about the progress of the war, about specific fighting that is taking place and the impact on communities—has been critical. There is a huge onus on both gathering this information and sharing it amongst one's community. A Juba resident described how this works:

> It is we South Sudanese who are feeding them with that news. For instance, [in 2013]: so, my auntie started calling me, personally, and she said that I found this in social media that there is killing in Juba, is it really true? We need to confirm from you. I told her yes, because I witnessed someone who was killed, so I told her here, yes that one happened, but I'm not sure whether, because I'm now not in one place, I'm really in a bad place, I won't tell you in detail. When I reach a place like UN House [the UN compound where many people fled for safety], I will tell you more. It seems like it is me who gives news to her. (DIP1, anonymous young woman, Focus Group 2, Session 1, University of Juba, 31 October 2017)

With easier online access, those in the diaspora then play a critical role in feeding back this information to others elsewhere, including other South Sudanese locations. Some respondents within South Sudan indicate that these feedback channels are critical for keeping people informed, calling their diaspora connections 'good followers' of news content from sources like Facebook and websites like the Sudan Tribune.

Because of their greater access to the internet, diaspora residents can better access news about rebel developments from media that is blocked from within South Sudan (such as Radio Tamazuj and the Sudan Tribune websites), or about events within local communities, especially in rural areas that might be discussed on forums and Facebook. Diaspora residents can feed this quite specific news back to their relatives in rural villages, for example to inform their movements on whether to travel to a specific area or not. This means that while the diaspora may be primarily 'consumers' of news, as described by the Juba resident above, some respondents argued that they use this role actively and effectively. One Juba-based respondent explained how this feedback of news and information helps decisions about matters of security because she does not have a TV or easy access to other forms of media; she relies on her family in Khartoum in Sudan to caution her about happenings in Juba, including news about checkpoints, localised gun violence, and major political events like the house arrest and detention of regime opponents. However, the gathering and sharing of this information have also had a traumatising effect.

This verification sharing, and re-sharing of news and information are exhausting for both Australian and South Sudanese residents. Many people are restricting their social media and news intake in both places, including youth in Australia quitting Facebook because of 'politics actually, in terms of the South Sudan conflict, and also the Australian reporting of young people. It was just negative' (DIP1, Anon., Consultation Group 2, Monash University, Melbourne, 11 November 2017).

This is part of the wider diasporic traumatisation caused by the war within South Sudan. One individual summed up this mental and emotional effect of the war:

> We were all affected by the war itself because South Sudan is a country that South Sudanese Australians have invested in. They've invested in [it] materially, they've invested in terms of ideas and ideals and human capital. So, when the country was at the brink of [war], it affected all of us here—and of course, unfortunately, the war took that ugly turn where our leaders selfishly used, you know, the innocent population [in the war], so somehow people that are here again are affected, people have families [involved]. [We have had] funerals every now and then around Melbourne, people have lost, people are losing people. ... So, we share in the trauma that is going on in South Sudan, the damage, the destruction, we are emotionally caught up in that. (DIP1, Anon., Consultation Group 1, Monash University, Melbourne, 28 October 2017)

Inevitably, the consequences of hearing so many traumatic stories of ethnicised conflict also led to polarisation among communities. A South Sudanese Australian participant commented, '[If] my tribe had a fight with another tribe and then maybe that tribe were defeated, automatically I shared it to my friend, it's like a football game'. (DIP1, Anon., Consultation Group 2, Monash University, Melbourne, 11 November 2017)

This trauma fed into the fragmentation of diaspora communities that had maintained an ethnic identity within a broader sense of unity created by the migration and settlement experience. This fragmentation is due to cumulative damage: the economic burden of supporting immediate family members in a sustained economic crisis in South Sudan; the instrumentalisation of ethnic division by political parties in the war to drive armed recruitment and target civilians in horrific violence; and the promotion of hate speech and inter-communal fear and suspicion to justify these brutal tactics. They have all worked to break inter-ethnic solidarity, organisation and trust in the diaspora as well as fracture collective identity along ethnic lines, causing tension and division (Barnes et al., 2018). A dual South Sudanese Australian national resident in Juba explained:

> the fragmentation that is here [in Juba] hit us so hard [in Australia]. Today you cannot talk about [anything]… even at funerals we don't meet these days. If there is a funeral among the Dinkas you don't see Equatorians there! You don't see people from Nuer community! We are so fragmented! … So as much as ten years ago there was a possibility of us coming together for a cause, today it is not possible. The Acholi would only make [financial] contributions to meet the issues in the Acholi-land. The Dinka Bor will only meet to make a case in the Bor area. So that's the most painful to me because when I went there [Australia] in 2000 there was nothing like that. I was a pastor to all, but today when I go to Australia—I'm not a pastor to all. I'm not. They will still respect me, but I'm not; I'm not. (DIP1, Interviewee, 30 October 2017, Juba)

Long-term Diaspora Financial Stress

Providing financial support, through remittances, to family and friends is typically a cultural or moral imperative for migrant and resettling people (Simoni & Voirol, 2020). But the 2013 conflict caused an often-unmanageable financial burden on communities throughout local and diaspora networks that intensified in line with the conflict itself. The conflict also precipitated rapid inflation and the depreciation of the South Sudanese pound, meaning that remittances in US dollars became increasingly financially powerful as local incomes were devalued and market prices rose. In Melbourne, young Nuer people described opting to work instead of study because of the intense need to generate income to send back to their family (Carver et al., 2020). Small individual payments made through money transfer agencies amounted to considerable sums. While the community as a whole struggled to meet a crisis-level demand for basic necessities, safety and security, let alone education and accommodation, they were able to collectively provide to varying degrees.

It is also essential to recognise the vast diversity of experience amongst different South Sudanese communities and their connections with the diaspora. South Sudanese displacement has been a complex, chaotic process. The mobility stories gathered for the Gambella-focused research illustrate the wide range of factors involved in whether or not an individual and their family move: the presence of relatives in other locations—and the ability to communicate with them at the right moment in time; the availability and accessibility of transport links; government policies on immigration and border management in the region and beyond (Carver et al., 2020). However, if one movement can be the somewhat random product of circumstance and chance, it can then lead to a trend or pattern that can last decades. In Akobo, there was a moment during the aid operation in the 1990s when Christian relief agencies began flying directly to the area from Kenya, allowing a part of the Akobo community to access Kenya in a way that has had far-reaching consequences still being felt in the area today (Carver et al., 2020, p. 25).

New dividing lines have emerged since the 2013 conflict. While the conflict is generally framed ethnically, class and power might be a better way of understanding the most significant divisions. For example, while it is true to say that Nuer communities now have less access to any government resources in Juba, these funds have shrunk considerably and, in some locations, have been offset by the need for aid agencies to recruit staff from these communities on relatively high US dollar salaries to work in those areas worst affected by conflict: the overall picture is highly complex, and is experienced as such in the Australian diaspora community.

Nevertheless, throughout this period, there have been groups with proximity to military powers that have continued to benefit significantly from the resources available in South Sudan, referred to by some analysts as the 'gun class' (Boswell, 2016; D'Agoot, 2018). These individuals have been able to entrench power and wealth and consolidate their positions, leveraging their transnational networks in support of their power base within the country.

PART 2: SOCIETAL CHANGES AND IMPACTS OF DIASPORA DEVELOPMENT

Our research has identified a complex inter-relationship between war, displacement and societal change. Environments in which violence becomes entrenched over long periods create a chaotic system of national, regional and international displacement, which is hard to predict and track. In turn, this displacement creates transnational networks that act as vectors for new kinds of societal change. South Sudan's recent history of a brief period of massive financial opportunity in the midst of violence and identity-based conflict has caused enormous changes, and the transnational networks have been a fundamental part of that.

While much analysis of transnationalism has focused on its political and economic effects, our work has confirmed that there is also a hugely significant emotional impact. This is especially the case given the nature of the pastoral communities dominant in so much of South Sudan. In our research on Nuer networks, the provision of mutual support amongst the community emerged as a prominent marker of Nuer identity, and—when feasible—transnational networks can be significantly constructive symbols of this, enabling communities to come together in mutually reinforcing ways. Institutions such as community associations—common through the diaspora—and churches have played critical roles in enabling this support beyond just the individual and family level.

Conversely, in more challenging times, the emotional impact of these networks can therefore be highly traumatising. When tragic and traumatic events are being communicated through the networks, this has a direct effect.

> Even though you are in a good place, sleeping is not easy with your children back there. ... We're here we sleep in a good place; we eat something good and you look behind you and you feel pain of what you've left behind. (Anon., Consultation Group 2, Monash University, Melbourne, 11 November 2017)

If the economic circumstances make it hard for individuals to provide support, this can easily translate into feelings of shame and guilt. Interviewees in Australia described not wanting to answer calls from their relatives in South Sudan because they know they can't do anything to assist. In such circumstances, the effects of this emotional trauma are liable to be enacted in the locations of resettlement, leading to tensions within communities, between communities, and with the wider societies where they have resettled (Koinova, 2016).

And the political dynamics in South Sudan, with those in power instrumentalising ethnic identity to mobilise communities, often through violence, make for a particularly challenging environment. In such circumstances, the functioning of transnational networks can be reinterpreted by others as a form of violence, whether these accusations are based on truth or not. *SBS Radio* and the *Sydney Morning Herald* have reported on growing incidents of South Sudanese Australians returning to South Sudan to participate in violence, with one interviewee stating that he was '100% certain that any man of Nuer or Dinka origin travelling to South Sudan between 2013 and 2016 had been travelling to participate in violence' (Cosier, 2016).

When paired with the effects of social media discourse on spreading disinformation and hate speech seen globally, this becomes a particularly toxic environment, with those in the diaspora liable to be accused of inciting violence. For those living in difficult conditions in South Sudan, and perhaps with idealised images of what diaspora life might be like, this can be particularly hard to accept. One respondent in Juba described their social media posts as 'vomiting', expressing disappointment that this is how they use their greater freedom of expression. Another respondent said:

> The South Sudanese in Australia do not have any authority to speak to us about reconciliation. Because I know them. I would rather say you reconcile first in Australia before you tell us how you reconcile. Because it is very toxic in Australia I know. So, the South Sudanese in Australia do not have moral authority to tell us how to reconcile. (Interviewee, 30 October 2017, Juba)

The combination of violence, trauma, economic hardship and division can lead to mistrust and open significant gaps between different parts of the transnational networks, limiting their abilities to play a constructive role in fostering community solidarity and inter-community reconciliation.

Our research also found increasing hostility towards those perceived as "elite" and navigating the transnational space for personal and political gain in a parallel dynamic. This was often linked to the notion of dual citizenship and having multiple passports:

My view, because I had a number of them South Sudanese from Australia, there is already divided loyalty that I could see, because especially during the conflict our airport was full with people with dual citizenship. They threw down our identity [referring to South Sudanese citizenship] and they raised up another identity in order to leave the country. So that alone to me is a divided loyalty. (Interviewee, 10 November 2017, Juba)

The possession of multiple passports has been commonplace in the region amongst political elites for many years, but the discourse around the role of the diaspora has allowed it to be weaponised more explicitly. On more than one occasion in recent years, an image of an Ethiopian passport registered to Riek Machar has been circulated on social media to undermine his authority as a South Sudanese politician.[3]

The end result of all these dynamics is to create an environment in which diaspora are painted by some as part of South Sudan's problems, undermining the social fabric of the new nation, engaging in hate speech and disinformation from positions of relative luxury and increasingly irrelevant to the future of the country. Such a position seems to be supported by the famous findings of economic study in the 1990s that the presence of a large diaspora was a key indicator of the likelihood of a return to war (Collier & Hoeffler, 2004).

But our research suggests that this is a misreading of the complexity of transnationalism and more a product of the failures of the South Sudanese governance environment than a cause of it. Transnationalism can clearly have both positive and negative effects—it has done so and continues to do so in South Sudan—but more importantly, it is now a fact of life for of a large proportion of the South Sudanese population. The question for national and international policymakers is not whether or not transnationalism is a good thing, but how their policies and programmes help bring out its best features and mitigate its most problematic elements. Unfortunately, these policymakers, locked into their state-centric perspectives on the world, are poorly placed to understand the chaotic, informal world of transnationalism and are also liable to see transnational mobility, especially of funds and young people, as another threat alongside terrorism and people trafficking. Far more work is therefore required to understand and engage with transnationalism more constructively.

---

[3] (https://hotinjuba.com/splm-io-explains-riek-machars-ethiopain-passport/)

178   S. MAHER ET AL.

Elites have a particularly important relationship with transnational networks as they have the resources to both build up assets in different locations and physically move themselves and their kin around the world as needed. As South Sudan's legal environment allows dual citizenship, this provides scope for individuals with the right connections to keep bases in multiple locations. It also enables capital flight, building different political alliances, and establishing a new internationalised South Sudanese class. The long-term effects of this on the country are yet to be fully seen and understood, particularly when power shifts to a generation that did not grow up fighting in the bush. However, this research did show dual citizenship, and the ease of international movement afforded to members of the elite classes, especially during conflict, as deepening divisions and emphasising diaspora privilege.

Many Juba residents noted that this ability to leave, and the distance of many South Sudanese living abroad from the daily realities and practicalities of living in Juba, meant that those in the diaspora have "another understanding" of events in South Sudan.

> 2013 before the war broke out, a lot of people in diaspora come to celebrate with their family Christmas, and also they come for independence and also keep in touch with the situation in their country. Most of us in here have witnessed bad things being committed against their tribal members. ... Ok, now you go there, when you have left somebody that has been killed, what do you expect from them? To be posting negatively and writing negatively because of the privileges that they have. And even here we don't have the access whereby you express yourself. There, it is open, as my brother said, they'll be talking; vomiting; saying how he feels. Sometimes the diaspora, they play negatively because they don't have a source of recognition. (Anon. young man, Focus Group 2, Session 1, University of Juba, 31 October 2017)

Juba residents often voice frustration that change is apparently not coming from outside the country within communities which might have more resources (social, financial, political, educational) to bridge these divides.

> For those of us who have returned to South Sudan, we are of different categories. There are those professionals who returned, and they want to [be] involved on the basis of their merits. But there are those who returned here, who [were] basically invited to jobs by their relatives in the government. That is a very sad part of it. That, they come knowing that they already have

positions, while there are those of us who come because we feel we want to be here and find opportunities for us to be involved. ... There are those who come here because they are comrades to the SPLM [Sudan People's Liberation Movement]. You in diaspora also have SPLM Chapters. So, there are those who left Australia, I can think of a few individuals who are now in the government. They are in the government because this is an SPLM government and so they are there on the strength of their experience or their roles in the diaspora. And there is another group. Again, I have met a few who have come here to invest because they have made dollars and now, they want to come here. (Interviewee, 10 November 2017, Juba)

Both Melbourne and Juba residents agreed that diasporic political pressure was more effective when applied, by petition or otherwise, at state, county and local levels, where their leverage (financially, and as prominent community members) could be used to best advantage.

Conclusions

South Sudanese transnational networks are both far-reaching and fundamental to many people's survival. The combination of thick kinship networks that exist in South Sudan (particularly in the absence of public safety nets) and extensive migration over many decades are at the heart of this. Our research suggests that this complex transnationalism is as much a product of the failures of the South Sudanese governance environment as a cause of it. This has become more explicit since the conflict (that began in 2013) has increasingly constrained economic opportunities within South Sudan. The research also suggests that the functioning of South Sudanese diaspora groups has changed over time, with greater levels of organisation occurring, for example, around the referendum or in initiating development projects such as school-building during the transitional peace period over 2005-2011. These efforts have been heavily eroded by political collapse and the economic crisis created by the financial burden of supporting family and kinship networks in need.

Transnationalism can clearly have both positive and negative effects—it has done so and continues to do so in South Sudan—but more importantly, despite its often chaotic and informal nature, it is now a fact of life for a large proportion of the South Sudanese population. The question for national and international policymakers is not whether this is a good thing or not, but how their policies and programmes could help bring out its

180   S. MAHER ET AL.

best features and mitigate its most problematic elements. Unfortunately, policymakers locked into state-centric perspectives are poorly placed to understand transnationalism of this kind. Far more work is therefore required to understand and engage with it constructively.

REFERENCES

African Union. (2015). Final Report of the African Union Commission of Inquiry on South Sudan. https://reliefweb.int/report/south-sudan/final-report-african-union-commission-inquiry-south-sudan

Barnes, C., Carver, F., Deng, S. A., Kiir, G., Kindersley, N., Lorins, R., & Maher, S. (2018). The Role of Transnational Networks and Mobile Citizens in South Sudan's Global Community: A Pilot Study Focused on Melbourne and Juba. *Rift Valley Institute.* https://riftvalley.net/publication/role-transnational-networks-and-mobile-citizens-south-sudans-global-community

Benier, K. J., Blaustein, J. B., Johns, D., & Maher, S. L. (2018). 'Don't drag us into this': Growing Up South Sudanese in Victoria after the 2016 Moomba 'riot'. *Monash University Research Report.* https://www.cmy.net.au/publications/dont-drag-me-into-this

Berry, J. W. (1997). Immigration, Acculturation, and Adaptation. *Applied Psychology, 46*(1), 5–34.

Boswell, A. (2016, 25 November). The Genocidal Logic of South Sudan's "gun class". *The New Humanitarian.* https://www.thenewhumanitarian.org/opinion/2016/2011/2025/genocidal-logic-south-sudan-s-gun-class.

Carment, D., & Calleja, R. (2018). Diasporas and Fragile States—Beyond Remittances Assessing the Theoretical and Policy Linkages. *Journal of Ethnic and Migration Studies, 44*(8), 1270–1288. https://doi.org/10.108 0/1369183X.2017.1354157

Carver, F., Chienien, J., Deng, S. A., Gidron, Y., Guok, D. R., Kindersley, N., & Wal, G. (2020). 'No one can stay without someone': Transnational Networks Amongst the Nuer-speaking Peoples of Gambella and South Sudan. *Rift Valley Institute.* https://riftvalley.net/sites/default/files/publication-documents/No%20one%20can%20stay%20without%20someone%20-%20RVI%20Report%20%282020%282029_282020.pdf

Collier, P., & Hoeffler, A. (2004). Greed and Grievance in Civil War. *Oxford Economic, Papers, 56*(4), 563–595.

Cosier, C. (2016, 14 July). Aussies in South Sudan Conflict Put Australian Law to the Test. *The Sydney Morning Herald.* https://www.smh.com.au/world/do-these-six-australians-have-a-case-to-answer-20160622-gpozja.html

D'Agoot, M. (2018, 29 May). Taming the Dominant Gun Class in South Sudan. *Africa Center for Strategic Studies*. https://africacenter.org/spotlight/taming-the-dominant-gun-class-in-south-sudan/

Délano Alonso, A., & Mylonas, H. (2019). The Microfoundations of Diaspora Politics: Unpacking the State and Disaggregating the Diaspora. *Journal of Ethnic and Migration Studies, 45*(4), 473–491.

Deng, S. A. (2017a). *Fitting the Jigsaw: South Sudanese Family Dynamics and Parenting Practices in Australia*. PhD, Victoria University, Melbourne.

Deng, S. A. (2017b). *South Sudanese youth acculturation and intergenerational challenges*. Paper presented at the Africa: Moving the Boundaries 39th AFSAAP Annual Conference, St. Catherine's College University of Western Australia.

Deng, S. A., & Marlowe, J. M. (2013). Refugee Resettlement and Parenting in a Different Context. *Journal of Immigrant & Refugee Studies, 11*(4), 416–430.

Deng, S. A., & Pienaar, F. (2011). Positive Parenting: Integrating Sudanese Traditions and New Zealand Styles of Parenting. An Evaluation of Strategies with Kids-Information for Parents (SKIP). *The Australasian Review of African Studies, 32*(2), 160–179.

de Waal, A. (2014). When Kleptocracy Becomes Insolvent: Brute Causes of the Civil War in South Sudan. *African Affairs, 113*(452), 347–369.

Duff, P. (2012). Identity, Agency, and Second Language Acquisition. In S. M. Gass & A. Mackey (Eds.), *The Routledge Handbook of Second Language Acquisition* (pp. 410–442). Routledge.

Ensor, M. (2013a). *Displaced Youth's Role in Sustainable Return: Lessons from South Sudan. International Organisation for Migration*.

Ensor, M. (2013b). Youth Culture, Refugee (Re)Integration, and Diasporic Identities in South Sudan. *Postcolonial Text, 8*(3), 1. https://www.postcolonial.org/index.php/pct/article/view/1729

Ensor, M. (2016). Refugee Girls and Boys and the Dilemmas of (Un)Sustainable Return to South Sudan. In M. Ensor & E. M. Goździak (Eds.), *Children and Forced Migration: Durable Solutions During Transient Years* (pp. 105–126). Springer International Publishing.

Erickson, J., & Faria, C. (2011). "We want empowerment for our women": Transnational Feminism, Neoliberal Citizenship, and the Gendering of Women's Political Subjectivity in Postconflict South Sudan. *Signs, 36*(3), 627–652.

Falge, C. (2015). *The Global Nuer: Transnational Life-worlds, Religious Movements and War*. Rüdiger Köppe Verlag.

Faria, C. (2010). Contesting Miss South Sudan: Gender and Nation-building in Diasporic Discourse'. *International Feminist Journal of Politics, 12*(2), 222–243.

Faria, C. (2013). Staging a New South Sudan in the USA: Men, Masculinities and Nationalist Performance at a Diasporic Beauty Pageant. *Gender, Place & Culture, 20*(1), 87–106. https://doi.org/10.1080/0966369X.2011.624591

Faria, C. (2014). Styling the Nation: Fear and Desire in the South Sudanese Beauty Trade. *Transactions of the Institute of British Geographers, 39*(2), 318–330. https://doi.org/10.1111/tran.12027

Faria, C. (2017). Towards a Countertopography of Intimate War: Contouring Violence and Resistance in a South Sudanese Diaspora. *Gender, Place & Culture, 24*(4), 575–593. https://doi.org/10.1080/0966369X.2017.1314941

Foltyn, S. (2017, 30 September). Meet an American Citizen Fighting with South Sudan's Rebels. *PBS NewsHour.* https://www.pbs.org/newshour/show/meet-american-citizen-fighting-south-sudans-rebels.

Getahun, S. F., & Dejene, S. (2021). Consequences of Covid-19 On Digital Economy in the Horn of Africa. *Review of Agricultural and Applied Economics, 24,* 21–26.

Grabska, K. (2011). Threatening Mini Skirts' or 'Agents of Development': Returnee Southern Sudanese Women and Their Contributions to Development. *The Nordic Africa Institute, 95,* 81–100.

Holtzman, J. (2007). *Nuer Journeys, Nuer Lives: Sudanese Refugees in Minnesota* (2nd ed.). Allyn and Bacon.

Horst, C. (2018). Making a Difference in Mogadishu? Experiences of Multi-Sited Embeddedness among Diaspora Youth. *Journal of Ethnic and Migration Studies, 44*(8), 1341–1356. https://doi.org/10.1080/1369183X.2017.1354161

Johnson, H. F. (2016). *South Sudan: The Untold Story from Independence to Civil War.* Bloomsbury Publishing.

Karabegović, D. (2018). Aiming for Transitional Justice? Diaspora Mobilisation for Youth and Education in Bosnia and Herzegovina. *Journal of Ethnic and Migration Studies, 44*(8), 1374–1389. https://doi.org/10.1080/1369183X.2017.1354165

Khawaja, N. G., & Milner, K. (2012). Acculturation Stress in South Sudanese Refugees: Impact on Marital Relationships. *International Journal of Intercultural Relations, 36*(5), 624–636.

Koinova, M. (2016). How Refugee Diasporas Respond to Trauma. *Current History, 115*(784), 322.

van der Linden, J., Blaak, M., & Andrew, F. A. (2013). The Contribution of the Diaspora to the Reconstruction of Education in South Sudan: The Challenge of Being Involved from a Distance. *Compare: A Journal of Comparative and International Education, 43*(5), 646–666. https://doi.org/10.1080/03057925.2013.821324

Maher, S., Deng, S. A., & Kindersley, N. (2018). South Sudanese Australians: Constantly Negotiating Belonging and Identity. *Sudan Studies, 58,* 53–64.

Marlowe, J. M. (2010). *'Walking the Line': Southern Sudanese Narratives and Responding to Trauma.* Flinders University.

Marlowe, J. M. (2011). South Sudanese Diaspora in Australasia. *Australasian Review of African Studies, 32*(2), 3–9.

Marlowe, J., Harris, A., & Lyons, T. (2014). *South Sudanese Diaspora in Australia and New Zealand: Reconciling the Past with the Present*. Cambridge Scholars Publishing.

Miller, M. J., & Kerlow-Myers, A. E. (2009). A Content Analysis of Acculturation Research in the Career Development Literature. *Journal of Career Development, 35*(4), 352–384.

Newhouse, L. (2012). *Urban Attractions: Returnee Youth, Mobility and the Search for a Future in South Sudan's Regional Towns*. UNHCR.

Quinn, B. (2017, 16 April). How Factions in South Sudan's War Took Shape on British Campuses'. *The Observer*. http://www.theguardian.com/global-development/2017/apr/2016/south-sudan-could-britain-create-peace-striking-how-close-they-feel.

Shakespeare Finch, J., & Wickham, K. (2010). Adaptation of Sudanese Refugees in an Australian Context: Investigating Helps and Hindrances. *International Migration, 48*(1), 23–46.

Shandy, D. J. (2002). Nuer Christians in America. *Journal of Refugee Studies, 15*(2), 213–221. https://doi.org/10.1093/jrs/15.2.213

Shandy, D. J. (2005). Nuer in the United States. In M. Ember, C. R. Ember, & I. Skoggard (Eds.), *Encyclopedia of Diasporas: Immigrant and Refugee Cultures Around the World* (pp. 1046–1054). Springer.

Steel, G. (2021). Going Global—Going Digital. Diaspora Networks and Female Online Entrepreneurship in Khartoum, Sudan. *Geoforum, 120*, 22–29. https://doi.org/10.1016/j.geoforum.2021.01.003

UNHCR. (2021). Report of the Commission on Human Rights in South Sudan. https://www.ohchr.org/EN/HRBodies/HRC/RegularSessions/Session46/Documents/A_HRC_46_53.pdf

Walters, L. (2016, 23 July). Australian Dual Nationals Face Life in South Sudanese Prison. *SBS News*. http://www.sbs.com.au/news/article/2016/2007/2023/australian-dual-nationals-face-life-south-sudanese-prison

Wilcock, C. (2018). Mobilising Towards and Imagining Homelands: Diaspora Formation Among U.K. Sudanese. *Journal of Ethnic and Migration Studies, 44*(3), 363–381. https://doi.org/10.1080/1369183X.2017.1313104

PART IV

Future Imaginings

CHAPTER 9

Interrogating Diaspora and Cross-Border Politics in Ukrainian Migration to Australia

Olga Oleinikova

Introduction

The world of democracy and cross-border mobility is experiencing a historic sea change, one that is taking us away from the nation state-based model of democracy and diaspora of past times towards a form of mutual alignment with no borders and frontlines (Keane, 2009). Many of the current 'hot topics' in international relations and migration research such as transnationalism, citizenship and voting rights, European disintegration, migration crises associated with the Covid-19 pandemic, the rise of cybercrime and global security threats, all challenging the 'container model' of the nation-state, are linked today to larger questions of democracy, democratic development, and the actors involved. In recent years, diasporas are becoming important actors in the democratic development of their sending states, as they are today better informed and connected to their home

---

O. Oleinikova (✉)
SITADHub (Social Impact Technologies and Democracy Research Hub) in the School of Communication, University of Technology Sydney, Sydney, NSW, Australia
e-mail: Olga.Oleinikova@uts.edu.au

© The Author(s), under exclusive license to Springer Nature Switzerland AG 2022
M. Phillips, L. Olliff (eds.), *Understanding Diaspora Development*,
https://doi.org/10.1007/978-3-030-97866-2_9

187

countries than ever before, with online news and social media linking them immediately with events, issues and discourses occurring in their homeland and around the world. This chapter aims to address not only the question of distribution, but also one that focuses on the relationship between the state and the diasporas and the role of the diasporas in democratic processes in their home country. Having the case study of the Ukrainian diaspora in Australia at its centre, this chapter asks how the modern diaspora diplomacy constitutes an important way by which diasporas influence the processes of democratisation, creating a noticeable impact from afar on the economic and political situation in their homelands.

This research question exposes an important ambiguity that rests at the heart of this chapter. On the one hand, I seek to probe how various actors and groups located across territorial space can affect political systems and, more specifically, influence democratic processes. In that sense, the chapter is driven by a post-territorial vision of politics (Oleinikova & Bayeh, 2019) and democratisation processes that privilege networks of affiliation and organising, rather than geographically bound political movements. It focuses on the nexus between one form of displacement, diasporas and a particular political system, democracy, to provide insights into how the former might impact democratic processes. On the other hand, this chapter explores that nexus principally in relation to the role of the multifaceted Ukrainian diasporas and their efforts to promote democracy and democratic building in contemporary Ukraine. It is clear, then, that this chapter cannot escape territory in its entirety, nor does it claim to. Rather it tries to theorise and apply the consideration of an overlooked yet crucial dimension to the study of democracy which is how it is formed, shaped and influenced from the outside, that is by actors and movements located externally to a particular territorial space. The sense of the crisis of territoriality proposed by Maier (2016) orients my research; I recognise the delocalising power of diasporic networks, of media technologies and space-time compression, while also acknowledging the continued potency of territory to define identity, nationality and, crucially, to act as a home for particular political systems. While democracy often means electoral politics and voting, and can also refer to government systems and principals of popular sovereignty, in this chapter by democracy we mean not only the set of democratic systems and principles, but also the development of a way of life committed to greater equality and to the public accountability of power that rests on history, civil society, shared memory and on diaspora communities and their involvement, which accelerate various structural shifts in contemporary Ukraine.

This chapter is organised as follows: firstly, it theorises the link between diaspora and democracy; secondly, it examines the case of Ukrainian migration to Australia and the active role of its diaspora in Australia as an important laboratory for understanding the modern diaspora-democracy connection beyond territory and nation-state borders. Finally, the chapter presents and discusses the empirical evidence of the increasing delocalising power of Ukrainian diasporic networks in Australia, of media technologies and space-time compression that have a positive impact on democratic efforts in Ukraine.

DIASPORA AND DEMOCRACY: NEW TERRAIN

Time would pass, old empires would fall and new ones take their place. The relations of classes had to change before I discovered that it's not the quality of goods and utility that matter, but movement, not where you are or what you have, but where you come from, where you are going and the rate at which you are getting there. (James, *Beyond a Boundary*, 2013)

Of particular concern to this chapter is the vision of 'territorial mentality' that seems to underpin studies of diaspora and democracy (Keane, 2018). Territory is a central component or is perceived as a necessary precursor for democracy to take shape (Keane, 2009; Merkel, 2014) and for diaspora to link community intrinsically to the space outside their natal (or imagined natal) country (Cohen, 2008). Indeed, as Therborn highlights, all 'politics begins with place' (Therborn, 2013, p. 509) and, as Maier elaborates, it is within territories that decisions are made, or as he states, 'territory is thus a decision space. It establishes the spatial reach of legislation ... collective decisions' (2016, p. 3) and of politics (2016, p. 6). And yet, studies of democracy, a form of political governance, have offered little reflection on its territorial dimension (Oleinikova & Bayeh, 2019).

A significant reason for this neglect, according to Cara Nine, is that 'democratic theory is exclusive to persons' located in a fixed geographical space, addressing 'how [these people] should be treated and how their associations should be organised' (Nine, 2012, p. 93), all the while 'ignoring' how a fixed territorial space anchors and circumscribes our understanding of democracy (Nine, 2012, p. 101). Even in more recent attempts to ameliorate the marginalisation of territory in democracy research, it is people and their co-habitation that remain the focus. For instance, in his 2016 examination of a political approach to understanding the development of democracy, David Miller hypothetically asks, considering 'the set of people who occupy the area defined by mooted boundary B, is it possible to create a well-functioning democracy within the area so defined?' (Miller, 2016, p. 40). This is one of the core questions that drive our research in this section. Using diasporas as the lens through which to wrestle with the issue is highly appropriate because, unlike democracy, theories of dispersal have, at times unwittingly, engaged significantly with territory and attempted to account for the ways various transnationally located social and political movements have contended with borders and fixed geographical spaces (Anderson, 1998). The reason for this high-level engagement stems both from the meaning of diaspora, as a form of dispersal from a set territorial space, and the timing of its emergence as a field of scholarly enquiry. Diasporas, as Bayeh (2019) suggests, are non-state-based political groups that can 'escape' or transcend boundaries and can work and connect across them, facilitated by macropolitical structures such as the bounded state. Regarding its etymology, 'diaspora' derives from the Ancient Greek verb *speirō* 'to scatter' and the preposition *dia* 'through or over'. As Judith Shuval argues, 'a critical component' of diaspora is that it entails a 'history of dispersal' and a 'collective ... cultural memory of the dispersion' (Shuval, 2000, p. 43). What is often said to have been scattered or dispersed are metaphorical seeds, which highlights the intrinsic reference to land and territory contained in the term. Historically, Robin Cohen (1997) distinguished five types of diasporas, one of which is the de-territorial diaspora, as in not connected with an actually existing state but rather an imagined/symbolic homeland, such as the Roma or Kurds. Safran (1991) likewise pointed out this characteristic (a common memory about the place of origin which could be an imagined one, as it was for centuries in the case of Jews or Armenians).

In his summary of current approaches to diaspora, Cohen (1997, pp. 135–136) suggests that 'diasporas are positioned somewhere between "nation-states" and "travelling cultures" in that they involve dwelling in a nation-state in a physical sense, but travelling in an astral or spiritual sense that falls outside the nation-state's space/time zone'. In this line, Cohen (2008) sees that theorising diasporas should begin by looking at the cases of people who live outside their places of origin rather than using a particular theory already established to portray them. Diaspora has been transformed (at least in a theoretical sense) from a descriptive condition applied largely to Jews in exile, to encompass a multitude of ethnic, religious and national communities who find themselves living outside the territory to which they are historically 'rooted'. This also points to the widely held assumption that diasporas are dispersed from a particular place or originary site. While this has been comprehensively debated within diaspora studies, some arguing against the importance of the territorial centre (Bayeh, 2019; Hepp & Couldry, 2009; Gamlen, 2019) and others asserting its enduring relevance (Zielonka, 2017), the significance of geographical space and land remains ever present and is inescapable within this field.

Another reason for the deep engagement with geographical space, related to the emergence of diaspora studies, is equally significant especially as it reveals of the kind of territory that seems to interest or orient diaspora research. It can be argued that even though 'state/country of origin', 'home' and 'homeland' are frequently used in diaspora literature, often, what is more than likely implied is the nation-state. Mishra (2006) highlights this point in his important study *Diaspora Criticism*. He argues that of 'the many supplementary terms that swirl in the orbit of diaspora criticism (hybridity, décalage, discontinuity, multilocality, nomadism, double consciousness and so on)' transnationalism and nationalism feature as the most prominent (Mishra, 2006, p. 131). Like Mishra, Jana Braziel and Anita Mannur contend that the nation is a key component in what they refer to as the practice of 'theorising' diaspora (Braziel & Mannur, 2003, pp. 3–4, 7–10). However, what is curious about the importance of the nation-state is not just its unquestioned frequency, but its emergence in the eighteenth and nineteenth centuries, post-date the occurrence of diaspora communities, from the perspective of the Jewish or Greek diasporas thousands of years ago. In light of this disjointed sequence of timing, what explains the centrality of the nation in diaspora research?

The answer to this can be traced to the timing of the emergence of diaspora studies as opposed to diaspora communities. Braziel and Mannur argue that the increased interest in diaspora research dates from 1991, with the inauguration of the journal *Diaspora*. Since then, 'debates over the theoretical, cultural, and historical resonances of the term [diaspora] have proliferated in academic journals devoted to ethnic, national and (trans) national concerns' (Braziel & Mannur, 2003, p. 2). This was reinforced more recently by Girish Daswani and Ato Quayson in their introduction to *A Companion to Diaspora and Transnationalism*. They write that, with the *Diaspora* journal 'the field progressively acquired scholarly coherence with a visible set of debates and practitioners' (Quayson & Daswani, 2013, p. 7). In other words, the institutionalised diaspora scholarship is a relatively contemporary field of inquiry. Tölölyan (1991, p. 4) highlights that 'dispersions, while not altogether new in form, acquired a different meaning by the nineteenth century, in the context of the triumphant nation-state'. The appeal of the nation-state in the last several decades has not waned (Brubaker, 2009) and, according to Massey, there has been an intense reconsolidation of the nation-state since the 1980s (Massey et al., 1994, p. 4). This is evident in the rise of exclusivist claims to territorial space, especially in the form of reactionary nationalisms opposed to new migrants and processes of globalisation (Massey et al., 1994, pp. 4, 151). Such claims of exclusivity are even more pronounced in a post-9/11 milieu, where states have strengthened their own powers in terms of homeland and border security in a bid to curtail the influx of undesirable and supposedly threatening outsiders. Thus, the displacement of people, especially in a context where the nation-state is being reconsolidated, means that the concept of diaspora studies needs to be understood as interacting with and even defining itself against nationhood.

According to Maier, territory is not just a 'decision space' but is also simultaneously 'constituted as an identity space or a space of belonging'. Territory specifies the 'domain of powerful collective loyalties', which is evidenced by how 'political and often ethnic allegiances' are supposedly 'territorial' (2016, p. 3). The notion of territory as both an 'identity' and 'decision' space resonates closely with the concept of the nation-state, where the nation is seen to reflect a common if not ethnic then cultural identity, and the state represents the geographical limits of legislation formation, political decision-making and sovereignty. But Maier, like so many diaspora theorists, has noted that the affiliations between territory, identity and decision-making, or between the state, nation and democracy, are not congruent—'Identity space and decision space have diverged' (2016, p. 3). For democracy research, this has significant implications aside from the assumption of territory as a necessary site for democracy to take shape, as mentioned above. Democracy scholarship has noted but also criticised the idea that the success of democracy is contingent upon the inhabitants of a democratic space sharing a common identity. As Carl Schmitt argued almost a century ago, 'Democracy requires … first homogeneity and second—if the need arises—elimination or eradication of heterogeneity' (1988, p. 9). Eliminating heterogeneity at odds with democracy, as noted by Seyla Benhabib who attempts in her article *Democracy and Identity* to address the perplexities of these two terms, 'of the tensions between the universalistic principles ushered in by the American and French Revolutions and particularistic identities of nationality, ethnicity, religion, gender, race and language' that cohabit the same democratic territorial space (1998, p. 85). Benhabib develops a typology of identity/difference movements to address this concern, a concern that had particular urgency after the political transition in Central and Eastern European (CEE) countries due to the '1989 decline of superpower polarism and the end of the Cold War [which] have bought with them a dizzying reconfiguration of the map of Europe' (1998, p. 86). Her study focuses on identities within nation-states and on how the development of a civic polity can help to accommodate difference within democracy. Benhabib's understanding of cultures as heterogeneous, dynamic, porous, hybrid, and as communities of dialogue fraught with power, helps to explore how diverse and dispersed communities interact with power institutions and influence the democratic processes.

This chapter benefits from the questions raised by scholars like Benhabib, but approaches the complexity of geographical space, territory, identity and democratic decision-making from a diasporic viewpoint to ask how a geographically dispersed national community shapes and influences democratic processes. The 'dizzying reconfiguration of the map of Europe', although initiated three decades ago in 1989, remains a prime site to propose this investigation, with a particular focus on Ukraine as a fledgling democracy that has suffered many shocks in the post-Cold War era and is a nation that is affected and shaped by a high coefficient of dispersal and diaspora.

Shaping Democracy from Afar: Insights from Ukraine

30 years of Ukraine's independence and the 2013/2014 Euromaidan protests showed Ukraine to be a state at a crossroads between East and West European paths. Ukraine's search for its identity and future is deeply rooted in historical fractures, which indicate its longstanding ties beyond its borders and territory that has shifted too many times. All these years since independence Ukraine still struggles to become a successful democracy, developing an active civil society as well as fighting the corruption, the oligarchisation of power and the nepotism that undermine Ukraine's democratic efforts. Diaspora dispersed communities have played an important role in this struggle, shaping the democratic Ukraine from abroad

through international media, the transnational roots of memory and the search for collective identity, as well as the transnational linkages of elites within the Ukrainian political and economic regimes. Having established themselves as active agents of democratic transition, galvanising the transnational interest-based politics to promote democracy, expanding claim-making from their local level to national, supranational, and global levels of engagement between their states of residence and Ukraine, Ukrainian diasporas have turned into a bridge to Western knowledge, expertise, resources, opportunities and global markets—all those that operate beyond the territory, time, space of a nation-state territory and at a most efficient deep level help to grow the seed of democratic change inside Ukraine. With the largest European population living outside the country (5.9 million) and the transnational embeddedness that has unexpectedly intensified in the Russian-Ukrainian political conflict, Ukraine makes a perfect case to examine and understand what democracy and diaspora mean in the twenty-first century.

Ukraine is characterised by transnational embeddedness and growing globalism and post-territoriality (Oleinikova, 2020). Modern Ukraine has never been that global before. Ranked the eighth country in the world for the largest number of people living outside the country's borders ('diaspora'), following India, Mexico, the Russian Federation, China, Bangladesh, Syrian Arab Republic and Pakistan, Ukraine ranks first place in Europe with the largest number of people living outside its territory (5.9 million) (Ahmadov & Sasse, 2016). The Ukrainian exodus was a series of mass migrations that mean today more than 20 million Ukrainians are living outside the country, according to the Toronto-based Ukrainian World Congress. That compares to 39 million still living in Ukraine. Canada and the United States have the biggest Ukrainian communities outside the former Soviet Union. Other significant long-standing communities are found in Brazil and Argentina, while more recent migration has settled an estimated 300,000 Ukrainians in Italy and 100,000 in Spain (Oleinikova & Bayeh, 2019).

The Ukrainian diaspora in Australia is one of the youngest centres of Ukrainian communities in the world. The first settlers (several dozen Ukrainian families) arrived in Australia in 1947 in response to the Australian Government's need for manpower to develop the country's post-war infrastructure. The mass influx of Ukrainian migrants to this country dates back to 1948–1949 (Chumak, 1991). This was the 'first wave' of emigration, known as 'political' (former 'displaced persons' and their descendants). Many of these migrants moved from Germany, from the so-called camps for displaced persons. In the late 1980s and early 1990s, a 'second wave' of ethnic Ukrainians migrated to Australia from Ukraine, but this time the reasons for migration were mostly economic. During the years of independence, some professionals in the field of Information Technology (IT), agriculture and STEM sciences also migrated from Ukraine to Australia. According to the 2016 census, the number of representatives of the Ukrainian community in Australia formally stands at only 4700 people. At the same time, these figures do not reflect the real situation because, at the time of conducting these sociological surveys, the number of Australians of Ukrainian origin included only persons whose place of birth was Ukraine, with Ukrainian as the primary language. According to the Australian Federation of Ukrainian Organisations (AFUO), a non-governmental organisation that coordinates the majority of Ukrainian organisations and represents Australian Ukrainians in their relations with the Australian state, the Ukrainian community in Australia includes 40,000 ethnic Ukrainians and occupies 35th position (0.18%) among ethnic groups living on the 'green continent'.

Empirically speaking, the dynamics of diaspora active involvement in the democratisation efforts of contemporary Ukraine presents something of a maze, containing at its centre normative contradictions as well as theoretical puzzles. As Ukrainian diasporas have become more involved and concerned with their homeland development, particularly in the past five years in the face of Euromaidan, dispersed communities in the digital, spaceless and fluid age have played a crucial role in the democratisation of the home state and have had a global impact. 'All Ukrainians in the diaspora and in Ukraine are in a struggle for freedom, for the values that those of us living in a democratic country hold dear', said Irene Mycak, a spokeswoman for the Toronto-based Ukrainian World Congress, in a telephone interview. As Kyivans froze on Maidan in 2013–2014, fighting for their European choice, Ukrainians in diasporas organised small 'Maidans' in their respective inhabited corners of the world. Ukrainians went out into the streets of London, Tokyo, Sydney, New York, Warsaw and Frankfurt. Through these actions, the Ukrainian diasporas fought for a wider global response. For example, in Australia, a 40,000-strong Ukrainian community urged the country to impose sanctions on Russia after its annexation of the Crimea. The small Ukrainian community in Hong Kong submitted a petition to the Russian Consulate, which later informed the embassy in Beijing.

Knowing of the mobilisation of Ukrainian diasporas, former president of Ukraine Petro Poroshenko stressed, when hosting the Ukrainian World Forum in Kyiv in August 2016, that Ukrainians all over the world should unite and protect their country. Sociologist Vic Satzewich (2002, p. 23) aptly pointed out that one of the positive outcomes of the conflict in Ukraine is 'the reinvigoration and reunification of Ukrainians globally'. According to him, the Ukrainian diasporas enhanced their ability to drive actions globally to the benefit of Ukraine by exerting valuable democratic influences. They lobbied foreign governments, organised countless protests, collected aid and reliably informed the world about events in Ukraine. Therefore, the involvement and the role of the Ukrainian diasporas in addressing the Ukraine crisis and their support towards the democratisation of the country are noticeable globally.

Despite its global scale, this transnational post-territorial dimension is under-examined, therefore modern Ukraine appears to be a perfect laboratory to explore the complexity of territory, identity and democratic decision-making from a diasporic viewpoint and to understand how a geographically dispersed national community shapes and influences the formation of democracy in the home country. The fact that Ukrainian diasporas play a significant part in the country's affairs exemplifies a unique formula for diaspora interaction with the home country that challenges the relevance of the self-contained unit in organising the political, economic or social life inside a country, as mentioned above. Taking the Ukrainian diaspora in Australia as an example, the following section discusses and showcases the empirical evidence of how a geographically dispersed national community acts beyond the territory of residence and has the capacity to mobilise politically from afar to influence the formation of democracy.

THE UKRAINIAN DIASPORA IN AUSTRALIA

Research into migration to Australia from Eastern Europe (Russia, Ukraine, Belarus, Moldova, Romania, Bulgaria, Hungary, Czech Republic, Poland and Slovakia) is almost non-existent. There are fragmented studies in the form of isolated articles and book chapters about: Polish migrants and diaspora in Australia (Kinowska & Pakulski, 2018); the linguistic integration of Russian migrants in Australia (Ryazantsev, 2014; Team et al., 2007); and Ukrainians in Australia (Oleinikova, 2016, 2017, 2020; Serbin, 2006). Specifically, there is a critical lack of systemic and comparative studies about the type of migrants who come from the most active donor-countries—Ukraine, Czech Republic and Hungary—as well as why they come, what they do upon arrival and which role they play in diaspora, as well as how they impact their home countries. During 2012–2016, I conducted the first systemic study of the modern wave of Ukrainian migration to Australia that had commenced since the 1990s (Oleinikova, 2020) and analysed how their lives have been shaped by structural factors (e.g. the crisis in Ukraine, the Australian migration system) and individual agency (e.g. personal values, needs, aims) before, during and after migration.

The Australian Ukrainian community traces its foundation to the arrival of post-World War II refugees from war-torn Europe. These refugees were termed 'Displaced Persons' and began arriving in 1948. Prior to 1948, only a small number had arrived and most of these were not nationally aware individuals. The most notable of these was Nicolai Miklouho-Maclay, an ethnographer and naturalist who visited Australia in 1878 and was responsible for the building of Australia's first biological field station at Watsons Bay in New South Wales (Serbin, 2006). Today, there is an active Ukrainian community of about 40,000 people, predominantly living in Melbourne and Sydney (Oleinikova, 2020). There are also Ukrainian centres in Geelong, Brisbane, Perth, Adelaide and Canberra. Smaller centres exist in Queanbeyan, Hobart, Newcastle, Moe, Albury-Wodonga and Northam.

In 2020–2021, I collected 20 semi-structured in-depth interviews with Ukrainians in Sydney and Melbourne. I talked to those community members who are active members of the Ukrainian diaspora, who have strong Ukrainian identity (as defined by themselves) and who became actively involved in Ukraine's democratisation efforts following the 2013–2014 Euromaidan protests. Participants were recruited through passive snowballing sampling, avoiding direct contact with potential respondents and recruiting through radio announcements, newspaper advertisements and introductions through friends and community. All respondents were assigned pseudonyms to maintain their confidentiality. The interviews were conducted in various settings: at the participants' residences, in offices, canteens, and sometimes even in bars and city parks. All participants were very open and willing to share their stories to assist in the research. On average, the interviews lasted for one-and-a-half to two hours.

The key roles of Ukrainian diasporas in post-Euromaidan Ukraine include being guardians of the democratic process, the transition to best democratic practices and raising political support for Ukraine in their countries of residence (Mulford, 2016). It can be noticed that the post-Euromaidan Ukrainian diaspora in Australia evolved together with Ukraine. A similar research conducted on post-Euromaidan diaspora organisations in Germany and Poland shows that many new Ukrainians abroad, unlike previous waves of diaspora, do not call themselves diaspora; however, they are widely engaged in many actions supporting Ukrainian transition to democracy and have assisted during the war in Donbass (Melnyk et al., 2016, p. 6). The research into the Ukrainian diaspora in Australia suggests that there was a substantial activation of the Australian Ukrainian diaspora after Euromaidan and the diaspora has been taking different roles in democratisation efforts in Ukraine.

By adopting the methods of semi-structured interview and online observation with 20 participants from Sydney and Melbourne in Australia, this section discusses three key findings. Firstly, it was found that social media technology is becoming a primary tool for establishing, maintaining and re-establishing social connections among diasporic Ukrainian communities, and the diasporic Ukrainians in Australia have their preference for adopting a specific social media platform, being heavy Facebook users. Secondly, there are several active diasporic organisations in Australia that have conducted a range of activities across the three areas of support—advocacy, financial support, and global awareness. Thirdly, there are three main challenges the Ukrainian diaspora is facing while trying to support democratisation in Ukraine—(1) lack of interest and support from the Ukrainian government; (2) the law on dual citizenship; and (3) complicated voting procedures.

Social media breathed new life into the cross-border connection between diasporas and their countries of origin (Fedyuk, 2019), placing diasporas and nation-states beyond the territorial dimension. In the same way social media played a role during Euromaidan (Onuch, 2015), they remained a great mechanism for Ukrainian diasporas to connect and communicate worldwide after Euromaidan (Melnyk et al., 2016). Social media became a ready-made tool to mobilise existing forms of networks and foster new ones, highlighting the pivotal role of social media in keeping dispersed Ukrainians informed of events unfolding on the ground. Facebook Euromaidan support groups in different countries evolved into new forums of scientific and political discussions about Ukraine's developments. They gave a chance to millions of Ukrainians and foreigners to stay informed about democratisation processes in Ukraine. Such global exchange of information plays an important role in a country's path to democracy.

The Ukrainian diaspora in Australia, being in the most distant geographical location from Ukraine, has significantly benefitted from the accelerated growth of social media usage on the continent. Facebook is Australia's third highest trafficked site after Google and YouTube (Alexa, 2021). 66%, or 16 million, Australians are monthly active Facebook users (Genroe, 2021). It was not a surprise to observe and also hear from respondents that 'Facebook is the number one platform for connection to Ukraine and the main platform that helps to coordinate events and run fundraisers' (Lesya, member of Sydney community). Each Ukrainian organisation in Australia has an active Facebook page; the most active Facebook groups include—Ukrainians in Sydney/Українці у Сіднеї!; Ukrainians in Australia; Aussie Ukrainians/АУ; Ukrainians of Diaspora.

There are several Ukrainian organisations in Australia that serve as a great visualisation of the active role the Ukrainian diaspora has been playing in Ukraine's democratisation efforts after Euromaidan. The biggest Ukraine's diasporic organisation in Australia is the Australian Federation of Ukrainian Organisations (AFUO). It is a peak body for 22 community organisations throughout Australia, such as churches, state community organisations, youth and women's organisations, and credit co-operative movements, as well as educational, returned service, language and other organisations. As such, it is widely regarded as the 'spokesbody' on matters concerning relationships within the Ukrainian community, between Australia and Ukraine. Our organisation is comprised of executive members who represent key facets of community life in Australia. The Australian Federation of Ukrainian Organisations is a member of the Ukrainian World Congress, the apex body for Ukrainian organisations in the diasporas; it works to promote a positive image of the Australian Ukrainian community, encouraging its members to maintain religion, language, culture and heritage whilst being active members in the broader Australian community.

AFUO's core initiative that is an 'ongoing success' (Marta, member of the Ukrainian community in Melbourne) is the Ukraine Crisis Appeal (UCA). UCA is a collaboration between the Australian Federation of Ukrainian Organisations (AFUO), Rotary Australia World Community Service (RAWCS) and Caritas Ukraine and it is the largest Australian tax-deductible fundraising effort for Ukraine. It has been operating since 2015 and runs two programmes—(1) Veteran Program, and (2)

Occupational Therapy (OT) Training. The Veteran Program aims to improve the living conditions of veterans and their families who were impacted by the Russian-Ukrainian war. Many of these veterans who are being assisted were injured and suffered disability as a result. With the aim of a holistic care programme, an in-depth assessment was completed by Caritas Ukraine qualified case workers to identify the specific needs of each of the veterans. These needs would not otherwise have been fulfilled due to financial circumstances and ineligibility for support from the state, as well as the lack of specialised treatment in their cities or villages. The project has succeeded in providing support and rehabilitation to 24 Veterans, with 52 of their family members as indirect beneficiaries, including 36 children. The OT Training Program is a new programme that will train hundreds of people to provide world class therapy and care to thousands of Ukrainians. The need for world class, evidence-based rehabilitation techniques to be utilised by Ukrainian health care professionals has existed for many years, however it has never been more needed than now, when many returning injured soldiers from the war in the east of the country have not been receiving adequate rehabilitation. Following the development of the Ukrainian Society of Ergotherapists and the first Training Program for OT Educators with World Federation of Occupational Therapists (WFOT) in 2018, several universities are working towards the development of Masters and Bachelor degree-level Occupational Therapy courses. Results of this initiative are yet to be seen.

Along with financial support through diasporic organisations, the individual financial support from Ukrainians abroad serves as an important mechanism for supporting economic and democratic developments inside the country. After Euromaidan, with the deterioration of the economic situation due to the war in Donbass, many Ukrainians had to emigrate. According to the Ukrainian Foreign Minister, Pavlo Klimkin, one million Ukrainians left the country in 2017. Some Ukrainians travel for work and later come back to Ukraine, while others move away for good. The role of both groups in the democratisation of Ukraine is important. Coming back to Ukraine with money earned abroad, Ukrainians can start new businesses and build sustainable households in the country. The ones who stayed away longer in foreign countries sent money home while they were abroad. It is wise to notice that money coming from Ukrainians abroad has been the largest foreign investment into Ukraine for years. According to estimates, Ukrainians abroad sent 11 billion dollars to Ukraine in 2018, which is five times more than direct foreign investments made during the previous five years (Oleinikova, 2019). The Ukrainian Government does not facilitate the growth of remittances from overseas, rather it has been actively discussed recently that the Ministry of Finance has strengthened its control over the taxation of funds transferred from abroad to individuals who are resident in Ukraine. In most cases, the discussion is around the money transfers to the homeland by so-called guest workers and, less often, about receiving payments under civil law contracts, inheritances, dividends or royalties.

Based on the collected data, there are three main challenges Ukrainian diasporas are facing while trying to support democratisation in Ukraine—(1) lack of interest and support from the Ukrainian government; (2) the law on dual citizenship; and (3) complicated voting procedures.

> We are patriots. We work on voluntary basis; give all our energy and all our free time to the initiatives that we know do good in Ukraine. Ukrainian government could involve us more; they could also establish a network of unofficial Ukrainian 'ambassadors', who will facilitate Ukrainian official diplomacy and improve external relations of the country. There is much more that the government could have done so far. (Bohdan, member of a Ukrainian organisation in Sydney)

The ability of a diaspora to cooperate with its country of origin is based on its ability to connect to this country (Carment & Sadjed, 2017, p. 5). It is not always easy to keep the connection (even despite the super power of social networks) and the Ukrainian Government does not facilitate the connection of Ukrainian diasporas to their country of origin. Although, diasporas have played a crucial role in Ukraine's democratisation, it is often neglected by the Ukrainian State (Malko, 2018). There is no special government body dealing with diasporas, although there were attempts to create one. Consequently, it is difficult for Ukrainians in emigration to fight for their rights, especially in the extreme cases of abuse from foreign employers. Furthermore, it is not easy for Ukrainians from diaspora to come back to Ukraine for work and study; there were attempts to introduce special quotas at universities, but they did not work well (Malko, 2018). When the Ukrainian Government wanted to introduce the law against dual citizens, thus taking Ukrainian citizenship away from the diasporas, foreign leaders and the Ukrainian diasporas protested widely (Moskalu, 2018) and the law was rejected. Such government actions can result in Ukraine's loss of its precious diasporic resource of 10–15 million Ukrainians (Malko, 2018).

Another challenge in the relations between the Ukrainian diasporas and the Ukrainian State is their participation in state elections. For years, Ukrainian politicians were not considering the need to engage diasporas in their political programmes. Voting procedures abroad remain complicated (voting only in a capital city, issues with registration, the need to have a long-term residence permit), which restrains many Ukrainian diasporas from taking part in elections. However, with more Ukrainians moving abroad and more of them becoming active participants in Ukraine's internal affairs after Euromaidan, Ukrainian politicians should rethink their approach to attracting the diasporas to take part in elections. When these people are denied closer and easier cooperation with Ukraine, it becomes challenging to transfer their valuable foreign experience and play their active role in democratisation in Ukraine.

> It would make perfect sense if there were some funding opportunities in Western Countries for Ukrainian diasporas. For example, while Ukrainian diaspora in the EU works for Ukraine's integration with the EU by accepting its values of democracy and human rights, the EU could develop new programs of support with better promotion and easier application mechanisms. Same can be replicated in Australia. (Antonina, member of a Ukrainian organisation in Sydney)

Conclusion

The case of Ukraine, with its high coefficient of dispersal and diaspora, teaches us empirically and theoretically to think of diaspora and democracy as post-territorial phenomena, because Ukraine's democratic development has happened not just inside the country but also from abroad (through its diasporas) and has entailed confronting questions about Ukraine's position in the European region, challenging the idea that an independent Ukraine must be a territorially bound and nationally exclusivist entity (Oleinikova, 2019). Similar to other cases discussed in this book, the case of Ukraine shows us that territory matters but so also does connectivity between diasporas and Ukraine, where the functioning of the dispersed communities has made promising strides over the last decade, playing an important role in the emergence of the Euromaidan protests 2013/2014 and continuing to remain vibrant since. Furthermore, diasporas are no longer limited in media consumption to the boundaries of the host nation. In fact, it has now extended beyond merely the reception of news to that of active involvement in discourses, and in turn democratic participation, thus even influencing internal politics within home countries. Social media has given diasporas more power than they previously had, and it would be interesting to see how this develops in the future within a post-territorial framework. Yet based on how recent developments have worked out, it seems that the connection between diasporas and their homelands will only increase and develop in different forms, cultivating the opportunities that communication technologies have to offer them.

REFERENCES

Ahmadov, A. K., & Sasse, G. (2016). A Voice Despite Exit: The Role of Assimilation, Emigrant Networks, and Destination in Emigrants' Transnational Political Engagement. *Comparative Political Studies, 49*(1), 78–114.

Alexa. (2021). https://www.alexa.com/topsites/countries/AU

Anderson, B. (1998). *The Spectre of Comparisons: Nationalism, Southeast Asia and the World*. Verso.

Bayeh, J. (2019). Diasporic Visions of Democracy and Territory. In O. Oleinikova & J. Bayeh (Eds.), *Democracy, Diaspora, Territory* (pp. 43–55). Routledge.

Benhabib, S. (1998). Democracy and Identity: In Search of the Civic Polity. *Philosophy and Social Criticism, 44*(2–3), 86–100.

Braziel, J., & Mannur, A. (2003). Nation, Migration, Globalization: Points of Contention in Diaspora Studies. In J. E. Braziel & A. Mannur (Eds.), *Theorizing Diaspora: A Reader* (pp. 1–22). Blackwell Publishers.

Brubaker, R. (2009). *Citizenship and Nationhood in France and Germany*. Harvard University Press.

Carment, D., & Sadjed, A. (2017). Introduction: Coming to Terms with Diaspora Cooperation. In D. Carment & A. Sadjed (Eds.), *Diaspora as Cultures of Cooperation* (pp. 1–26). Springer International Publishing.

Chumak, Y. (1991). *Memories of Lyandek*. Ukrainska Knyzhka.

Cohen, R. (1997). *Global Diasporas*. UCL Press.

Cohen, R. (2008). *Global Diasporas: An Introduction*. Routledge.

Fedyuk, O. (2019). The Digital Power of Ukrainians Abroad: Social Media Activism and Political Participation. In O. Oleinikova & J. Bayeh (Eds.), *Democracy, Diaspora, Territory* (pp. 145–162). Routledge.

Gamlen, A. (2019). *Human Geopolitics: States, Emigrants, and the Rise of Diaspora Institutions*. Oxford University Press.

Genroe. (2021). Social Media Statistics for Australia. https://www.genroe.com/blog/social-media-statistics-australia/13492

Hepp, A., & Couldry, N. (2009). What Should Comparative Media Research Be Comparing? Towards a Transcultural Approach to 'Media Cultures'. In D. K. Thussu (Ed.), *Internationalizing Media Studies* (pp. 32–48). Routledge.

James, C. L. R. (2013). *Beyond a Boundary*. Duke University Press.

Keane, J. (2009). *The Life and Death of Democracy*. Simon and Schuster.

Keane, J. (2018). *Power and Humility: The Future of Monitory Democracy*. Cambridge University Press.

Kinowska, Z., & Pakulski, J. (2018). Polish Migrants and Organizations in Australia. *Cosmopolitan Civil Societies: An Interdisciplinary Journal, 10*(2), 33–45.

Maier, C. S. (2016). *Once Within Borders: Territories of Power, Wealth, and Belonging since 1500*. Harvard University Press.

Malko, R. (2018). Ukrainska Diaspora: Ne Rozghubyty Sebe (In Ukrainian. Ukrainian Diaspora: Not to Lose Itself). *Tyzhden*. Retrieved January 26, 2019, from https://tyzhden.ua/Politics/218965

Massey, D. S., Arango, J., Hugo, G., Kouaouci, A., Pellegrino, A., & Taylor, J. E. (1994). An Evaluation of International Migration Theory: The North American Case. *Population and Development Review, 20*(4), 699–751.

Melnyk, L., Patalong, M., Plottka, J., & Steinberg, R. (2016). *How the Ukrainian Diasporic Community in Germany Contributes to EU's Policy in Its Home Country*. IEP Policy Paper on Eastern Europe and Central Asia. Institut für Europäische Politik, (9), 13–21.

Merkel, W. (2014). Is There a Crisis of Democracy? *Democratic Theory, 1*(2), 11–25.

Miller, D. (2016). Boundaries, Democracy, and Territory. *The American Journal of Jurisprudence, 61*(1), 33–49.

Mishra, S. (2006). *Diaspora Criticism*. Edinburgh University Press.

Moskalu, V. (2018). Violeta Moskalu: Bill Aims to Strip Ukrainians Living Abroad of Citizenship. *KyivPost*. Retrieved February 2, 2019, from https://www.kyivpost.com/article/opinion/op-ed/violeta-moskalu-bill-aims-strip-ukrainians-living-abroad-citizenship.html

Mulford, J. P. (2016). Non-State Actors in the Russo-Ukrainian War. *Connections, 15*(2), 89–107.

Nine, C. (2012). Compromise, Democracy and Territory. *Irish Journal of Sociology, 20*(2), 91–110.

Oleinikova, O. (2016). Moving Out of Their Places: Migration into Australia. *Journal of National Taras Shevchenko University of Kyiv: Sociology, 1,* 54–58.

Oleinikova, O. (2017). Moving Out of 'Their Places': 1991–2016 Migration of Ukrainians to Australia. In A. Pikulicka-Wilczewska & G. Uehling (Eds.),

Migration and the Ukraine Crisis: A Two-Country Perspective, an E-IR Edited Collection.

Oleinikova, O. (2019). Democratic Transition Research: From Western to Post-Soviet East European Scholarship. *East/West: Journal of Ukrainian Studies, 6*(1), 147–167.

Oleinikova, O. (2020). *Life Strategies of Migrants from Crisis Regimes: Achiever or Survivor*. Palgrave Macmillan.

Oleinikova, O., & Bayeh, J. (2019). *Democracy, Diaspora, Territory: Europe and Cross-Border Politics*. Routledge.

Onuch, O. (2015). EuroMaidan Protests in Ukraine: Social Media Versus Social Networks. *Problems of Post-Communism, 62*(4), 217–235.

Quayson, A., & Daswani, G. (Eds.). (2013). *A companion to diaspora and transnationalism*. John Wiley & Sons.

Ryazantsev, S. V. (2014). The Lingual Integration of Migrants in Russia: Declarations and Realities. *Life Science Journal, 11*(8s), 139–143.

Safran, W. (1991). Diasporas in modern societies: Myths of homeland and return. *Diaspora: A Journal of Transnational Studies, 1*(1), 83–99.

Satzewich, V. (2002). *The Ukrainian Diaspora*. Routledge.

Schmitt, C. (1988). *The Crisis of Parliamentary Democracy*. MIT Press.

Serbin, S. (2006). Ukrainians in Australia. *Ukrainian Studies, 2*, 304–313.

Shuval, J. T. (2000). Diaspora Migration: Definitional Ambiguities and a Theoretical Paradigm. *International Migration, 38*(5), 41–56.

Team, V., Markovic, M., & Manderson, L. (2007). Family Caregivers: Russian-Speaking Australian Women's Access to Welfare Support. *Health & Social Care in the Community, 15*(5), 397–406.

Therborn, G. (2013). Why and How Place Matters. In R. E. Goodin & C. Tilly (Eds.), *The Oxford Handbook of Contextual Political Analysis* (pp. 509–533). Oxford University Press.

Tölölyan, K. (1991). The Nation-State and Its Others: In Lieu of a Preface. *Diaspora: A Journal of Transnational Studies, 1*(1), 3–7.

Zielonka, J. (2017). The Remaking of the EU's Borders and the Images of European Architecture. *Journal of European Integration, 39*(5), 641–656.

CHAPTER 10

Diaspora Policy: A Missing Plank in Australia's Multicultural Policy Portfolio

Melissa Phillips

INTRODUCTION

Governments attend to the needs of diasporas and diaspora communities in varied ways including through structured policies, provision of funding, and programmes, which in turn enable the development of networks and a thriving environment for the development of diasporas. Ensuring responsive and effective arrangements for diaspora members resident in Australia on either a temporary or a permanent basis, and for Australian nationals living overseas, is an area of public policy that has been consistently recommended by leading scholars and in multiple Parliamentary Inquiries over many decades. Measures such as policies, funding and targeted programmes would also offer a systematic and predictable approach to diaspora management across all levels of government. However, there has been a general reluctance to put in place permanent systems at federal, state or local levels to coordinate or manage diaspora affairs, as has been done in many other contexts including in countries that rely on

M. Phillips (✉)
Western Sydney University, Penrith, NSW, Australia
e-mail: melissa.phillips@westernsydney.edu.au

© The Author(s), under exclusive license to Springer Nature Switzerland AG 2022
M. Phillips, L. Olliff (eds.), *Understanding Diaspora Development,*
https://doi.org/10.1007/978-3-030-97866-2_10

207

immigration, for instance Canada and the USA, as well as in countries of sizeable out-migration, such as India and the Philippines. This chapter considers the implications of this inaction and queries the logic of lauding Australia as a highly diverse multicultural nation when it is unable to attend to the needs of diasporas beyond ad hoc funding. The impacts of keeping diaspora at arm's length have become more pronounced during the Covid-19 pandemic and times of national attention on critical matters, such as Australia's relationship with China.

This chapter utilises a secondary data analysis methodological approach and draws extensively from a wide range of sources, including government statistics, policy documents and reports from relevant government inquiries and key inter-governmental agencies. It starts by setting out what is understood from the literature as to how diaspora development can be fostered through policy settings and the provision of platforms and spaces for meaningful engagement. As a country that relies heavily on immigration, Australia has developed numerous policies and programmes to address the needs of migrant and refugee communities to determine the size and composition of the immigration programme itself as well as efforts to support people to settle in the country. Many migrant and refugee communities go on to form associations that are involved in diaspora activities, as this edited collection highlights and as has been acknowledged in the most recent 2020 Senate Inquiry. In comparison with migration policy, the diaspora policy domain in Australia is less regulated and is characterised by an uncoordinated and ad hoc approach. There have also been moments of focus on the significant rates of out-migration of its nationals, but what remains is an absence of strategic governance of diasporas despite the potential areas for quick wins in the future to capitalise on the proven strength and reach of diaspora organisations. This chapter reviews these critical milestones and maps current institutional arrangements for handling diaspora affairs. The chapter then goes on to offer some international comparisons to show how other countries have formulated their responses to diasporas, and it notes some key programmes established by multilateral entities, such as the World Bank. It argues that for Australia to have a greater foreign policy impact, diaspora organisations should be recognised as key assets and be consulted on a more systematic basis.

Engagement and Policy Arrangements: Necessary Precursors for Diaspora Development

Diaspora engagement can be fostered through a number of mechanisms including policies that Gamlen cautions 'should not necessarily be seen as part of a unitary, coordinated state strategy. Rather, they form a constellation of institutional and legislative arrangements and programmes that come into being at different times, for different reasons, and operate across different timescales' (2006, p. 4). Three main forms of diaspora engagement are top-down engagement initiatives (consultation, funding etc.), bottom-up approaches led by diaspora communities and organisations seeking spaces for inclusion themselves, and thirdly, iterative approaches that emerge from informal networks and collaboration (Ong'ayo, 2016, p. 15). All of these approaches to engagement are predicated on migration policies that offer integration into countries of residence as well as participation in countries of origin (Faist, 2000; Gamlen, 2006). In this way, diaspora communities can be truly transnational in the spaces they participate in and influence (see e.g. Chap. 2). Drawing on the work of Faist, Ong'ayo proposes four political opportunity structures in the countries of destination that are relevant to this chapter as they support diaspora engagement across a range of geographical locations and can further a number of foreign policy, development and migration goals. The first political opportunity structure is a policy environment that is conducive to the participation of non-state actors in policy processes; followed by the type of policies that target migrant involvement; then the availability of resources, subsidies or activities in policy priority fields; and finally, local networks (Ong'ayo, 2016, pp. 23–24). All of these are necessary precursors for an enabling policy environment, which is what many diaspora communities and other stakeholders have continually identified as necessary for the Australian context. The next part of this chapter evaluates the presence and effectiveness of these four planks or structures in the current Australian policy landscape and analyses how emerging gaps can be filled, drawing on best practice in other sites.

Diaspora Policy—A Missing Plank in Australia's Multicultural Policy Portfolio

Australia contributes to diaspora-formation in two distinct ways. The first is through Australians departing the country to work, travel or migrate overseas in a pattern that has a long history and is often seen as a rite of passage for younger Australians, many of whom go on to remain overseas for work, personal reasons or to stay in a country where they may have family links. This estimated one million Australians includes highly skilled professionals and return migrants, as well as young Australians working and travelling overseas (Tan et al., 2021). As such, they are members of a highly diverse diaspora community who may have varying needs over the duration of their time as residents outside the country. The second way is that through Australia's temporary and permanent skilled migration programme, as well as a sizeable proportion of international students coming to study in the country, there are large groups of migrants residing in Australia who can be defined as diaspora community members. Temporary and permanent migrants (hereafter migrants) are usually young, skilled and highly mobile individuals and families, who are encouraged to settle in Australia to study and work. They are also relied upon by industry as employees of choice both in sectors facing skills shortages, and to work in locations that may find it harder to attract skilled workers, such as in regional and rural areas. Migration policy settings at the federal level, such as temporary skilled and regional sponsored visas, have been specifically designed to attract migrants to Australia and, while not all would identify as diaspora members, they would often have needs similar to those of other diaspora communities during their time of residence in Australia. Each of these specific categories of diaspora groups will be discussed next.

An estimated one million Australians abroad, comprising what Hugo terms a 'contemporary diaspora', have been overlooked in population studies and to a certain extent have not received wide policy attention or visibility within the migration portfolio (Hugo, 2006, p. 110). The 2020 Covid-19 pandemic has brought into sharp relief the number of Australians living overseas who maintain links with Australia and are an underutilised resource (They still call Australia home: Inquiry into Australian Expatriates, 2005).[1] It has also presented a situation where Australian expatriates are often in dire need of services such as consular assistance and support that they may not be able to access readily. Tan et al. (2021) have suggested that pre-existing conceptions of expatriate diaspora as highly skilled, young professionals are outdated, driven in part by the fact that data is lacking as to where Australians reside overseas and what activities they are engaged in. Despite substantive evidence, there remains a perception that the Australian expatriate diaspora represent a source of human capital that

[1] https://advance.org/.

could drive innovation and foster greater international collaboration (PricewaterhouseCoopers & Advance, 2018). This has largely been driven by business which has identified specific ways in which diaspora skills can be harnessed to capitalise on growing markets in Asia, for example (PricewaterhouseCoopers & Advance, 2018).

Such a phenomenon is what is commonly referred to as people-to-people links, whereby personal links are seen as a crucial factor for developing positive international relations (Phillips, 2013). Countries with large diaspora communities, such as India and the Philippines, tend to understand better the need to harness diaspora skills, networks and financial resources by establishing dedicated government ministries, offering dual citizenship and facilitating the transfer of funds (Ragazzi, 2014). Australia remains at a nascent stage of harnessing its own diaspora; the lack of a focused policy framework targeting this so-called global community of Australians group perpetuates the paucity of information as to their size, role and potential. While groups such as Advance.org provide a professional network for overseas Australians they cannot be a substitute for government and do not have a mandated role to play at times of national emergencies, for instance. A call made in the 2005 Senate Inquiry into Australian Expatriates for the 'the establishment of a policy unit within the Department of Foreign Affairs and Trade, to facilitate the coordination of policies relating to Australian expatriates' remains a critical gap in the policy landscape for the management of Australia's diaspora (p. 123) that mirrors a similar lack of attention to diaspora groups resident in Australia. The situation of this latter group will be discussed next.

Policies Targeting Diaspora Communities

As the Introduction notes, Australia is a country of immense cultural diversity, comprising migrants and refugees who come to the country on a temporary and permanent basis. The Australian Human Rights Commission (AHRC) submission to the DFAT Inquiry states that, with 49% of the Australian population either born overseas or having a parent born overseas, there is 'a large proportion of Australian citizens [that] could be considered 'diaspora' communities in Australia' (AHRC, 2020, p. 3). However, not every Australian born overseas or with migrant ancestry will necessarily identify as being part of a diaspora, or multiple diaspora communities, and so the AHRC also calls for a clearer definition of diaspora to aid policy development and a common understanding of this phenomenon in Australia. Diasporas can include groups who have settled in Australia over a long period of time as well as newer, more recently arrived migrants and refugees. Given the immense heterogeneity of diasporas based on country of origin, age, gender, ethnicity and languages spoken, it is more accurate to refer to diaspora communities in the Australian context, although most government departments tend to refer to culturally and linguistically diverse (CALD) communities, which would include diaspora communities as a subset of this group. Given the relatively scant attention paid to diaspora communities as a discrete category of Australia's CALD population, it necessary to hone in on the policy arrangements that might address diaspora concerns and needs in order to understand better how they are perceived as subjects for policy attention.

Diaspora policy rarely explicitly features in discussions of multiculturalism, migration or foreign policy, which are the three key federal government portfolios with which it intersects. In many ways, this invisibility of diaspora policy is indicative of a wider invisibility about diaspora in Australia, which has been detailed above. This is despite the fact that Australia's cultural diversity is lauded as an asset in countless policy statements, such as the 2018 multicultural policy statement (Home Affairs, 2018). While federal responsibility for multicultural affairs rests with the Department of Home Affairs (hereafter Home Affairs), which in turn engages with diaspora communities through peak bodies and various networks, the Department of Foreign Affairs (DFAT) has a commitment to working with diaspora communities to promote Australia abroad and to support its foreign policy objectives, with a particular emphasis on diaspora communities support for the government's development assistance programme (2017 Foreign Policy White Paper). Another government agency that has a relationship with diaspora communities is the Australian Security Intelligence Organisation (ASIO) which focuses on 'threat assessments, strategic analysis, border integrity, special events, counter-espionage and foreign interference and counter-terrorism matters, as well as providing community-based situational awareness' (Submission to Senate Inquiry). A number of peak groups, such as the Refugee Council of Australia, Settlement Council of Australia, Multicultural Youth Advocacy Network, Australian Human Rights Commission, and the Federation of Ethnic Communities' Councils, provided submissions to the Senate Inquiry highlighting the number of groups that have a focus on diaspora within their scope or mandate. This responds to a point noted earlier about the value in having a constellation of available arrangements to assist diaspora at different points in time, notwithstanding the merits of clearly outlining the inter-relationships between different actors and specific areas of policy focus. Returning to the framework for diaspora engagement, alongside established agencies and peak groups there must be an availability of resources that diaspora communities can readily access to fund their initiatives. This aspect is discussed next.

FINANCING FOR DIASPORA ENGAGEMENT

As will be discussed later, appropriate funding for diaspora activities and supporting organisations is a necessary prerequisite that complements the provision of an enabling policy environment. Both DFAT and Home Affairs have key remits on diaspora communities; in the most recent Senate Inquiry, Home Affairs identified its specific interests in diaspora communities as being related to social cohesion, community safety and social, economic and civic participation, while DFAT singled out support to diaspora community associations as also communication and partnership as being most relevant to its work. Home Affairs utilises its network of community liaison officers and funds community organisations through Fostering Integration Grants as part of A$62.8 million in funding for social cohesion. It also works through the Australian Multicultural Council and the Refugee and Migrant Services Advisory Council, as well as other peak bodies noted above. DFAT provides specific funding to diaspora bodies and community groups through an International Relations Grant Program allocated across seven Foundations, Councils and Institutes (FCIs), as well as funding projects based in diaspora communities and a friendship grants scheme. Through these schemes and engagement with peak bodies, it seeks to engage with diaspora communities on matters of common interest, including development and humanitarian issues.

Some submissions to the Senate Inquiry identified smaller funding needs specific to diaspora communities, such as training for diaspora professionals to volunteer in their countries of origin, that may be overlooked in these larger grants, especially those focused on domestic issues related to social cohesion (see e.g. Advisory Group on Australia-Africa Relations (AGAAR) Submission). Other submissions highlighted that smaller diaspora community organisations often lacked governance and administrative capacity to apply for grants competitively. This relates to the fourth enabler of diaspora engagement, which is the presence of local networks. While groups such as the now defunct Diaspora Action Australia (DAA)

214   M. PHILLIPS

have played a coordination role to the extent permitted by resources, there is no peak coordination body for diaspora communities in Australia that can facilitate the development of local networks. Such an entity would also serve as a focal point for government and could also support diaspora development initiatives utilising existing models, some of which are described later in this chapter. As DAA's submission concluded, 'the scarce funding to diaspora support organisations [...] also makes it difficult to upskill, build capacity and strengthen the capabilities of diaspora to play their best role' (DAA, 2020). Until the question of adequate funding, specifically targeting diaspora communities alongside support for coordination and the building of local networks is resolved, many diaspora communities, especially from new and emerging communities, will unfortunately struggle to realise their goals. This is a feature raised in the Senate Inquiry that also related to a whole-of-government policy approach.

With ninety submissions made to the Senate Inquiry that raised a wide range of issues related to diaspora communities, the Inquiry has offered a window into the immense capacity within Australia's diaspora communities, the issues they face and where they sought greater support from the Australian Government. However, despite the need for a whole-of-government policy on diaspora being raised by some witnesses and mentioned in submissions, this was not reflected in the final recommendations of the report. Instead, the recommendations of the Inquiry stopped short of proposing any systemic changes at policy level and focused instead on aspects such as the need to have multicultural policy statements reinforce the recognition and celebration of the contribution of diaspora communities to Australia (Recommendation 1), and that DFAT develop an internal policy on diaspora community consultation (Recommendation 15). In order to understand what policy arrangements may foster diaspora engagement across all elements of funding, coordination, building of networks and policy development, it is useful to scope the situation in similar countries of immigration.

How have Similarly Diverse Multicultural Countries Dealt with Diaspora Engagement

The focus of this section are the settings for diaspora engagement (broad policy environment, diaspora-focused policies, availability of resources, and local networks) in countries with similar conditions as Australia and how they are being utilised to manage the needs of multiple diaspora communities; this is sometimes referred to as host-state foreign policy (Singh, 2012). Most research on diaspora policy is from the perspective of diaspora-producing countries and the policies they implement for their populations abroad. This is because, as Ragazzi observes, 'sending states are increasingly using their diaspora as a multiplier for foreign policy' (2014, p. 76), which includes lobbying for improvements in countries of origin (Carment & Calleja, 2017). Countries with high levels of emigration have a number of tangible mechanisms to manage relationships with their diaspora. These encompass a wide spectrum of initiatives, from consular services within Ministries of Foreign Affairs, responsibilities within domestic ministries (for instance the Philippines' Overseas Workers Welfare Administration sits in the Ministry of Labour), inter-ministerial agencies or stand-alone ministries (Ragazzi, 2014). Yet Ragazzi (2014) also found that states with high GDPs do not tend to focus on diplomatic efforts with diaspora, despite the fact that diaspora communities themselves express a desire for systematic policy platforms and opportunities for developing strategic alliances. This aligns with the situation in Australia, as outlined in this chapter. The case studies that follow are examples taken from other sites that can inform the Australian context in order to enhance diaspora engagement.

Canada offers a useful comparison to Australia as a country of immigration with a stated commitment to multiculturalism. A policy review on the Canadian diaspora context completed in 2011 highlighted the gaps in diaspora policy and the need to develop relationships further between diaspora communities and policy makers (Olyan & Smith, 2011). It suggested that the growing presence of diaspora communities in Canada, the number of Canadians living abroad, and the volume of remittances being sent out from the country warranted a 'comprehensive diaspora policy … to address three overarching objectives: improving Canada's international standing and promoting Canadian interests, facilitating transfers of knowledge between diaspora groups and the Canadian government, and systematically addressing the concerns of diaspora groups' (p. 2). In 2013, when the Canadian International Development Agency merged with Foreign Affairs and International Trade Canada to become the Department of Foreign Affairs, Trade and Development (DFATD, known as Global Affairs Canada) its Departmental Plan made scant reference to diaspora, with the exception of consultation with them on human rights issues of concern (Global Affairs Canada, 2021). However, there are reference groups at local level, such as the Ontario Council for International

216   M. PHILLIPS

Development Diaspora Engagement Networking Group that could be replicated in contexts such as Australia.[2]

European actors have invested in similar consultative mechanisms, such as an Africa-Europe Diaspora Development Platform (ADEPT). Others use existing platforms, such as the Global Forum for Migration and Development (GFMD), to engage with diasporas and use their expertise to inform policy debates. The Swiss Development Cooperation (SDC) has a Global Programme Migration and Development (GPMD) that has three areas of work targeting diasporas. These are improving conditions in countries of origin to facilitate diaspora as agents for development, supporting migrant organisations to improve organisational skills for development cooperation and project based cooperation. SDC has also implemented a Swiss Civil Society Organizations Platform on Migration and Development, which brings together government officials, civil society organisations (CSOs) and the private sector with a focus on diaspora for development aligned with the 2030 Agenda for Sustainable Development.[3] At a country level, some non-government organisations (NGOs) also have programmatic areas of work specifically focused on diaspora. For instance, the DAA Senate Inquiry submission highlighted the Diaspora Emergency Action and Coordination (DEMAC), an initiative aimed to improve diaspora emergency response capacity and coordination with the humanitarian system funded by the European Civil Protection and Humanitarian Aid Operations (ECHO) and implemented by the Danish Refugee Council, AFFORD-UK, and the Berghof Foundation. The Danish Refugee Council is also a co-founder of DiaGram, a network of organisations across Europe that supports diaspora engagement in country of origin and has programmes for diaspora business entrepreneurs and small grants for diaspora organisations.[4] One of the most evident ways in which diaspora engagement can happen is through policy consultation and volunteer programmes, as will be discussed next.

Targeted approaches towards specific diasporas can realise policy and development benefits, as Chap. 4 highlights. For example, in the United States of America, there have been consultations held with Darfurian diaspora that fed into wider engagement with diaspora in other countries on issues related to conflict in Darfur, through groups such as the United

[2] https://www.ocic.on.ca/what-we-do/multi-sectoral-dialogue/diaspora/.
[3] https://www.eda.admin.ch/deza/en/home/themes-sdc/migration/diaspora-migrant-communities.html.
[4] https://drc.ngo/our-work/what-we-do/civil-society-engagement-cse/diaspora/.

States Institute for Peace (USIP) (Hayward, 2008). USIP has also convened South Sudanese leaders and advocates to address issues such as online hate speech. Through such forums, diaspora are able to liaise with key government representatives and offer a coordinated approach to advocacy and policy development. Going beyond mobilising diaspora for peace through consultation and engagement, there are a number of programmes that actively support diaspora volunteers to return to their countries of origin. UN-led endeavours include a United Nations Development Programme (UNDP) project called Transfer of Knowledge through Expatriate Nationals (TOKTEN), and the International Organization for Migration (IOM) Temporary Return of Qualified Nationals (TRQN). A review of diaspora volunteer programmes found that 'there is little doubt that diasporas constitute a significant pool from which to draw volunteer manpower and talent for international development agencies' (Terrazas, 2010, p. 35). It goes on to recommend consideration of mainstream volunteering programmes recruiting diasporas, utilising organisations with links to diaspora communities, and where appropriate, focusing on highly skilled diaspora volunteers who can support specific projects.

To implement successfully the projects noted above, there needs to be a clear understanding of who constitutes the diaspora—their size, attributes, skills and experience. This is a finding that IOM and the Migration Policy Institute (MPI) have also reiterated as being important for countries of destination, to know their diasporas through census and survey data (IOM/MPI, 2012). This has more recently been referenced in the 2018 United Nations Global Compact on Safe and Orderly Migration (GCM)—the first significant international agreement on migration—that made reference to diasporas or diaspora organisations 25 times in the final agreement. Objective 1 of this Global Compact is to 'Collect and utilize accurate and disaggregated data as a basis for evidence-based policies', including through cooperation 'with relevant stakeholders in countries of origin, transit and destination to develop research, studies and surveys on the interrelationship between migration and the three dimensions of sustainable development, the contributions and skills of migrants and diasporas, as well as their ties to the countries of origin and destination.' (Objective 1, Para 17 (k)). An innovative approach to diaspora mapping was displayed in New Zealand through a public-private partnership called Kea New Zealand that was formed to mobilise and register New Zealanders overseas (Kea New Zealand, 2011). A 2006 exercise known as 'Every One Counts' was a survey of expatriates that coincided with the National Census, which was repeated in 2011 and attracted 15,297 responses from

New Zealanders aged 16 years and over living abroad (Kea New Zealand, 2011). There are also examples of diaspora snapshots, such as research undertaken by RAND Europe in partnership with the Institute for the Study of Labor (2014). This diaspora mapping focused on 25 diaspora communities' resident in Europe and the US and was commissioned by the European Commission's Directorate General for Home Affairs (DG Home), but its broad scope limited the potential for drawing diaspora engagement strategies from the data. It also does not lend itself to ongoing diaspora engagement, for example, Kea New Zealand has also played a role in encouraging diaspora members to vote in national elections and has attracted government funding and private sector sponsorship. Overall, this points to the immense value of coordination efforts either through government agencies and non-government organisations or, in the above case, through private-public partnerships that can offer ongoing coordination and development of diaspora databases.

In countries with large and diverse diaspora communities, such as the US, as IOM/MPI note 'the US government, for example, has encouraged the formation of several diaspora foundations to encourage unified action on the part of diverse immigrant communities: these include the American Irish Foundation (now merged into The Ireland Funds), American India Foundation, US-Mexico Foundation, and American Pakistan Foundation. Such bodies help articulate the goals of diaspora communities both to the governments of their countries of origin and to the governments of the countries where they have settled' (2012, p. 29). Other models for diaspora engagement include centres such as the African Diaspora Policy Centre based in the Netherlands, and the Diaspora African Forum (DAF) which has been established in Ghana with endorsement from the African Union (AU). Models for coordination need to factor in the relative size of diaspora communities and the breadth of government counterparts in the country of destination and countries of origin. The next section returns to the conditions for diaspora engagement in Australia and then develops recommendations for future policy arrangements.

Discussion

Returning to the four political opportunity structures outlined above that countries of destination can implement to support diaspora engagement, it is clear that Australia meets the first requirement of having a policy environment that is conducive to the participation of non-state actors in policy processes. This is evidenced by decades of multicultural policy and systematic engagement with CALD communities on issues such as the refugee intake, settlement services and the Senate Inquiry itself. With regard to policies that target migrant involvement, the second attribute in the political opportunity structure framework, this chapter has already shown that diaspora groups may be involved in discussions on multicultural policy more broadly; however, there is no federal diaspora policy that speaks to the needs of diasporas. In the Australian context, the stated focus of diaspora support is largely on amplifying development assistance, which is a rather limiting approach to diaspora engagement and does not address multiple issues raised by diasporas and raised in the Foreign Policy White paper. As the DAA notes:

> The Foreign Policy White Paper recognises diaspora communities as one of Australia's development partners. It identifies the diaspora diplomatic role to assist Australia to deepen ties with other countries, facilitate trade and investment and influence how Australia is perceived overseas. The Foreign Policy White Paper also acknowledges the value of diaspora's networks and knowledge to help improve Australia's understanding of development and humanitarian issues in other countries. Also, the White Paper marks Australia's clear commitment to work with diaspora communities, However, there are few interventions from the decision making process to practically achieve Foreign aid and development towards the fulfilment of diaspora as aid partners. Two of the direct consequences of the policy vacuum seems to be inadequate and the current policy development framework requires an adjustment according to diaspora's needs. Lastly, the existing funding schemes and programs are unsuitable to systematically build diaspora capability and capacity. (2021, p. 10)

The last point made by DAA above relates to the third political opportunity structure, which is the availability of resources, subsidies or activities in policy priority fields. Funding issues were raised by diaspora communities in a number of Senate Inquiry submissions, including the need for sustainable ongoing funding, support to enable enhanced remittance delivery, and funding for diaspora to carry out development work in their countries of origin (see e.g. Advisory Group on Australia-Africa Relations (AGAAR), 2020). As the Refugee Council of Australia (RCOA) noted in its submission (2020, p. 3):

220   M. PHILLIPS

Refugee diaspora associations are often multi-mandate organisations that respond to changing priorities within communities and do not fit easily within siloed funding programs, particularly where a 'community' is dispersed and the organisation may be engaged in support work at local, national and international levels simultaneously. Funding that is more accessible to these types of organisations tends to be situated at a local level, project-based and small scale, such as funding to run cultural festivals or events. This type of funding does not allow diaspora associations to invest in their governance, sustainability and capacity to respond flexibly to community-identified needs and priorities.

RCOA also references the Danish Refugee Council programmes, amongst others, as a 'promising model' of support for diaspora associations and diaspora-led activities that recognises the need also to strengthen leadership and governance structures. The final political opportunity structure is that of local networks. Although there is a multiplicity of local diaspora community organisations, the gaps in coordination are evident. On the side of government, multiple submissions to the Senate Inquiry noted the value of having a Diaspora Liaison Unit within DFAT, while others highlighted coordination platforms such as DEMAC as a necessary framework in diaspora architecture. This aligns with Carment and Calleja, who suggest that developing relationships between home countries, host countries, and diaspora communities are predicated upon creating a viable diaspora engagement framework; having diaspora-centred institutions; and managing programmes that target diasporas as development actors (2017, p. 239).

CONCLUSION

Well-engaged and empowered diasporas are an important resource for resolving crises and aiding recovery, and diaspora members are often among the very first responders to humanitarian crises. William Lacy Swing, former Director-General of the IOM.

This chapter has shown, following Ong'ayo, that conditions in countries of origin and destination play a role in shaping diaspora communities, with 'the ability of diaspora to organise collectively in the country of destination depend[ing] on characteristics such as the size of the community, the political and policy environment and individual attributes, i.e. leadership, experience and legal status' (2016, pp. 1–2). In countries of destination, frameworks and policies offer an effective way to support inclusion and participation whilst at the same time giving diaspora communities themselves clarity over their role and the objectives of engagement with government. This is critical not only to maximise the contribution diaspora can make in countries of origin and destination, but also to ensure alignment with Australia's commitment to the 2030 Agenda for Sustainable Development, which has migration as a cross-cutting theme.

The context in Australia indicates there are the necessary policy preconditions for consultation and engagement with diaspora communities, such as a well-established multicultural policy framework and government departments tasked with specific roles and responsibilities in relation to culturally and linguistically diverse communities. It is recommended that similar attention be paid to diaspora communities through the creation of a DFAT-level diaspora desk, or staff tasked with responsibility for diaspora engagement that has clearly defined liaisons with government departments such as Home Affairs and ASIO. A community-level coordination organisation would provide a vital counterpart to the Australian Government as well as to governments seeking to engage with their diaspora members resident in Australia. This should be bulwarked with a diaspora engagement statement or policy and transparent accountability measures, such as key performance indicators. The absence of targeted and sustainable funding in the diaspora sector should also be urgently addressed in order to reap the benefits from diaspora communities, which have been showcased in this edited collection. From this, it would be expected that a thriving and active diaspora network would develop for the benefit of Australia, the countries of origin, and for the diaspora communities themselves.

References

Advisory Group on Australia-Africa Relations (AGAAR). (2020). *Submission to the Foreign Affairs, Defence and Trade References Committee: Issues Facing Diaspora Communities in Australia*. Retrieved November 24, 2020, from https://www. aph.gov.au/Parliamentary_Business/Committees/Senate/Foreign_Affairs_ Defence_and_Trade/Diasporacommunities/Submissions

Australian Human Rights Commission. (2020). *Submission to the Foreign Affairs, Defence and Trade References Committee: Issues Facing Diaspora Communities in Australia*. Retrieved November 24, 2020, from https://www.aph.gov.au/

Parliamentary_Business/Committees/Senate/Foreign_Affairs_Defence_and_Trade/Diasporacommunities/Submissions

Carment, D., & Calleja, R. (2017). Diasporas and Fragile States Beyond Remittances: Assessing the Theoretical Linkages. In *Diaspora as Cultures of Cooperation* (pp. 223–260). Springer.

Commonwealth of Australia. (2017). Foreign Policy White Paper. Retrieved September 13, 2021, from https://www.dfat.gov.au/publications/minisite/2017-foreign-policy-white-paper/fpwhitepaper/index.html

Department of Home Affairs. (2018). *Australian Government's Multicultural Statement*. Retrieved February 17, 2021, from https://www.homeaffairs.gov.au/about-us/our-portfolios/multicultural-affairs/about-multicultural-affairs/our-statement

Diaspora Action Australia. (2020). *Submission to the Foreign Affairs, Defence and Trade References Committee: Issues Facing Diaspora Communities in Australia*. Retrieved November 24, 2020, from https://www.aph.gov.au/Parliamentary_Business/Committees/Senate/Foreign_Affairs_Defence_and_Trade/Diasporacommunities/Submissions

Faist, T. (2000). Transnationalization in International Migration: Implications for the Study of Citizenship and Culture. *Ethnic and Racial Studies, 23*(2), 189–222. https://doi.org/10.1080/014198700329024

Gamlen, A. (2006). *Diaspora Engagement Policies: What Are They and What Kinds of States Use Them?* COMPAS Working Paper. 06-32. Retrieved June 4, 2021, from https://www.compas.ox.ac.uk/2006/wp-2006-032-gamlen_diaspora_engagement_policies/

Global Affairs Canada. (2021). Departmental Plan 2021–2022. Retrieved September 30, 2021, from https://www.international.gc.ca/transparency-transparence/departmental-plan-ministeriel/2021-2022.aspx?lang=eng

Hayward, S. (2008). Engaging the Darfur Diaspora for Peace. *United States Institute for Peace*. https://www.usip.org/publications/2008/02/engaging-darfur-diaspora-peace

Hugo, G. (2006). An Australian Diaspora? *International Migration, 44*(1), 105–133.

International Organization for Migration & Migration Policy Institute. (2012). *Developing a Road Map for Engaging Diasporas in Development: A Handbook for Policymakers and Practitioners in Home and Host Countries*. Retrieved October 12, 2020, from https://diaspora.iom.int/iommpi-diaspora-handbook

Kea New Zealand. (2011). *Everyone Counts Survey*. Retrieved September 30, 2021, from https://www.keanewzealand.com/

Olyan, H., & Smith, P. (2011). *Diasporas: A Policy Review Prepared for the Privy Council Office*. Carleton University. Retrieved February 14, 2021, from https://carleton.ca/cifp/wp-content/uploads/1357.pdf

Ong'ayo, A. O. (2016). Development Potentials of Diasporas Collective Organising: The Case of Ghanaian Diaspora Organisations in the Netherlands. In A. Adepoju (Ed.), (2014) *The Diaspora Decade: Some Perspectives on African Migration-Related Issues*. NOMRA.

Phillips, M. (2013). Migration and Australian Foreign Policy Towards Africa: The Place of Australia's African Transnational Communities. In D. Mickler & T. Lyons (Eds.), *New Engagement: Contemporary Australian Foreign Policy towards Africa*. Melbourne University Press.

PricewaterhouseCoopers, & Advance. (2018). *Out of Sight, Out of Mind? Australia's Diaspora as a Pathway to Innovation*. Retrieved January 12, 2021, from https://www.pwc.com.au/publications/pdf/the-australian-diaspora.pdf

Ragazzi, F. (2014). A Comparative Analysis of Diaspora Policies. *Political Geography, 41*, 74–89.

Refugee Council of Australia. (2020). *Submission to the Foreign Affairs, Defence and Trade References Committee: Issues Facing Diaspora Communities in Australia*. Retrieved November 24, 2020, from https://www.aph.gov.au/Parliamentary_Business/Committees/Senate/Foreign_Affairs_Defence_and_Trade/Diasporacommunities/Submissions

Senate Legal and Constitutional References Committee. (2005). *They Still Call Australia Home: Inquiry into Australian Expatriates*. Retrieved May 14, 2021, from https://www.aph.gov.au/Parliamentary_Business/Committees/Senate/Legal_and_Constitutional_Affairs/Completed_inquiries/2004-07/expats03/report/index

Singh, A. (2012). The Diaspora Networks of Ethnic Lobbying in Canada. *Canadian Foreign Policy Journal, 18*(3), 340–357.

Tan, G., Taylor, A., & McDougall, K. (2021). *COVID has Made One Thing Very Clear—We Do Not Know Enough about Australians Overseas*. Retrieved November 10, 2020, from https://theconversation.com/covid-has-made-one-thing-very-clear-we-do-not-know-enough-about-australians-overseas-159995

Terrazas, A. (2010). *Connected Through Service: Diaspora Volunteers and Global Development*. Washington, DC: Migration Policy Institute.

United Nations Global Compact for Safe, Orderly and Regular Migration. (2018). Retrieved October 5, 2021, from https://undocs.org/A/RES/73/195

INDEX[1]

A
Acculturation, 165
Activism, 14, 29, 30, 32, 37, 38, 156, 196
African diaspora, 62
Art, 50–52
Australian diaspora, 209–211
Australian Government, 13, 48–50, 70, 81, 149, 208, 214

B
Belonging, 19, 24
Bosnian diaspora, 13–32
Brain drain/gain, 71, 74, 131
Businesses, 20, 21, 26, 71, 76, 78, 126, 165, 169, 200, 216

C
Celebrity, 38, 40–42
Chain migration, 15, 25

Churches, 76, 165, 168, 175, 199
Citizenship
    Australian, 18, 19, 102
    dual, 19, 64, 70, 176, 178, 198, 201, 211
Civic participation, 147, 213
Commemorations, 30–32
Communication technologies, 32, 65, 168, 171, 188, 198, 203
Communities
    translocal, 16, 25, 27–29
    transnational, 146
Community associations, *see* Diaspora organisations
Community leaders, 150, 152
Conflict, 139, 144–146, 170–171

D
Darfurian diaspora, 216
Decolonialism, 112, 120, 121
Democracy, 48, 189–193, 202

---

[1] Note: Page numbers followed by 'n' refer to notes.

© The Author(s), under exclusive license to Springer Nature Switzerland AG 2022
M. Phillips, L. Olliff (eds.), *Understanding Diaspora Development*, https://doi.org/10.1007/978-3-030-97866-2

225

226 INDEX

Democratisation, 49, 187, 188, 194–196, 198–202
Development assistance, 20, 21, 52, 71, 142, 212, 219
Development projects, 179, 200
Diaspora-centred development, 63, 79, 80
Diaspora diplomacy, 188
Diaspora humanitarianism, 20, 97, 103, 104, 113, 115–117, 123, 220
  Pacific, 111–132
  refugee, 97–105
Diaspora institutions, 43, 63, 70, 81, 177, 201, 207, 220
  policy, 208, 211, 219
Diaspora organisations, 17, 20, 48, 65, 67, 97, 99, 130, 131, 140, 145, 150, 157, 163, 165, 168, 198, 199, 208, 213, 216, 220
Diaspora visits, 21
Diasporisation, 88, 93
Dispersal, 89, 91–97, 167, 190, 193, 202
Dwelling, 91–97, 190

E

Economic development, 200
Economic engagement, 61, 64–68, 70, 76–79
Elites, 162, 164, 170, 176–178, 194
Emotions, 175
Emplaced experts, 38, 45, 52
Employment, 26, 78, 169, 170
Exchange networks, 130
Experts, 22, 38, 45, 47, 51–54

F

Family obligations, 138
Fijian diaspora, 124, 128–130
Foreign Policy White Paper, 212, 219
Fragmentation, 173

Funding, 213, 220
Fundraising, 20, 26, 27, 102, 129, 199

G

Genocide, 13, 14, 22, 28–32, 30n2
Ghana diaspora, 69
Global intimacy, 25
Governance, 96n7, 115, 116, 177, 208, 213, 220

H

Hazara diaspora, 102
Home, 15, 24, 26, 31, 164, 191
Homeland activism, 37, 38, 195
Homeland politics, 37
Hometown associations, *see* Diaspora organisations
Humanitarian, 20
Humanitarian-development nexus, 116, 131
Humanitarianism, 112, 114
Human rights, 32, 50, 142, 157, 215

I

Identity, 22, 24, 27, 32, 38–40, 42, 43, 47, 90, 115, 118, 125, 127, 128, 131, 138, 139, 144, 163, 165, 173, 175–177, 188, 193, 196
  collective, 23, 28, 111, 125, 144, 194
  translocal, 25
Imagined community, 25, 91, 103, 125, 126, 128
Information-sharing, 171, 198
Integration, 18, 19, 65, 78, 93, 96, 97, 138, 140, 164, 209
Inter-ethnic harmony, 138, 140–146, 149, 152, 176
Investment, 26, 64, 65, 67, 70, 71, 75–78, 169, 200, 219

K

Kenyan diaspora, 69
Kinship networks, 161, 179
Knowledge and skills transfer, 22, 67, 75, 76, 78
Knowledge bearers, *see* Experts

L

Leadership, 220
Lobbying, 71, 196
Localisation, 114, 131, 132
Local knowledge, 45, 47, 52, 105, 129
Long-distance nationalists, 43

M

Mapping, 217
Media, 27, 30, 31, 47, 53, 142, 144, 163, 164, 171, 188
  social, 19, 46, 47, 102, 145, 171, 172, 176, 177, 198, 199, 203
Memory, 24, 25, 27, 28, 194
  collective, 15, 32, 190
Migrant associations, *see* Diaspora organisations
Mobility, 21, 152, 157, 170, 174, 177, 178, 187
Money transfer, 166, 168, 169, 173
Multiculturalism, 19, 95, 96, 143, 148, 152, 208, 212, 215
Myanmar diaspora, 37–54

N

Nation-state, 23, 189–192
Near diaspora, 90

P

Pacific diaspora, 111–132
Peacebuilding, 65, 137–157

Philanthropy, 71
Pluralism, 143, 148
Political activism, 91
Political movements, 188, 190
Post-territorial, 188, 194, 196, 202

R

Racism and discrimination, 164
Refugee diasporas, 89–91, 94, 104, 150n3
Refugees, 14, 17–20, 23, 27, 39, 40n1, 40n2, 43n5, 53, 87, 104, 162, 164
Remittances, 20, 21, 27, 65, 67, 71, 72, 75, 91, 115, 117–118, 120, 124, 147, 168, 169, 173, 200, 201, 211
  collective, 104, 168
  reverse, 73
Resettlement, 15, 16, 87, 88, 92–94, 92n3, 100n10, 104, 162–164, 167
Return migration, 74–77, 81, 200
Rhizomatic networks, 103

S

Social networks, 22, 27, 93, 102, 116, 117, 198, 201
  of care, 101–105
  translocal, 25, 26, 102, 126, 157
  transnational, 88, 90, 102–105, 118, 126, 127, 164, 174–176, 178, 179, 198
Social punishment, 45–47, 52
Solidarity, 17, 26, 28, 31, 32, 101, 115, 127, 130, 131, 168, 173, 176
South Sudanese diaspora, 64, 67, 137–157, 217
Sri Lankan diaspora, 137–157

T

Territoriality, 32, 103, 188, 189
Territory, 189, 191–193, 196, 202
Tourism, 66, 78
Trade, 76–78, 97, 165, 219
Translocalism, 23, 144, 156
Transnational exchange networks, 118, 127
Transnationalism, 23, 38–43, 61, 63, 64, 88, 90–91, 97, 121, 131, 138, 175, 177, 179, 180, 187, 191, 209
Trauma, 17, 172, 173, 175
Troublemaker, 38, 42–43
Trust, 26, 116, 129, 150, 152–154, 156, 167, 168, 173, 176

U

Ukrainian diaspora, 203–205
Unsolicited bilateral donations, 120–121, 124, 131

V

Victim, 38–40
Volunteer programs, 216, 217

W

Wider diaspora, 90, 91, 102, 111, 147

Y

Young people, 138, 172, 177

Printed in the United States
by Baker & Taylor Publisher Services